THE FRIDAY BOOK

BOOKS BY JOHN BARTH

The Floating Opera
The End of the Road
The Sot-Weed Factor
Giles Goat-Boy
Lost in the Funhouse
Chimera
LETTERS
Sabbatical

John Barth

THE
FRIDAY BOOK

Essays
and Other Nonfiction

A PERIGEE BOOK

Perigee Books
are published by
The Putnam Publishing Group
200 Madison Avenue
New York, NY 10016

Several pieces in this book have been published previously, and the author
gratefully acknowledges the following sources: *Antaeus* for "Tales Within Tales
Within Tales"; *The Atlantic* for "The Literature of Exhaustion" and for "The
Literature of Replenishment: Postmodernist Fiction"; *The Boston Globe* for
"Speaking of *LETTERS*"; *Esquire* for "Revenge"; The Johns Hopkins Press
for the foreword to *Western Wind, Eastern Shore: A Sailing Cruise Around the
Eastern Shore of Maryland, Delaware, and Virginia* by Robert de Gast; The
David McKay Company, Inc., for *"Writer's Choice"* from *Writer's Choice,*
edited by Rust Hills; New American Library for the afterword to *Roderick
Random* by Tobias Smollett; The New York Times, Inc., for "Some Reasons
Why I Tell the Stories I Tell the Way I Tell Them Rather Than Some Other
Sort of Stories Some Other Way," which appeared as "The Making of a
Writer," and for "Getting Oriented"; The Pennsylvania State University Press
for *"The Ocean of Story"* from *Directions in Literary Criticism,* edited by
Weintraub and Young; *The Washington Post Sunday Magazine* for "Historical
Fiction, Fictitious History, and Chesapeake Bay Blue Crabs, or, About
Aboutness."

Designed by Helen Barrow

The text of this book is set in Times Roman and Helvetica Light.

Library of Congress Cataloging-in-Publication Data

Barth, John.
The Friday book.

I. Title.
[PS3552.A75F7   1984b]   814'.54   85-12128
ISBN 0-399-51209-8

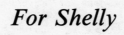

For Shelly

THE FRIDAY BOOK,
OR,
BOOK-TITLES SHOULD BE STRAIGHTFORWARD AND SUBTITLES AVOIDED

Essays and Other Nonfiction

The Title of This Book

Book-titles should be straightforward. *Book-Titles Should Be Straightforward* is not quite straightforward (see below)—nor is it quite the title of this book. *The Canterbury Tales, A Cruising Guide to the Chesapeake, The Trial, The Idiot, Moby-Dick, The Anatomy of Melancholy, The Friday Book*—those are straightforward.

Comic works need not bear comic titles. *The Frogs. The Birds. Don Quixote. Tom Jones.* A catchy title may serve a catchy book (*Catch-22* is not a title with a catch to it; it is straightforward): Two truly catchy books by the logician Raymond Smullyan—*What Is the Name of This Book?* and *This Book Needs No Title*—have appropriately catchy titles. But better a book more engaging than its title (*The Adventures of Huckleberry Finn*) than a title more engaging than its book (*Steal This Book*, by Abbie Hoffman).

Later in the course—the course of this arrangement of miscellaneous nonfiction by a habitual novelist and occasional short-storyteller who has also for three decades professed the reading and writing of fiction in American universities and along the way has entertained a couple of ideas at a time about literature—we may touch upon other principles and categories of literary titling and upon titling errors to be avoided.

Indeed, let us touch upon them now and have done with it: I mean such misdemeanors as Titles Quoted From Even Better Works Than One's Own (*The Sun Also Rises, The Winter of Our Discontent, Tender Is the Night*), Hokey-Romantic Titles (*How Green Was My Valley, Winter Blood, Not as a Stranger, The Executioner's Song*), especially Tacky Tandems (*War and Peace* is straightforward; *Pride and Prejudice* and *Sense and Sensibility* are nearly so, but for the alliteration. *The Beautiful and Damned, The Naked and the Dead, The Agony and the Ecstasy*—these are the Tacky and the Poshlost: see below), Poetical Inversions (*By Love Possessed, Too Late the Phalarope, After Many a Summer Dies the Swan*), and other varieties of what the late Vladimir Nabokov called by the Russian word *poshlost:* a word adequately defined for our purposes by the samples given. Such titles may happen to entitle works otherwise innocent of hoke, affectation, pretentiousness, tack, poshlost; such works are not better for their titles.

Then there is the Self-Referential Title, which refers not to the subject or to the contents of the work but to the work itself. The Bible. Samuel Beckett's film *Film;* his play *Play.* Fulton Oursler's *The Greatest Story Ever Told* is not mainly self-referential and therefore is not essentially boastful: It refers less to the book it entitles than to the book that that book is about: i.e., The Book. Its element of ironic or at least amused self-referentiality is, however, part of the title's point, as it is in the title of Philip Roth's novel *The Great American Novel.* Quite all right.

The Canterbury Tales refers not primarily to Chaucer's book thus named but to the tales told in it, the Canterbury tales, and thus is not self-referential; the same is true of Boccaccio's *Decameron,* Marguerite of Navarre's *Heptameron,* Giambattista Basile's *Pentameron,* Somadeva's *The Ocean of Story,* the *Panchatantra,* the *Vetalapanchavimsata* (*25 Tales Told by a Vampire*), and most other tale-cycle titles. The title of the ancient Egyptian *Book of the Dead,* like that of the modern *Guinness Book of World Records,* is semi-self-referential: It names both the container and the thing contained, as if one were to label a jar of apple jelly not *Apple Jelly* but *Jar of Apple Jelly.* The *Kitab Alf Laylah Wah Laylah,* or *Book of the Thousand Nights and a Night,* would seem to be in this category as well, but in curious fact it refers immediately neither to the book thus titled nor to the period of Scheherazade's liaison with King Shahryar, but rather to a book *described* by the book thus titled, itself entitled *The Marvels and Wonders of the Thousand Nights and a Night,* which book in turn, the text itself explains, is a popular edition of yet another book (in thirty volumes) called *The Stories of the Thousand Nights and a Night. That* is the original book of the scribes' transcription of the tales told by Scheherazade to the king, plus the tale of Scheherazade telling those tales to the king. The book we hold in our hands is a book about a book about that book; it might properly be entitled *The Book of the Book of the Book of the Thousand Nights and a Night.*

Rather, it is a *copy* of a translation of that book about that book about that book, just as that innermost book is a written copy of Scheherazade's spoken tales, themselves recited from her memory of the "thousand books of histories" in her personal library and the "works of the poets," which she knew "by heart." Such several removes between us and the original tales—removes acknowledged in many cases explicitly, if in passing, by the text itself—suggest an awareness among the ancients in many cultures of what in Hebrew tradition is implied by the Cabalistic notion of The Original of the Book: an original we can only infer from however "authoritative" a copy, even the author's manuscript. I have for example revised this paragraph a number of times on a number of Friday mornings here in my workroom overlooking Langford Creek on the Eastern Shore of tidewater Maryland and have not got it quite right yet, have not got it right quite yet, have not yet got it right, quite, but like the tide I shall move on now and later return. More about tales within tales and tales about tales in the pages to follow, and considerably more about Scheherazade. Also tides.

The difference between Self-Referential Titles like the Bible or *Film,* Self-Reflexive Titles like *The Title of This Book,* and Self-Demonstrating Titles like *Book-Titles Should Be Straightforward* is that the first name the thing they name (at least a copy of that thing), the second name the name of the thing, as the name *name* names itself, and the third exemplify not only what they are but what they say. Inasmuch as the names of things are also members of the class of things, things in the world, a perfectly self-reflexive sentence such as *Adjective adjective subject adverbially verbs adjective adjective object* is as meaningful, though its content is not in itself so moving, as the sentence *Old King Priam tearfully kisses Achilles's bloody hands.*

The late John Gardner was pleased to argue that sentences like the latter make up what he called Primary Literature—literature about "life"—whereas the former add up to Secondary Literature: literature about literature, or in this case language about language. One understands what he meant (Homer's powerful scene in Book XXIV of the *Iliad,* of Priam kissing Achilles's hands, still bloody from Hector's slaughter, in vain supplication to return his dead son's body, was one of Gardner's favorite examples of Primary Literature). But since one may write stirring sentences about matters in themselves unstirring or even nonsensical ("And hast thou slain the Jabberwock? Come to my arms, my beamish boy!"), and unstirring sentences about stirring matters ("Homer's powerful scene in Book XXIV of the *Iliad* . . ." above), the issue is far from simple. Such distinctions as Primary and Secondary Literature, particularly when they become value judgments, do more to becloud than to clarify the manifold processes of language and literature, which, like many other processes both "natural" and artificial, from walking upright to welding automobile frames by computerized robot, depend upon more or less subtle and intricate "feedback loops" for their success. Surely we do better to acknowledge that literature, like language, is seldom simply but always also about itself. Titles too, about which this is enough.

Four mornings a week from September through May I have for some years been privileged to make up and set down my stories in a pleasant white house in the city of Baltimore, where in the afternoons I teach at the Johns Hopkins University. On normal Thursday evenings my wife and I drive across the Chesapeake Bay Bridge to a pleasant red house on Langford Creek, off the Chester River, off that same Bay, where on Friday mornings (unless the story in progress asserts the priority reserved to it) I refresh my head with some other sort of sentence-making, preferably nonfiction, while Shelly does schoolwork. Two English teachers. Most of the pieces here edited, revised, and assembled were in fact composed before I was blessed with this tranquil work-rhythm, from which only the later ones proceed. But I find that rhythm so agreeable that in the summer months too, when teaching and weekend-commuting are suspended and we live and work only in our creekside house, hoping the world will not soon end, I still reserve the last weekday morning for whatever "Friday-piece" is in hand, and I hope to do so until the period of my life's sentence.

Though I am far from regretting that sentence—which in the main has been thus far a serene, productive, and rewarding one—if I could revise it to my preferences, the pieces here collected would all have been written on Friday mornings on Langford Creek; then *The Friday Book,* itself conceived and executed over a year's Fridays, would be my Friday book indeed.

Prefatory notes and other introductory material should be avoided wherever possible. See "Author's Introduction."

The Subtitle of This Book

Subtitles—like printed dedications, notes on titles, author's introductions, forewords, sonnets and epistles dedicatory, and the rest—should be avoided. Get on with it. Get on with it.

But if you must use a subtitle, at least eschew the archaizing *or,* followed by cutesy fake earlier-centuryisms. *Or, the Whale* is quite all right for *Moby-Dick,* or was in the nineteenth century. Erica Jong's *Fanny: Being the True History of the Adventures of Fanny Hackabout Jones,* can be justified as the title and subtitle of a twentieth-century novel humorously imitative of eighteenth-century fiction—a category of humorous twentieth-century fiction one would have thought exhaustible by a single instance, but its appeal seems to be as perennial to Americans as other fake colonialisms.

Subtitles are usually made necessary by titles with more "grab" than straightforwardness. *The American Heritage Dictionary of the English Language* requires no subtitle. *Book-Titles Should Be Straightforward* is intelligible but requires at least the subtitle *Essays and Other Nonfiction* to make it meaningful. Sub-subtitles like *Subtitles Should Be Avoided* should be avoided if only because though fairly straightforward they necessitate a sub-sub-subtitle, in this case *Essays and Other Nonfiction,* which, had it been used as the book's title in the first place, would have been perfectly straightforward and required no subtitles.

This is not to say that no straightforward title requires subtitling. It is useful to know whether the title *Baltimore* is subtitled *A Picture History* or *Telephone Directory.* Straightforwardness, moreover, while a virtue, is not the only virtue; therefore one sees titles which sin against no other principle of titling than straightforwardness and are doubtless more arresting or engaging than *Fifty Stories* or *Tales of the Chesapeake,* but may require subtitling. Should you perpetrate such a title, follow it with a subtitle which not only is straightforward but manages also to avoid the *as* fetish worshipped in particular by literary critics: *Literature as Equipment for Living. Language as Gesture. Subtitles as Literary Genre.*

Say it straight. Get on with it.

Author's Introduction

The chief purpose of introductions (I like to say when introducing guest authors to their public audiences at Johns Hopkins, in whose Writing Seminars I preside over advanced, unadvanced, and backward apprentice writers of fiction, coaching the first, instructing and encouraging the second, and gently hoping that the third will find another métier) is to test the public-address system. Introductions ought therefore to extend beyond a single breath, but not much beyond. They also permit latecomers to be seated and the guest author to size up his/her house and perhaps make appropriate program adjustments.

There are a number of Rules for Public Introducing, of which the first is Do not upstage the introducee by introducing him/her with cleverer remarks than he/she is likely to make him/herself and the second is Never introduce either a speaker or a text with an attempted parody of him/her/it, for if your attempt is successful you have broken Rule One, and if it is not you have been at least faintly foolish.

Introduction to a course of study is better done by a straightforward syllabus, to a body of assorted nonfiction by a straightforward table of contents, than by one more nattering text-before-the-text. Eschew introductions wherever possible. What cannot be eschewed, swallow hard and abbreviate. Above all, avoid any version, especially any *clever* version, of the introduction "This author [course, text, whatever] really needs no introduction."

If you yourself are the author/teacher, and your presentation is after all largely self-explanatory—an arrangement of your essays and occasional lectures, some previously published, most not, most on matters literary, some not, accumulated over thirty years or so of writing, teaching, and teaching writing, interstitched with little lessons on the manufacture of fiction, presentations to sundry symposia, remarks upon your work and your life as an American writer in the second half of the twentieth century, and other "continuity" material (not to be confused with "filler": Continuity, like discontinuity, has its place in writing which takes its readers seriously; "filler" does not), and here as they say collected for the first time—you should dispense with introductions and get on with the job.

Ms. Katha Pollitt, reviewing in the *New York Times* a 1983 volume of essays by Ms. Cynthia Ozick, writes, "This is not your typical collection of essays by an eminent middle-aged writer of fiction. You know what sort of book I mean—a graceful miscellany of book reviews, introductions, and speeches, all wrapped up and offered to the public less as a book, really, than as a kind of laurel, a tribute to the author's literary importance." Okay: This book *is* that sort of book, except that it contains no book reviews—my vows to the muse, made long ago and reasonably well kept, prohibit among other things the giving or soliciting of advertising testimonials and the reviewing of books—and I offer it to the public after all less as a kind of laurel than as an honest-to-goodness book.

J.B.

Baltimore/Langford Creek, Md., 1983/84*

---

* James Joyce made these subscripts fashionable with his *Trieste-Zurich-Paris, 1914-1921* at the foot of *Ulysses:* a kind of navigational fix on literary high modernism. It is a practice of no artistic value whatever and therefore better eschewed, though in the case of American writers the dates of composition may be of interest to the Internal Revenue Service.

*Table of Contents**

The Title of This Book • *ix*
The Subtitle of This Book • *xiii*
Author's Introduction • *xv*
Table of Contents • *xvii*
Epigraphs • *xix*
Some Reasons Why I Tell the Stories I Tell
the Way I Tell Them Rather Than Some Other Sort
of Stories Some Other Way • *1*
How to Make a Universe • *13*
More on the Same Subject • *26*
An Afterword to *Roderick Random* • *30*
Mystery and Tragedy • *41*
Muse, Spare Me • *55*
The Tragic View of Recognition • *60*
The Literature of Exhaustion • *62*
More Troll Than Cabbage • *77*
The Role of the Prosaic in Fiction • *80*
The Ocean of Story • *84*
A Poet to the Rescue • *91*
Aspiration, Inspiration, Respiration, Expiration • *97*

---

* But see the caveat regarding even tables of contents, in "Epigraphs," below.

The Tragic View of Literary Prizes • *99*

Praying for Everybody • *101*

Doing the Numbers • *106*

Intelligent Despisal • *110*

Writer's Choice • *122*

Western Wind, Eastern Shore • *124*

The Spirit of Place • *127*

Getting Oriented • *130*

My Two Problems: 1 • *141*

My Two Problems: 2 • *144*

My Two Problems: 3 • *151*

My Two Uncles • *153*

My Two Muses • *158*

The Future of Literature and the Literature of the Future • *161*

Algebra and Fire • *166*

Speaking of *LETTERS* • *172*

Historical Fiction, Fictitious History, and Chesapeake Bay
Blue Crabs, or, About Aboutness • *180*

The Literature of Replenishment • *193*

The Self in Fiction, or,
"That ain't no matter. That Is nothing." • *207*

Revenge • *215*

Tales Within Tales Within Tales • *218*

The Prose and Poetry of It All, or, Dippy Verses • *239*

The American New Novel • *255*

Don't Count on It • *258*

Epigraphs

... *should be avoided. There is something hokey about an epigraph, even a straightforward epigraph: a posture of awe before some
palimpsestic Other Text; a kind of rhetorical attitudinizing.* Poshlost. *It
may be true, as the critic Wayne C. Booth has observed, that epigraphs
and titles assume a particular importance in modernist writing, where
"... they are often the only explicit commentary the reader is given. ..."
All the same, they are hokey: one more bit of window-dressing before
we get to the goods.*

*Hokier yet are comic-ironic epigraphs. If you must lay on an epi-
graph, take it from some neutral text of a sort entirely different from
your own. To quote other writers in the course of a lecture, an essay, a
story—even writers better than yourself—is properly to give credit
where credit is due and to marshal authority in defense of your argument. But to preface your text with an epigraph from a superior author
in the same genre is to remind the reader that he might better spend his
time with that author than with you. Such epigraphs are tails that wag
their dogs, but from in front, like an awkward figure of speech. They
make the works that follow them an anticlimax. Walter Scott did better
to fake his epigraphs (e.g., at the head of Chapter XXXVI of* Ivanhoe:
*"Say not my art is fraud—all live by seeming. ..." OLD PLAY); Er-
nest Hemingway likewise, without attribution, in* The Snows of Kili-
manjaro;* *F. Scott Fitzgerald best of all, by taking the epigraph to* The
Great Gatsby *from a fictitious poet in his early novel* This Side of
Paradise.

Do not borrow epigraphs from better works than yours in hand,
or from better writers than yourself.
                        —J.B.: "Epigraphs," in *The Friday Book*

---

* But see his lapses in e.g., *The Sun Also Rises,* where, as elsewhere, he
compounds the epigraph misdemeanor with the quoted-title one.

. . . worse than an epigraph is a brace of epigraphs, especially when the second is deployed in Tantalizing Ironic Counterpoint to the first, as it will almost always be. Dispense with epigraphs, comrades, *as with quoted or kitschy titles, subtitles, printed dedications (unless love and gratitude blow away the rules), acknowledgments, prefaces, forewords, introductions, tables of contents, and all other throat-clearings and instrument-tunings, except where they are quite necessary or* very *useful,* and for the love of God get on with the story.*

—Ibid.

---

* The same, it goes without saying, goes for footnotes.

Some Reasons Why
I Tell the Stories I Tell
The Way I Tell Them Rather Than
Some Other Sort of Stories
Some Other Way

THE FOLLOWING apology for my life is a Friday-piece of fairly recent date, written for a *New York Times Book Review* series inaugurated about 1981 and still ongoing under the general and hokey title "The Making of a Writer." Thus its opening sentence. Thus also its counter-hoke title, above, which the editors of the *NYTBR* kindly permitted me to set under their own when the piece appeared in the May 9, 1982, issue of that organ. The version below is slightly amended.

Of the making of writers there is no end till The End unmakes them. Here's how Yours Truly tells his Once upon a time:

TWINS

It is my fate, and equally my sister's, to have been born opposite-sex twins, with an older brother and no younger siblings.

Much is known about "identical" (monozygotic) twins, less about fraternal (dizygotic) twins, less yet about us opposite-sexers (who, it goes without saying, are always dizygotic). But twins of any sort share the curious experiences of accommodating to a peer companion from the beginning, even in the womb; of entering the world with an established sidekick, rather than alone; of acquiring speech and the other basic skills *à deux,* in the meanwhile sharing a language before speech and beyond speech. Speech, baby twins may feel, is for the Others. As native speakers of a dialect regard the official language, we twins may regard language itself: It is for dealing with the outsiders; between ourselves we have little need of it. One might reasonably therefore expect a twin who becomes a storyteller never to take language for granted; to be ever at it, tinkering, foregrounding it, perhaps unnaturally conscious of it. Language is for relating to the Others.

Now, most opposite-sex twins come soon to shrug the shoulders of their imaginations at that congenital circumstance; to regard it as a more or less amusing detail. They can do so because it was not their additional fate to have a three-year-older brother who, upon hearing the unlucky news that he had suddenly not one but a *team* of rivals for his parents' thitherto undivided attention, gamely and fatefully remarked: "Now we have a Jack and Jill."

Poor firstborn: Thy day in the family sun wast shadowed from that hour, but thou hadst in advance thy more than justified revenge. Jack and Jill we became, and up childhood's hill we went—in scrappy East Cambridge, a crab-and-oyster town on the Eastern Shore of Maryland—lugging between us that heavy pail. Our grade school teachers oohed and aahed (doubtless privately ughed) at the awful cuteness of our names, while alleywise classmates reddened our innocent ears with every bawdy version of the nursery rhyme. I can recite them still, those scurrilous variations; my ears still redden.

Language, boyoboy, c'est pour les autres: My sister and I were by it not let to forget our twinness. Until circumstance and physical maturation differentiated and tumbled us toward our separate fates—a fair benchmark is the fall of '43, when we approached both puberty and public high school in an unaffluent, semirural, semi-Southern eleven-year county system further impoverished by the war: no school band, few varsity sports, an attenuated faculty, reduced course offerings, and three curricula: the Agricultural for most of the farm boys; the Commercial for nearly all the girls and some of the boys, those who expected to go neither back to the farm nor on to college; and the Academic for the small percentage of us in that time and place whose vague ambitions did not necessarily preclude higher education (the two or three whose parents were already of the professional class were whisked out of that system and off to private preparatory schools for at least their eleventh grade and a proper twelfth)—until the Commercial course and biological womanhood befell Jill, the Academic course and biological manhood Jack, we were a Jack and Jill indeed, between whom nearly everything went without saying.

With those closest since, I have had sustained and intimate conversation, but seldom in words except at the beginning and end of our connection. Language is for getting to know you and getting to unknow you. We converse to convert, each the other, from an Other into an extension of ourself; and we converse conversely. Dear Reader, if I knew you better, what I'm saying would go without saying; as I do not, let me tell you a story.

Once upon a time, in myth, twins signified whatever dualisms a culture entertained: mortal/immortal, good/evil, creation/destruction, what had they. In western literature since the Romantic period, twins (and doubles, shadows, mirrors) usually signify the "divided self," our secret sharer or inner adversary—even the schizophrenia some neo-Freudians maintain lies near the dark heart of writing. Aristophanes, in Plato's *Symposium*, declares we are all of us twins,* indeed a kind of Siamese twins, who have lost and who seek eternally our missing half. The loss accounts for alienation, our felt distance from man and god; the search accounts for both erotic love and the mystic's goal of divine atonement.

I have sometimes felt that a twin who happens to be a writer, or a writer who happens to be a twin, might take this *shtik* by the other end and use schizophrenia, say, as an image for what he knows to be his literal case: that he once was more than one person and somehow now is less. I am the least psychological of storytellers; yet even to me it is apparent that I write these words, and all the others, in part because I no longer have my twin to be wordless with, even when I'm with her. Less and less, as twins go along, goes without saying. One is in the world, talking to the Others, talking to oneself.

My books tend to come in pairs; my sentences in twin members.

MARSHES, TIDES

Jack-and-Jilling was not easy in Dorchester County, Maryland, of which Cambridge is the seat. Eighty percent of that county is sub-sea level: estuarine wetlands all but uninhabited by men, but teeming like bayous and everglades with other life: the nursery of Chesapeake Bay. No hills down there to go up; and your pail of water will be salt.

More exactly, it will be brackish, turbid, tidal, and tepid: about the same salinity and summer temperature, I am persuaded, as the fluid we all first swam in. Unlike lake water on the one hand or ocean on the

---

* It may be that in fact as many as 70 percent of us are. See e.g., the chapter "The Vanished Twin," in Kay Cassill's *Twins: Nature's Amazing Mystery* (New York: Atheneum, 1982).

other, this will not sting your eyes. Dorchester Countians sensibly nowadays prefer swimming pools, to avoid the medusa jellyfish, or sea nettle (and the watermen, like watermen everywhere, seldom swim at all); but as summer youngsters we played in the natural element for hours and hours, eyes always open. We were often nettled but never chilled; on the other hand, we could see little farther than in the womb.

As a grown-up I've spent agreeable years on a mountain lake and come to enjoy the clear Caribbean, where you can see your anchor on the bottom full fathom five. Yet both seem artificial: the one a backyard pool, be it Lake Superior itself; the other a vast lighted aquarium. Only our warm green semisaline Chesapeake estuaries strike me (strike that: *caress me*) as real, for better or worse.

North across the Choptank from Dorchester is nearly marshless Talbot, the Gold Coast county of tidewater Maryland. Hervey Allen, author of the bestselling *Anthony Adverse,* used to live over there; James A. Michener, author of the bestselling *Chesapeake,* lives over there. A little train nicknamed The Millionaires' Special used to connect *its* county seat to New York City. Almost anyone with sense and money would prefer Talbot to Dorchester. But my father used to say that the real Eastern Shore begins on the south bank of the Choptank; and Mr. Michener himself, tisking his tongue at population-pressure problems on the upper Shore, once declared to me his confidence that our lower-Shore rivers will survive "to the end of the century."

Eighteen more years.

Nearly all who took the Academic course, and many who didn't, left Dorchester County for good after graduation. Before I joined their number, I used sometimes to stand in those boundless tidal marshes, at the center of a 360-degree horizon, surrounded in the spring by maybe a quarter-million Canada geese taking off for home, and at least by age nine or ten think two clear thoughts—never clearer than upon our returning from a visit to my one connection with the larger world, a New Jersey aunt who took us marshlings to the top of the Empire State Building and *all over* the New York World's Fair of 1939/40—(1) This place speaks to me in ways that I don't even understand yet; and (2) I'm going to get out of here and become a distinguished something-or-other. My wife shakes her head at the apparent vanity of that latter. But in a landscape where nothing and almost nobody was distinguished; where for better or worse there was no pressure from nature or culture to stand out;

where horizontality is so ubiquitous that anything vertical—a day beacon, a dead loblolly pine—is ipso facto interesting, the abstract wish to distinguish oneself somehow, anyhow, seems pardonable to me.

In Civil War times Maryland was a Border State. Mason's and Dixon's Line runs east-west across its top and then, appropriately, north-south down the Eastern Shore, which was heavily loyalist in the Revolution and Confederate in the War Between the States. Marsh country is a border state, too, between land and sea, and tide-marsh doubly so, its twin diurnal ebbs and floods continuously reorchestrating the geography. No clear demarcations here between fresh and salt, wet and dry: Many many square miles of Delaware happen to be Delaware instead of Maryland owing to a seventeenth-century surveyors' dispute about the mid-point of a line whose eastern terminus is the sharp Atlantic coast but whose western peters out in the Dorchester County marshes, where the "shoreline" at high tide may be a mile east from where it was at low, when reedy islets muddily join the main. Puberty is another border state; also twinhood, Q.E.D. Your webfoot amphibious marsh-nurtured writer will likely by mere reflex regard many conventional boundaries and distinctions as arbitrary, fluid, negotiable: form versus content, realism versus irrealism, fact versus fiction, life versus art. His favorite mark of punctuation will be the semicolon.

He will also carry a perpetual tide clock in his blood. My father, never a waterman but never far from tidewater, on his one visit to the cottage I owned for years on Lake Chautauqua in west New York, could neither accept nor remember that the water level there remained the same hour after hour, day after day. Three lunchtimes into the visit he would still wonder how it could be high tide *now* when it had been at breakfast. He was polite about it, but landlocked water bored him, as it does me. How can water that doesn't chase the moon speak to the imagination? I had rather watch tides come and go from the merest muddy fingerling of a cove off a creek off a river off a bay off an ocean than own Golden Pond.

What mattered to me as a boy was the fact that the scruffy water in Cambridge Creek was contiguous with, say, Portugal. Years later, standing where Prince Henry the Navigator's navigators' college was, I was helped to get my bearings by the reciprocal of that fact.

My books and their author first located themselves in tidewater-land, then moved outside it; have lately returned; may drift off again, or not.

The tide goes out, comes back, goes out, comes back. As many metaphors as boats are carried on it.

MUSIC

Between Cambridge Creek and Cape St. Vincent I broke my crown in New York City at the Juilliard School of Music, into whose summer program I tumbled after high school, 17, with money I'd earned playing drums in a homegrown jazz band for the two years prior. No union rules in marshville.

About music my sister knew next to nothing and I less than my sister, though we'd been given piano lessons in vain right through the end of the Depression and beginning of the War; duets were thought especially apt for Jill and Jack, and we went along, she primo, I secondo. Along about V-E Day we were permitted to quit those lessons, and at once I became passionately interested in playing jazz.

Never a distinguished drummer (though a steady), never a soloist (a twin solo?), I was modest and middle-class enough to aspire to neither composition nor performance as a musical career, but too ambitious to consider teaching. In 1947 the big bands were still swinging; orchestration was what I went up the flyway to Juilliard to study, but we jazzfolk knew the word was *arranging*. My heroes became Pete Rugolo, Sy Oliver, Eddie Sauter, Billy Strayhorn. I would be a distinguished arranger: The term suggested something less glamorous but more dignified, daytime, and regular than *jazz drummer,* with its aura of sweat, alcohol, and "tea," as marijuana was then called. Though my father's dead brother had aspired to sculpture and my New Jersey uncle's to tournament tennis, there had never been a professional musician in the family; yet no eyebrows were raised at my ambition. There is a wonderful freedom in having parents whose schooling ended with the eleventh grade or earlier: Merely to finish public high school is to be successful in their eyes; anything beyond it is a triumph. I could have declared that I was going to be a distinguished metaphysician, even a distinguished *poet,* and they wouldn't have minded. My New Jersey aunt spoke hopefully of, you know, studio orchestras.

I moved into a cockroach-and-cabbage walk-up where the subway roared out from underground near the old Juilliard on 123rd Street, took the requisite placement tests, and found myself assigned to Elementary Theory and Advanced Orchestration: rather like an apprentice writer's being assigned Bonehead English and a master class in novel-writing. I managed A's in both, learned a little about music, and for the first time confronted my limitations clearly and discovered something useful about myself.

My New York neighborhood, though dirty, was in 1947 wonderfully safe. I spent my best time wandering about it day and night in gritty June and grimy July, listening to black jazz blaring from the record shops on Lenox Avenue and rather enjoying my first acute loneliness. Illinois Jacquet, overblowing his tenor sax, was very big that season. Teddy Wilson was on the Juilliard summer faculty, and a number of my new classmates were young jazz players. They wore pegged pants and lapel-less jackets and saxophone straps, and they spoke hip language in New York accents, which I imitated. It impressed me that several of them were Jewish and some even black: my first real extraethnic acquaintances. They were not unfriendly.

Within a week I came to understand that they would be the professional musicians of their generation. I observed them; I observed me. Theirs was genuine apprentice talent, large or small; mine was makeshift amateur flair. No false modesty here: The news was nowise traumatic, but it was as unequivocal as a high-jump bar that others clear with ease or difficulty but you can't even approach. For this as well as other things, there had simply been no real standards of measurement down there in the marsh. I played with jazz groups for twenty-five years thereafter— for money in college and early teaching days, for mere pleasure later— but never after my Juilliard summer took myself seriously in that line.

Anyhow, I *was* lonely, even commuting in on the E L & W from my New Jersey aunt's house as I did in the latter part of my term. To have gone a whole summer without swimming in the Choptank River, to be as pale in August as I'd been in May, seemed incredible. I went home to think of some other way to be distinguished.

Playing jazz was agreeable for some of the same reasons being twins was: conversation in non-verbal language, the annexation of oneself to the lively organism of the group—pleasures the opposite of writing's. At heart I'm an arranger still, whose chiefest literary pleasure is to take a received melody—an old narrative poem, a classical myth, a shopworn literary convention, a shard of my experience, a *New York Times Book Review* series—and, improvising like a jazzman within its constraints, reorchestrate it to present purpose.

LEARNING

I came back crack-crowned down the flyway to find that I'd lost my tidewater girlfriend and won a scholarship I'd forgotten I had competed for, to the Johns Hopkins University. Well, now.

One was expected to select a major; I hadn't thought about it. Career counseling in our high school consisted of a ten-minute conversation with the phys ed teacher some time before graduation. Girls were counseled to be nurses, teachers, secretaries; boys, the farmers excepted but myself included, business administrators. As I'd been going to be a distinguished arranger, I'd dismissed that counsel. Now I shopped through the Hopkins arts and sciences catalogue, ruled out the sciences, and shrugged my shoulders at such academic majors as literature, history, philosophy, economics. A new department called Writing, Speech, and Drama listed a major in journalism; I put down Journalism and took the bus to Baltimore to become a distinguished journalist, understanding only vaguely that journalism meant newspaper work, which I had no interest in. I think I thought it meant, like, free-lancing and, uh, keeping a journal.

In a week I found that the Hopkins journalism major (we no longer offer it) was a hasty improvisation consisting of a guest-lecture course by a Baltimore *Sun* editor and a general curriculum in the arts and sciences, including the department's offerings in the writing of fiction and poetry. No matter: That same week I found musicians to job with for the next many seasons and settled into the task of surviving my freshman year in a serious university for which nothing since kindergarten had prepared me. (My parents had sent their children—at some sacrifice in those Depression years—to Cambridge's only kindergarten, a private, one-room affair which we loved at the time and which I see in retrospect to have been quite good. Miss Ridah Collins's Kindergarten was no playschool: we were taught reading and writing there. All my schooling between it and Johns Hopkins was a more or less benign blank of which I remember next to nothing.)

What the aristocrats take for granted, Anton Chekhov wrote to his brother, *we pay for with our youth.* What my better educated Hopkins classmates took for granted—especially the good-private-schooled ones—I paid for with my underclass years, at least. They had *heard* already about the Renaissance, the Enlightenment, and the rest; I was lost in the dark ages. They were as it were discussing the architecture while I was trying to find the men's room. Everything was news.

The university was small, the faculty distinguished; all of them taught us undergraduates as well as their graduate students. While looking for the men's room I found the aesthetician and historian of ideas George Boas, the philologist Leo Spitzer, the poets Pedro Salinas and Elliott Coleman, and many another inspired, inspiring teacher: never condescending, nowise palsy, utterly serious, impersonal, good humored, intellectually generous. Splendid role models every one, who can seldom have had in their hands such unformed Silly Putty as my then mind. They were nice about it, if they noticed at all; it was their way, and I approve it, not to talk to us through Homer and Dante and Cervantes and Proust and Joyce, but to talk through us to those great ones, with whom they were at home.

I also found and happily lost myself in the library, a book-filer in the stacks of the Classics Department and William Foxwell Albright's Oriental Seminary, and set about the impossible task of Catching Up. No happier happenstance could have happened to me: not just the physical fact of those canyons of ancient narrative—which I managed somehow to find more inspiring than intimidating, and which it excites me still to prowl through—but the particular discoveries upon my cart of Burton's annotated *Book of the Thousand Nights and a Night,* Petronius's *Satyricon,* the *Panchatantra,* Urquhart's (misfiled) Rabelais, the eleventh-century Sanskrit *Ocean of Story.* Tales within tales within tales, told for the sake of their mere marvelousness. My literary education was, excuse me, *à la carte:* much better for a writer, maybe, than any curricular table d'hôte. I was permanently impressed with the *size* of literature and its wild variety; likewise, as I explored the larger geography of the stacks, with the variety of temperaments, histories, and circumstances from which came the literature I came to love. Book-filing made me a critical pluralist for life.

Finally, still looking for that men's room, I found my way into an elementary fiction-writing class presided over not by one of the gray eminences but by a gentle marine combat veteran, Poe scholar, and Faulkner fan who permitted us to call him Bob; whose Southern tongue charmed "write" into "rot," our department into Rotting Speech and Drama. Bob's course was a whole year long and repeatable; one simply turned in a story every two weeks. I wrote a story for Bob every two weeks for two years, starting from absolute scratch, trying everything and doing it all wrong over and over and over again. D's, C's, the odd B, C's, D's, through the first of those years at least. Perhaps if Bob had been a professional rotter himself, I'd have been intimidated (perhaps not; perhaps I'd have learned more, sooner, about the craft of rotting). But he was by his own confession a scholar pressed into service by a shorthanded department, and he was an excellent teacher for one who had *everything* to learn.

By the beginning of my junior year I was writing not much better—at best I'd climbed from absolute to relative scratch—but I had by then taken on some freight of literature both curricularly and off the cart. In particular I had discovered Faulkner, Scheherazade, Joyce, Cervantes, and Kafka, and a thing had happened curiously different from what had happened at Juilliard. I was beating my head against a wall, but not breaking my crown; I was toiling uphill with much slippage and misstep, but not quite falling. Almost imperceptibly I had found my vocation, even in that term's religious sense. That I was still doing everything wrong (whereas at Juilliard I'd done some things right) scarcely mattered. As unequivocally as I'd realized I was *not* a genuine apprentice distinguished musician, I realized I was going to—well, not be a distinguished writer, maybe; that adjective was losing its importance; but devote my life to the practice of literature.

In retrospect I am impressed at the strength and depth of my then conviction, especially in the face of what I was composing. The work I did even two and three years later, in the graduate-level workshops (we were all reading *Finnegans Wake* then and had changed the department's name from Rotting Speech and Drama to Writhing, Screech, and Trauma), would not admit me today to the Hopkins seminar I preside over, some of whose members are already publishing their homework. By the time I left Baltimore in 1953 to begin a long circumstantial self-exile from home waters, I had begun to find my general subject matter, but it took me two years beyond that—of imitating Faulkner, imitating Joyce, imitating Boccaccio imitating the *Arabian Nights*—to get a bona fide handle on it: to book Ulysses and Scheherazade aboard a tidewater showboat with Yours Truly doubling at the helm and the steam calliope, arranging language no longer for the Others but for others.

TEACHING

All of us writhers, screechers, and traumers took for granted that we'd do something else for a living while we practiced our vocation. I make that clear to my students today, at our first meeting, though it

would doubtless go without saying: that even the gifted apprentice novelists among them had better plan their economic lives the way poets have
had to do since the Romantic period.

I myself chose teaching, by a kind of passionate default or heartfelt
lack of alternatives: Though demanding, it was less abusive and exhaust-
ing of my resources than the other things I'd tried—manual labor, office
work—and the hours, pay, and future seemed better for a family man,
which I had become, than those of a small-time pick-up musician. One
last late afternoon in Baltimore, a like-minded friend and I discussed how
we might honorably spend our professional academic lives while doing
with our left hands the thing that mattered to us most. Ben decided he
would spend his answering all rhetorical questions: If someone should
ask, with a bored smile, "Who's to say, after all, what's Real and what
isn't?" he'd say "Check with me" and run the questioner rigorously
through the history of metaphysics. I decided I'd spend mine saying all
the things that go without saying: staring first principles and basic distinctions out of countenance; facing them down, for my students' benefit
and my own, until they confess new information. What is literature?
What is fiction? What is a story?

One of those things is that some things a writer dislikes (at least
wouldn't have chosen) may nevertheless be good for him, as a writer. I
am an inert sort who, left to himself, might never have exited the
womb—I was as comfortable there as in turbid-tidal-tepid Langford
Creek, off the Chester River, off Chesapeake Bay, where I live now, and,
unlike most folks, I had company—though it is doubtless better for me, as
a writer, that I was obliged to do so (a full hour and a quarter after my
primo sister). I had as leave stayed on in Baltimore, but the exigencies of
the academic job market took me north of Mason's and Dixon's for
twenty years: first to Penn State, where I learned to love the vast multifariousness and rough democracy of big American state universities, and got
so thirsty for open water that I cleared my throat and published my first
three books, all set in Maryland; then to SUNY/Buffalo, where I published the next three and learned to like cities again and to savor (especially in the noisy late 1960s) another sort of border state: the visible
boundary of our troubled republic and the comforting sight of great
Canada across the river, where the geese come from: haven for dispos-
sessed Americans in every upheaval since the States united. I had rather
been back at Penn State (where I had rather been back at Johns Hopkins
[where I had rather been back in the womb]), but as a writer I'm glad to

have sniffed tear gas and to have heard—if only like Odysseus tied to the mast—the siren songs of Marshall McLuhan and my friend Leslie Fiedler.

It goes without saying that what the original sirens sang to that canny other sailor must have been something like "You can't go home again," and that that song ain't so very far from wrong. As with Heraclitus's man standing by the river, into the same which he cannot step twice, it isn't only the Home that changes, but the You, too, and so you can't and can.

I did, sort of, some years back. The tidewater I returned to was not, 30,000 tide-turns later, the tidewater I'd left, nor was the leaver the re-turner, though to protect the innocent no names had been changed. If between twins as they get older less and less goes without saying, in a good marriage between a man and a woman or a writer and his place so much more every season goes without saying that should I grow as old and wise as Sophocles I'll never get it all said.

But I intend to try.

How to Make a Universe

THE REST of these Friday-pieces are arranged more or less in the order of their composition, presentation, or publication.

The semi-expatriate American writer Gore Vidal has denigrated American universities as "a branch of show business." Most non-American writers I've met, whatever they think of our universities in general, are either politely amused by or openly contemptuous of our "creative writing" programs—virtually non-existent outside the U.S.A., as they were *inside* the U.S.A. before World War II. The raw numbers involved in that quixotic enterprise certainly invite some skepticism: See my Friday-piece "Doing the Numbers," farther on in this book.

But I share neither of these attitudes and do not admire the judgment of those who do. One of the considerable pleasures, for this writer, of working full-time in various American universities has been the opportunity to hear other writers—foreign, domestic, "academic," nonacademic, anti-academic, even anti-rational—perform and talk about their inventions, as well as lecture upon other matters, well or badly, but seldom unrevealingly.

Writing well and reading or discussing well are separate talents. Some of those who contemn "the writer in the university" have also maintained that the best writers are not likely to be good performers of their work, much less good discussers of it, even if they are willing to field questions from students and apprentice writers about their own productions. This opinion—most often held by writers ill at ease with live audiences or defensive for one reason or another about the general academic-intellectual enterprise of higher education—is as untrue as is its opposite: There is simply no correlation either way between the two (or among the three) competencies.

My own pleasure for the past twenty years or so has been to visit overnight, on the average of once a month during the academic year, some campus other than home base. Such a visit normally entails an informal seminar with students of literature and (if the college offers fiction-writing courses) with apprentice writers, as well as a public lecture or an hour's reading from work in progress. These annual nine or ten overnighters help pay the rent and interfere in no way with my responsibilities to either my muse or my students. On the contrary: They provide me with a change of scenery, an inside look at every sort of academic institution and writing program from the Ivy League to Southwest Succotash Vo-Tech (it is a rule of thumb, with many exceptional fingers, that the prestige of a college correlates inversely with its lecture fees), and an outside look at most of our republic. The sovereign states of Alaska, Idaho, Montana, Nevada, New Mexico, and Utah, as of this writing, are the only ones in which I have yet to set lectorial foot. These flying junkets also alarm my wife, whose faith in gravity exceeds her confidence in aerodynamics; and they oblige me to meet and talk and listen to many more strangers than I otherwise would. Nine times out of ten I enjoy the excursion. American colleges and their students and faculties, especially the less distinguished ones, are so unalike except in their democracy that but for the lower class of criminals I think few segments of our society are unrepresented there (many offer extension courses for convicts). Certainly the poor, the dull, the ignorant, the mad, the merely cranky, the inarticulate, the illogical, the illiterate, and the unlettered have their campus contingents, as do their contraries.

Except for a 1979 swing through German and Austrian universities with William Gass, John Hawkes, and our spouses—a sort of postmodernist road show—I have never done a campus "tour," and I am not tempted to do one. Fewer than one overnight per month would defamiliarize the material and leave me vulnerable to platform jitters, which I never normally suffer; more would make me feel in show business indeed, and as a former musician I fear I'd come to like the feeling. Anyhow I enjoy staying home.

So: Once a month times ten months times twice ten gives a couple hundred lecture-readings per twenty years, a number I regard as neither large nor small. Those readings have taught me some differences between fiction for the eye and fiction for the ear and have sharpened my appreciation of both the oral and the printed narrative traditions. More important, they have relieved the essential solitariness of writing and have given me the chance to hear how my stories and opinions play in the provinces as well as in the academic capitals.

One wintry white interval between two periods of my life, I lived alone in a summer cottage on Chautauqua Lake, in far western New York—deserted in that deep-snow season—and commuted up the terminal stretch of the New York State Thruway to my classes at SUNY/Buffalo. The temporary solitude was not disagreeable, and I was shown that the second loneliest job in the world is that of the single ticket-taker in the Westfield toll plaza, that minor last exit on the great Thruway. Second loneliest, because even he or she, in that moment when your fingers hold one end of the Thruway ticket and his/hers hold the other, enjoys a simulacrum of direct human contact.

But the writer's sentences are written into the void. Even when all three hundred passengers on an A-300 Airbus are reading the same bestseller-of-the-moment, its author's transaction with them is individual, mediated, solitary, anesthetic. A spooky art, writing, when you think about it.

A writer needn't think about it, or may well simply shrug his shoulders if he does. In any case, it can be refreshing—for one who enjoys college students and their teachers and their schools; who after thirty-five years of professoring is still mildly excited by blackboards and mortarboards and the strains of *Gaudeamus Igitur*—once a month to put by for a day his practice of the Solitary Virtue, fly off to an off-campus campus, and share his fabrications with a live audience instead of a merely living one.

Among the first places ever to invite me to do that was Hiram College, a pleasant, small mainly-liberal-arts campus in the town of Hiram, in the pleasant-small-college-abounding state of Ohio. Hiram College was principally philanthropized by Hoover vacuum-sweeper money and maintains a benevolent connection with a Protestant denomination called The Disciples of Christ, the Hoover heirs being of that persuasion. On December 1, 1960, when I was thirty years old and had published my first three novels—*The Floating Opera, The End of the Road,* and *The Sot-Weed Factor*—I was invited by a friend on the Hiram faculty to fly out from Penn State, where I then taught, and address one of the college's periodic faculty-student convocations. I had given a few readings here and there from my fiction, but this was my first proper public lecture. Gentle present editing disguises neither its brashness nor its naïvety, but I continue to believe the main things it says.

Everybody knows that nowadays many of our American poets and writers and some of our painters and composers of "serious" music work in our colleges and universities. People who concern themselves with the state of the arts occasionally worry whether this is a good thing. Can great art come from a person who works decent hours for a decent wage and owns an automobile and supports a family? Aren't artist types supposed to stay up all night, grow beards, take lovers, get cirrhosis of the liver, and in general astonish the bourgeoisie?

Personally, I like Tonio Kröger's remark in Thomas Mann's story ("Tonio Kröger," 1903):

> Do you want me to go about in a ragged velveteen jacket and a red waistcoat? Every artist is as bohemian as the deuce, inside! Let him at least wear proper clothes and behave outwardly like a respectable being.

But I've never been able to get very interested in the question of what sort of person an artist should be and what sort of life he ought to lead. For one thing, a glance around shows us that magnificent work can come from just about any kind of person and circumstance, however much we might prefer to believe that the great artist is also a great human being. Publicly nasty fellows like Richard Wagner, privately nasty ones like Robert Frost; coarse ones like François Rabelais, delicate ones like Marcel Proust; worldly ones like Honoré de Balzac, naïve ones like Lewis

Carroll; demi-lunatics like Ezra Pound, businessmen like Wallace Stevens; fascists, perverts, politicians, customshouse clerks, Jew baiters, humanitarians, athletes, pediatricians, private secretaries, habitual criminals—the art we admire seems to spring from anywhere.

It is curious and touching that whenever people speak of the association between artists and universities, their concern is always for the artist, that the university might corrupt him. It seems to me they might worry whether the universities won't be the ones that get corrupted. The motto of Johns Hopkins University, for example, is St. Paul's notion that the truth will make you free; but five centuries before St. Paul, Sophocles was already showing us in *Oedipus the King* that truth is morally ambivalent at its best, and at its worst catastrophic. Socrates bids us know ourselves, but Shakespeare shows that at the end of the road of self-examination and insight may very well lie paralysis of the will like Hamlet's, and abdication of one's personality. Plato regards poets as enemies of the republic. Mann declares that in the artist there's something of the sinister mountebank, something hostile to life and health and virtue. Think of Samuel Beckett's schizoid-geriatric narrators, Franz Kafka's artist-as-anorexic, or as bug. Leslie Fiedler declares (in his essay "*No!* in Thunder") that all good writers say *no* to life, *no* to order, *no* to right and wrong, justice and injustice, and all the pious categories that constitute the world.

Is it right to support such monsters at the public charge? Is it prudent to expose honest scholars to them, to say nothing of young women and men? The prospect of allowing card-carrying Communists on our faculties seems wholesome by contrast: *They* want no more than to overthrow our government and our capitalist way of life, as Senator McCarthy tells us, but the artist on this view is a cosmic subversive, an overthrower of Knowable Reality, an altogether dangerous fellow—the more so because he may look and act like an English teacher or anybody's next-door neighbor. He may actually believe himself a responsible citizen.

But don't be fooled, just because he or she might be. At Penn State, for instance, where I work, I teach three things—"humanities," literature, and fiction-writing. Of these three, my only real specialty is fiction-writing, and I'm not altogether persuaded yet that that can be taught; or, if it can, that it ought to be; or, if it ought, that I know how to teach it. So before I offer any views of mine on the construction of universes, I'll make to you the same disclaimer I make to my students: that I'm not an expert either in literature or in philosophy, but a mere storyteller. Which is to say, a professional liar.

Having established that, I don't mind pointing out that many of the makers of literature and philosophy might be regarded as professional liars, too. Perhaps it takes one to know one. What's more, you may hope with me, as not with some, that *my* lies, at least, will be of professional caliber; there's something to be said for that. I look at the history of western culture the way Kafka looked at "Amerika": His statue of Liberty, with her sword held high, may not resemble exactly the lady we've seen on Bedloe's Island, but she's arresting and piquant in her own right. Similarly, the Leibnitz or William James or Buddha I refer to this hour may not resemble the ones you know, but I can hope they'll be clever enough chaps to serve my purpose.

The question before us is, How does one make a universe?

I can't explain how. The storytellers' trade is the manufacture of universes, which we do with great or little skill regardless of explanations and interpretations. Rightly or wrongly, we had rather make things that we can't explain than explain things that we can't make. You hear it said that the novelist offers you an attitude toward life and the world. Not so, except incidentally or by inference. What he offers you is not a *Weltanschauung* but a *Welt;* not a view of the cosmos, but a cosmos itself.

Consider the great immodesty of art, compared to science and philosophy. Ortega y Gasset deplores the arrogance of the middle-class man of science, that Boeotian who has mastered one subcompartment of knowledge and therefore feels qualified to pass judgment on politics, morals, and art. Ortega is right, no doubt, and rightly extends his criticism to specialists of every ilk and stamp. But forgetting the scientists themselves, I don't know which I admire more about science, its poetry (which I'll speak of later) or its modesty. All the scientists hope to do is describe the universe mathematically, predict it, and maybe control it. The philosopher, by contrast, seems unbecomingly ambitious: He wants to *understand* the universe; to get behind phenomena and operation and solve the logically prior riddles of being, knowledge, and value. But the artist, and in particular the novelist, in his essence wishes neither to explain nor to control nor to understand the universe: He wants to make one of his own, and may even aspire to make it more orderly, meaningful, beautiful, and interesting than the one God turned out. What's more, in the opinion of many readers of literature, he sometimes succeeds.

What a botch Nature is. It's true that for some people its splendors have been testimony of God's existence. "How can anyone be agnostic?" they ask down the ages, at least since the invention of windows: "Just look out the window!" But it's equally true that Nature's indifferent cruelty and monstrous waste have led others for ages to quite different conclusions. For Lucretius the very sloppiness of the cosmos argued that the gods had had no hand in it. Dostoevsky's Ivan Karamazov cannot accept a divine program which allows for the torture and death of even one sinless little child, let alone the millions and millions who have gone that route. Robert Louis Stevenson stands aghast at what he calls "our rotatory island loaded with predatory life, and more drenched with blood, both animal and vegetable, than ever mutinied ship. . . ." To these observers, at least—who cannot be charged with insensitivity or lack of fellow feeling—our lives have neither order nor purpose; our values are cruel illusions; our conversations are tedious beyond appraisal; our bodies are preposterous, our minds a bad joke. On their view, the kindest judgment we can make upon the universe is that of the nihilists, that it is absurd. Or that of a friend of mine, a believer, who assures me that God *did* make the universe, but only by way of a heavenly graduate-school project, which may well fail to earn Him His Master's degree. Or that of Stendhal: "God's only excuse is that He doesn't exist."

By comparison, the universes of our good novelists might be said to come off well indeed. In the worlds of Henry Fielding, Jane Austen, Charles Dickens, Gustave Flaubert, James Joyce, there is nothing but has its place in an order luminously knowable to the beholder, however difficult to explain. The lives of the characters have shape and point and relationship; their conversations and actions are purposive, significant—or if dull and clumsy, they are artfully dull and clumsy. Objects and landscapes glow in their rendered essences like side-lit trees in late afternoon; through it all there breathes a beautiful economy, such as certain old philosophers dreamt of in their cosmologies.

Metaphysicians no longer subscribe, I imagine, to Aristotle's doctrine of the entelechies: the notion that everything is striving to realize its essence, the acorn to be an oak, the oak to reach absolute oakhood, the fool to be a perfect fool, and so forth. Even less popular today, I should think, would be Leibnitz's elaboration of this doctrine: his notion of the pre-established harmony of the cosmos. Leibnitz—my Leibnitz—asserts that in order for me to be absolutely and perfectly me in my quintessential mehood, I may very well require you in your very youness, and this hall in its perfect hallity; at the moment of my biography when the heavenly script calls for me to punch you in the nose, your nose, says Leibnitz, takes an ardent yearning to be punched, and the floor where you fall—or

I—has a yen to be covered up by one of us, and the air we shout into was itching to be vibrated, and so on, and so on: the music of the spheres. We may not accept Leibnitz these days as a serious describer of the universal process, but I point out to you (as Kenneth Burke has observed) that the doctrine of pre-established harmony exactly describes how Trollope's universe works, or Conrad's, or Dickens's. We speak of the "inevitability" of an excellent plot, by which we mean far more than a bleak determinism. Would Don Quixote be so quixotic if Sancho Panza were not so pragmatic? For Matt Dillon to be his Matt-Dillonest requires that Chester be absolutely Chestrian, and conversely.* Moreover, the protagonist's mere essence virtually calls into existence his antagonist, as in Hegelian dialectic: Marshal Dillon's very expertise at slinging gun creates the envy that will summon up adversaries to try his strength, and the ritual Western commences. If Oedipus did not make his vow to discover who he is, he wouldn't *be* who he is; given the vow and the circumstances, everything follows.

Does life ever work so perfectly? The Buddhists sometimes picture the universe as a cobweb strung with beads of dew, each drop reflecting all the others. In the novelist's world, not only does every thing imply every other thing and each event every other event, as Leda's egg hatched the history of Troy; but the egg itself, the dew-strung web, is an artistic whole—distinct, harmonious, and radiant—as the actual real world is not.

We now reflect on a further fact: There are no *problems* in the universe of a well-executed novel, however much it may raise problems in our own, or dramatize them, or even attempt incidentally to solve them. Consider Goethe's novel *The Sorrows of Young Werther.* Certainly it raises moral and metaphysical questions about the phenomenon of passion in *our* lives, in *our* society; it raised them acutely enough in Goethe's own time to bring numerous would-be Werthers to commit suicide like their hero. But in the novel itself, the problem is no *problem:* It's part of the plan, so much so that the story (that is to say, the universe of the novel) would be meaningless and incomplete without it. Werther's suicide is the climax and "inevitable" conclusion of a completely meaningful series of events; it is the focus of an imaginary and entirely relevant eighteenth-century German universe. The suicide of one of Goethe's readers is more likely to have been the messy termination of an incoher-

---

* Hero and sidekick, respectively, of the popular 1950s television series *Gunsmoke.*

ent string of mostly accidental causes and effects: a meaningless phenomenon in a blind universe that existed perhaps infinitely before the fellow's
birth and continues irrelevantly to exist even yet. That thought alone has
driven men to suicide; in an existentialist play like *Hamlet,* their death
would have a *point,* if merely the point of pointlessness like Hamlet's
own, or like the death of the nihilist Bazarov in Turgenev's *Fathers and
Sons.* In real life, as far as many of us can see, it has none whatever.

Consider even the fundamental problem of being, that starting-place
of ontology and religion, and no doubt the profoundest brain-teaser in
human thought. It is a problem which takes us, I think, to the very giz-
zard of art, and it shall bring us to the point of this lecture.

The problem is twofold: Why does the universe exist at all, when, as
Schopenhauer says, we can not only conceive of its nonexistence but perhaps even wish it? Such is the sentiment of Paul Valéry when he calls the
universe "a blot on the perfection of nonexistence." And second, granting
the existence of being, why is anything in the universe the way it is instead of some other way, which we can readily imagine? Why must every
action have an equal and opposite reaction, instead of, say, a proportion-
ate one, or in every tenth instance none at all? Why must falling bodies
accelerate at just thirty-two feet per second per second, and not thirty-one
or thirty-three? Why must Jupiter have twelve moons and Italy be shaped
like a boot and the date of the Norman Conquest be A.D. 1066 and all
Gaul be divided into three parts and one's wife have a freckle on her
elbow? Except to True Believers, all the "reasons" are proximate, contingent on earlier and equally arbitrary facts; but the question is ultimate.
Look at ourselves—"the disease of the agglutinated dust," Stevenson
calls us—

> . . . lifting alternate feet or lying drugged with slumber; killing, feed-
> ing, growing, bringing forth small copies of ourselves; grown upon
> with hair like grass, fitted with eyes that move and glitter in the face;
> a thing to set children screaming. . . .

How arbitrary it all is! Even if one sees much beauty in it, as I do,
how arbitrary! I have never liked the idea that art is the product of neuro-
sis, of a spiritual wound—the pearl–oyster theory of imaginative creation.
It may be true—in fact, it probably is—but I don't like it, and anyhow it
isn't the *whole* truth, or the most prior truth. It seems to me that it is in-

sight into the blind arbitrariness of physical fact, together with the gross finality of it, that upsets the thoughtful young person and sometimes makes him or her an artist. Look at it: that there is *this* man speaking at this time to these people (all with ear-bones shaped like stirrups and anvils)! One doesn't mind, really, but why must that be the only way it is?

Grübelsucht, the Germans call this wonder: the sickness of brooding curiosity. But if it is decadent, I maintain that it is a decay which feeds the root of artistry. Perhaps the artist's reaction to this unreasonable "thinginess" of things will indeed take the form of a nausea, as in Sartre's novel of that name; or perhaps of sober awe, as in Stevenson's essays. Or perhaps—and this seems more often the case with the great ones—if our chap is of hardier nervous stuff and artist to the bone, he may not even discuss the philosophical question as such, but intuitively embrace it and set to making universes of his own, transforming the apparently blank givens of existence "in the smithy of his soul" to something ordered and fine and pregnant with human significance.

There is on the coast of California, or used to be, or I wish there had been, a big *camera obscura,* of the sort that once fascinated Leonardo da Vinci. A long-focus lens on the roof of the building receives the image of the ocean and projects it by means of mirrors onto a large ground-glass plate inside the darkened room. You can stand outside and see the ocean firsthand for free, but people pay money to step inside and see it on the screen. I quite understand them: It's not the same thing at all. There is something about the dark chamber and the luminous plate that makes the commonplace enchanting. Things that may scarcely merit notice when seen directly—a tree, a rock, a seagull—these things are magically displaced, recomposed, and represented. Like the drowned man Ariel sings of in *The Tempest,* the scene is familiar and yet transfigured; things shine serene by their inner lights and are intensely interesting.

A novel works like the *camera obscura.* The arbitrary facts that make the world—devoid of ultimate meaning and so familiar to us that we can't really see them any longer, like the furniture of our living room— these facts are passed through the dark chamber of the novelist's imagination, and we *see* them, perhaps for the first time. More, we hang upon them, often with a passion—characters and events that in real life might bore us or simply escape our notice. We stand before them rapt, entranced, like the spectators at the panther's cage in Kafka's "Hunger Artist" story; we do not want ever to go away. . . . And then, because as ordinary men and women we dwell after all in *this* universe, not that one, we leave the chamber, blinking as the pupils of our eyes contract to normal. After a bit we light a cigarette, speak of something else, and proceed through a cosmos invisible to us because we're in it.

There's the point: The problem of being, so difficult in our own universe, resolves itself as if by magic in the luminescent universes of fiction, because as we read an excellent novel we are all endowed temporarily with a sort of oriental insight. I've heard it said that the Zen master who has had his *satori,* or mystic awakening, refuses to analyze his insight into Truth. If you ask him what ultimate reality is like, he may holler "Boo!" or throw his fan at you. He will not say, like Kierkegaard, that the self is a relation which relates itself to itself, and in relating itself to itself relates itself to another. Not at all. If he says anything, it will be perhaps that the crops need a good rain; on the other hand, he may burp in your face. This response is called *upaya,* or "direct pointing"; the sense of it is that as soon as Being is *conceived of*—that is, as soon as it's represented as a concept (opposed to not-Being) and therefore made problematical—the problem can't be solved. Even to say "Being simply *is*" is to impose upon Reality the human conceptions of noun, verb, and adverb, the human logic of grammar and syntax, and thus to falsify it, since there are no categories in Nature's warpless, woofless web. Therefore the Buddhist burps: He does not describe reality; he points to it. He gives you a little piece of it.

But this is just about what the artist does; this is the high philosophy of novels and statues and poems. Standing like God and the author *outside* the cosmos of a fine novel or play, we don't finally wonder why things happen as they do or why the characters are as they are. Hamlet may analyze himself (and the critics may analyze his analysis, and the critic's psychoanalyst may analyze the critic's analysis of Hamlet's analysis of Hamlet, until everything starts to sound like Kierkegaard's definition of the self), but you and I, from outside, we sense that within the story everything's existence is its own justification; we feel the harmony, the necessity, the truth of it all, noumenal and glowing like the *camera obscura.*

This is perhaps a clue to our universe that the novelist offers in his immodest and subversive resemblance to God. Consider all art for a moment as *upaya:* an enormous burp in the face. Consider that if the novelist is like God and a novel like the universe, then the converse ought to have at least some metaphorical truth: The universe is a novel; God is a novelist! (I have observed elsewhere that the trouble with God is not that He's a *bad* novelist; only that He's a realistic one, and that dates Him.)*

We've all heard the commonplace, from atheists as well as believers, that the universe is a work of art. But look what happens to some of the "agonizing questions of our time," of all times—the Freshman Anthology questions—if that proposition is regarded rigorously instead of sentimentally. Take the great Search for Meaning and Purpose in Life, for instance—the ostensible theme of so much modern literature. On this view, those who seek an *idea* in the universe are like those who demand ideas in a work of art, and the fact is (I'm paraphrasing the aesthetician George Boas), while you can't really keep ideas *out* of a poem, say, as Amy Lowell wanted to do, nevertheless the ideas are never the main thing. The *idea* of many of Shakespeare's sonnets is "When I am blue, I think of you." Archibald MacLeish declares that a poem must not mean, but be; we may now declare that the universe must not mean, but be.

And we may bid good-bye to the problem of value, for if the values of the universe are like the values of a novel, the truest thing about them is that they're by no means necessarily shared by the characters, or even comprehensible to them. There is a grand dramatic irony in the world. Our search for meaning, even our dialogues with God, are like those interactions between characters and author in the novels of Unamuno and Gide, or Pirandello's famous play; the author is in charge even when challenged by his creatures, and the Author who thus participates as a character isn't the real author at all. The real author lives and works in a dimension quite other than that of his creatures (but reminiscent of theirs—he has made them in his image). By what equipment can Tom Jones perceive Henry Fielding? His reason, his technology if he has any, are *absurd,* as ours are absurd. Even a dogged faith on his part that there is a Henry Fielding would be absurd. Did Alexey Karamazov's universe "begin" at a point in time, or has it existed infinitely? The fact that Dostoevsky wrote the novel in 1880 seems clearly irrelevant; the whole question is unintelligible.

Even the problem of God's "intention" in creating the universe becomes rather beside the point. An artist may quite fail to reach his goal, for one thing—Faulkner tells us that all novels are failed poems. Or he may not even know what his deepest intentions are until some critic (or theologian) tells him. The novelist's intention may escape us altogether—

---

* But also keeps bringing Him back into fashion.

at least the characters can't guess it!—and anyhow we're all aware of the "intentional fallacy" the critics speak of: If we see a meaning in the universe different from the author's intended one, ours may be quite as valid as his, other things being equal. The fact is, a work of art has a life of its own, and so in this sense does the universe. Different people, including the author, see different things in it, and all may be right in a way and wrong in a way, for the universe "means" many things and nothing, like a great novel (though it may not mean just any old thing a freshman reader wants it to mean).

I conclude that the nihilism of the kind of artist I have been describing is not the nihilism of Lucretius or John Dewey or Jean-Paul Sartre; it is God's nihilism. Artists are ethical nihilists in that, however passionate their commitments as people and citizens, as artists they are indifferent to values exterior to their work, which is in this respect morally neutral. But they are anti-nihilists in that, like God, they make pieces of art, universes which *are,* and (relatively speaking) nothing can be absoluter than that. Art ends up being for art's sake no matter what the artist had in mind; reality is for its own sake regardless of God; and so finally even the question of God's existence and nature, like the question of Homer's or Shakespeare's existence and nature, becomes academic.

This criticism of the universe sounds a little like the old New Criticism of literature, and may lie open to some of the same objections. But literary critics, both New and Old, are after all seeking to *explain* works of literature by means of analysis, and I'm not. The critic operates as a more or less skillful anatomist of literature; I'm regarding the universe here as a novelist reading another fellow's novel. There are some Godawful boners in it—yet, as Horace reminds us, even good Homer sometimes slept. There are master strokes as well, to make any other novelist envious: The first law of embryology, for instance—that ontogeny recapitulates phylogeny—is as poetic a fancy as anything in literature. I wish I'd thought of it. And the second law of thermodynamics, the principle of universal entropy, informs the whole show with a splendid dying fall. My point is that this grand and complex entity after all *is,* as *Huckleberry Finn* finally is, beyond philosophy, theology, literary criticism, and the sometimes torturing attempts of its inhabitants to understand it and their place in it.

Now, it goes without saying that this view of God and His fellow fabricators implies nothing whatever about the way you should run your life. It aims at no direct bearing on the problems and desires that harass you, whatever they may be, any more than art does—and yet, of course, like art, it has every relevance to those problems. The hero of my first novel begins by believing that "nothing makes any ultimate difference," and decides to end his life; he ends by realizing that if nothing makes any difference, that truth makes no ultimate difference either, and so rather than committing suicide he predicts that he'll go on living in much the same manner as before. Yet obviously there *will* be a kind of difference from then on. It's the same difference experienced by Kierkegaard's man-who-has-come-through: He goes about his daily round as always, but he is "every moment leaping perfectly and surely into the infinite, the absurd, and every moment falling smoothly and surely back into the finite." Similarly, that which is attained by the final enlightenment of certain Buddhists is called *wu-shih,* a term that means "nothing special": Alan Watts, the student of Zen, quotes Professor Suzuki, the Zen master, on the subject of how it feels to have attained *satori,* or awakening: "Just like ordinary everyday experience," Suzuki declares, "except about two inches off the ground."

So. If you ask a novelist to explain his novels, don't be surprised if he merely cries *"Boo!"* If I were God, that's how I'd answer my theologians.

More on the Same Subject

ON THE AFTERNOON before or the morning after one's public lecture comes the Informal Open Seminar With Interested Students of Writing or Literature. In the course of that aforementioned maiden lecture-trip to Hiram College, I opened my maiden IOSWISOWOL thus:

How many of you are familiar with W. H. Auden's sonnet "The Novelist"?

[*Show of hand.*]

Let me refresh your memories:

THE NOVELIST

Encased in talent like a uniform,
The rank of every poet is well known;
They can amaze us like a thunderstorm,
Or die so young, or live for years alone.

They can dash forward like hussars: but he
Must struggle out of his boyish gift and learn
How to be plain and awkward, how to be
One after whom none think it worth to turn.

For, to achieve his lightest wish, he must
Become the whole of boredom, subject to
Vulgar complaints like love, among the Just
Be just, among the Filthy filthy too,
And in his own weak person, if he can,
Must suffer dully all the wrongs of Man.

This poem helps account for the famous fact that young people's fiction—I mean fiction written by, not for, young people—is seldom very good. At least not as often as good as their poetry is. A look through almost any undergraduate literary magazine will bear out this painful truth, as will a review of literary biography: The actuarial profile of fiction-writers, especially of novelists, shows a slower maturation curve than that of lyric poets, theoretical physicists, mathematicians, and chess players.

The last two lines of Auden's poem also imply one famous view of what the novelist's *function* is: a view echoed before the fact in Stephen Dedalus's celebrated vow (in James Joyce's *A Portrait of the Artist as a Young Man,* last chapter) "to forge in the smithy of [his] soul the uncreated conscience of [his] race."

Well. I have come from State College P A to Hiram O in order to wonder aloud in your presence what a novel is and what it's for—an activity suspicious at best and pernicious at worst. Pernicious because in the artist's worst case, talking about his art may become a substitute for making it; suspicious—let's say suspect—because what artists say about their art must often be taken with a grain of salt. They may speak vaguely of "inspiration," for example, when the fact is that their assiduously practiced discipline has become such second nature that they're no longer conscious of its complex operation. They may truly not understand their own work, in the critical-analytical way in which a professional talker-about-art understands it. Or they may be pulling the public leg: I think of Robert Frost's insistence that his poem "Stopping by Woods on a Snowy Evening," which has to do with a muted and deferred death wish, has nothing to do with a muted and deferred death wish, as John Ciardi and others insist it does, but is merely and literally about stopping by woods on a snowy evening. I think of William Faulkner's reportedly replying—to an interviewer who asked him whether *The Sound and the Fury* is not "on one level" a debate among the Id, the Ego, and the Superego—"Wouldn't s'prise me atall."

This foot-shuffling, shit-kicking, finger-in-the-collar, I'm-just-a-pore-country-cracker pose is Mister Mark Twain's legacy to American writers. I can't imagine Hawthorne, Emerson, Poe, Melville, or even Thoreau indulging in it. I myself find it unbecoming, though I understand the impulse. I am no friend of anti-intellectuality; anti-intellectuality, even anti-intelligence, has enough friends already, and does not need me. Yes-

terday I remarked that it's no doubt better to be able to make wonderful
things that you can't explain than to be able to explain wonderful things
that you can't make. I affirm that opinion today; but as a writer who also
tries to teach literature (I mean teach students; I'm not likely to teach literature anything), and who happens to admire and respect good scholarship, I here go on record as believing that neither talent—the talent for
making or the talent for explaining—is to be sneezed at. The gift of explaining wonderful things that you can't yourself make—novels, paintings, trees, animal courtship rituals, planetary movements—is also a
wonderful thing. Better, certainly, than being able *neither* to make nor to
explain.

So: The question before us this December 1960 morning is What are
novels for? And the answer is Any damn thing you want to use them for.
For their readers, collectively, they may be public psychotherapy, as
Aristotle seems to say Greek tragedy was: I take that to be the general
sense of Auden's poem. For their readers individually, novels may function as extensions of or alternatives to their single mortality: Even the
Bonapartes evidently found it tiresome to be *just* Bonapartes; they all
read novels, and most of them wrote novels, too. Novels may function as
criticisms of life, as criticisms of society, as ideological or moral propaganda. They may function as aphrodisiacs, soporifics, items of interior
decoration, doorstops. The Doubleday hardcover first edition of my
novel *The Sot-Weed Factor* happens to weigh almost exactly two pounds
and has a dust jacket drawn by the wonderful artist Edward Gorey; you
might frame that dust jacket for your Edward Gorey collection and use
the text as a kitchen-scale counterweight to tell whether your roast of beef
weighs more or less than two pounds. You might also read the book.

As for the novelist himself, his motives may be as multifarious as his
readers'. To be sure, he may be out to forge racial conscience in the
smithy of his soul or to suffer dully in his own weak person all the wrongs
of man. On the other hand, he may aim for nothing more nor less than
aesthetic bliss—that's what Vladimir Nabokov says *his* pure and total aim
is. But the journals and biographies of the great novelists teach us that
their novels also served for them such important functions as sources of
income, of prestige, of social or sexual or career advancement; as outlets
for their smart or cranky ideas or their mere spleen; as escape from their
spouses, their kids, their chores. In short, as just about anything imaginable.

This being the case, we must allow that what a novel is may be more than or different from what it's for. I propose we drop the *for* and address the *is*.

My contention, as some of you heard yesterday, is that a novel is not essentially a view of this universe (though it may reflect one), but a universe itself; that the novelist is not finally a spectator, an imitator, or a purger of the public psyche, but a maker of universes: a demiurge. At least a semidemiurge. I don't mean this frivolously or sentimentally. I don't mean it even as a figure of speech (as Joyce does, elsewhere in the *Portrait,* when he speaks of the artist as God, standing in the wings of his creation, paring his fingernails). I mean it literally and rigorously: The heavy universe we sit in here in Hiram, Ohio, and the two-pound universe of *The Sot-Weed Factor,* say, are cousins, because the maker of this one and the maker of that one are siblings.

This contention will strike you as immodest. It is.

Questions?

An Afterword to *Roderick Random*

I AM NO SCHOLAR. Because my 1960 novel *The Sot-Weed Factor* betrays some familiarity with Colonial America and the eighteenth-century English novel, some readers have reasonably but mistakenly inferred that I must know a good deal about those subjects. For the purposes of fiction, however, a novelist can become sufficiently knowledgeable about almost anything in a hurry. To authenticate a mere passing metaphor—one drawn from sailing, say, or medieval siege warfare—the writer may read a whole book on the subject; on the other hand, two chapters on testamentary law may enable him to do a courtroom scene upon which his whole plot turns.

To be sure, many novels are written out of long and deep acquaintance with their materials, and all great novels, one supposes, out of deep acquaintance with their subject. The distinction is useful: more upon it in the Friday-piece "About Aboutness," farther on. With the *subject* of *The Sot-Weed Factor*—innocence—I was guilty of much experience, but its eighteenth-century materials I worked up ad hoc and promptly afterwards forgot. In this respect a novelist may be the opposite of an iceberg: Nine-tenths (Or is it four-fifths? Six-sevenths? It is eight-ninths: I have just looked it up for the purposes of this metaphor) of what he knows—about icebergs, say—may be right there on the surface of the page for which he learned it.

Thus when the editors of the Signet Classics invited me in 1963 to write an introductory essay (published as an afterword in the format for that series) to their edition of Tobias Smollett's 1748 novel *Roderick Random**, they innocently assumed me to be something of an eighteenth-century specialist. I responded that I had in fact neither read anything at all of Smollett's nor ever written a literary essay. *They* responded, in effect, Why not try both? I did.

Rereading the result twenty years later, I hear what we call the 1960s beginning to rumble in its latter pages. And I confess to being tantalized by how nearly I uttered, at the end, the now talismanic word *postmodern*. Oh, well.

---

* New York: Signet Books, 1964.

Among the pleasures of Smollett is that one swift reading does him. He wrote quickly and not too carefully, and might as well be read that way; close and repeated goings-over of *Roderick Random, Peregrine Pickle,* and the rest will add little to what one gathered the first time through, and are likely to prove somewhat tiresome, like a second ride on the same roller coaster.

No use looking in *Roderick Random* for "deeper meanings," for example, or any significances beyond the obvious. After its brilliant opening, in which Roderick's mother dreams herself delivered of a tennis ball by the devil, the story is as literal and explicit as its hero-narrator, who reports his extremes of mood as glibly as if they were external events, like his shifting fortunes: *I am seized with a deep melancholy and become a sloven—I am more and more happy—I am treacherously knocked down—I am married.* Even the remarkable dream is explained at once, lest we dally over it, and however teasingly inadequate the Highland seer's analysis, it is characteristic that the dream turns out to mean exactly and unironically what he says it means: that Roderick will travel a great deal, suffer adversity, return, and flourish. We later readers may wonder why that tennis ball buried itself at Mrs. Random's feet, say, and why it was the perfume of the blossoms, exactly (of the shrub the ball then turned into), that woke her up, and whether the "strong operations" of that perfume were pleasant or disturbing. Readers in a good many earlier centuries might have shared our curiosity. But Smollett does not, nor apparently did most of his contemporaries. To give a name like "Captain Weazel" to a loud-mouthed little coward is about as far as he ventures in the extra-meaning way—blithely forgetting even so that two sentences earlier he'd likened the captain to "a spider or grasshopper erect," called him "a . . . coxcomb," and dressed him in "a frock of what is called bearskin." Some weasel! For the rest, the action of this "first and greatest of all sea stories," as *Roderick* has been misbilled (ignoring not only the *Odyssey,* for instance, but the fact that little more than a third of the book has anything to do with seafaring), is played out strictly on the surface.

And a bawdy, glistering surface it is, eighteenth-century England! The Scyllas and Grendels whom earlier heroes dealt with have been evicted by the Age of Reason, to be replaced by Crampleys and Mackshanes; only a more-or-less mad intelligence like Blake's saw clearly that the dragons weren't exterminated at all but had merely retired, into caves and deeps inaccessible to the Enlightenment, there to change costume and await the next act. Formerly the monsters came after *us,* or met us at the threshold of their realm, and we did our best with magic weapons and magic words. Latterly, armored in bathyscaphes and the formulas of depth psychology, we go down after them. In either case, and as foe or quarry, the adversary is acknowledged and the issue joined. But the world of Fielding and Smollett, if treacherous enough, is nowise mysterious; their heroes' way is stormy but never dark; Roderick voyages out to Paraguay and Guinea, but not to that place where, Homer tells us, "East and West mean nothing"—where form and time, reason and identity, all go by the board. When Aeneas hears the wingbeats of a bird, it turns out to be Celaeno the Harpy; when Roderick and Strap are beset by a demon, it turns out to be somebody's pet raven—Ralpho by name. Nice ladies aforetime not infrequently proved to be witches; Mrs. Sagely, who shelters Roderick after the shipwreck, is suspected of witchcraft but turns out to be a nice lady. Although in both instances the appearance differs from the reality, to the eighteenth-century storyteller it was the reality for a change that appeared less awesome and more interesting, however rough in some features. *Divine,* for better or worse, no longer meant goddish, merely sexy (e.g., "that divine creature" Narcissa, a "gift of Providence" whose "angelic charms" include an "Elysian" décolletage). *Devilish* no longer meant diabolical, either literally or figuratively, but devil-may-care: The fellow mistaken for Old Nick in Chapter XXXVII is Roderick himself. To the rough-and-ready rationalism of the time, the devil is only a scapegrace, and the deep blue sea is only wide. A kind of outer darkness, so to speak, which formerly had shadowed the surface of things, was dispersed for good and all; their inner darkness had yet to be reappreciated. Dante's Beatrice and the ghost of Hamlet's father lay behind; Moby-Dick and Kafka's bug-man lay ahead; in the meanwhile, fetching or foul, hurrah for the literal skin of things! Homer's Penelope is more than a wife: She's Destination. Joyce's Molly Bloom is among other things a Female Principle. But Fielding's Sophie Western is only a woman, and Smollett's Narcissa is scarce even that: Not truly a body, much less an embodiment, she's a mere bright-skinned reflection of the hero's self-esteem: a comely face, a fetching bosom, and an utterly noncosmic womb.

In short, *Roderick Random* is a novel of nonsignificant surfaces—which is not to say it's a superficial, insignificant novel, any more than the age that produced it, the age that invented the English novel, was superficial or insignificant.

And while you're not looking for implicit meanings, don't look for niceties of structure, either. There *is* no structure to *Roderick Random* beyond the most official sort of long-range suspense, dutifully laid on. We know very well, and could hardly care less, that Roderick will wind up with Narcissa, who in any case doesn't enter the tale until more than halfway through. As to the how of his getting her—the long-lost wealthy parent who turns up like Daddy Warbucks in the nick of time—perhaps the less *said* about that clanking device the better. The particular nature and order of Roderick's encounters, unlike those of Candide or Don Quixote, are without consistent point, incremental meaning, "inevitability," relevance to character, or cumulative force; they are—precisely—random, and could lightly be extended, abridged, or re-arranged without much loss of effect. Moreover, Smollett never delays us with complexities (or beauties) of language, nor with very subtle insight into character, nor with subtle paradox, subtle ambivalence, subtle analysis, or subtle wit. There is no subtlety in the man, any more than there is breadth of vision, breathtaking artistry, masterful psychology, or dazzling invention. To the moral and metaphysical limitations of the eighteenth century he adds the artistic limitations of the picaresque mode at its most undisciplined, and flavors the mixture with various shortcomings of his own.

Thus Roderick's indignation at cruelty, hypocrisy, affectation, ingratitude, and dishonesty, for example, is unfailingly acute when he is their victim; otherwise it's not to be counted on, despite the pious advertisement of the Preface, for he is himself capable of most of these vices—though he seldom *approves* of them, even while enjoying them. We see him at one moment stirred to compassion for hapless prostitutes, whose wretched lot is described by his fellow-gonorrhetic Miss Williams; at another his spirits are "so much elevated, that nothing [will] serve [him] but a wench," and he looks on unmoved while the drunken Bragwell kicks "half a dozen hungry whores" in Moll King's coffeehouse, just for the hell of it. He can be charitable to those who have injured him, if fortune has well punished them already—thus he cures Miss Williams of her venereal infection and forwards ten pistoles to Mackshane in prison—but more typically he'll hold a grudge for sixty chapters, and as he himself cheerfully admits, he's not above maltreating even the faithful Strap: "In spite of all the obligations I owed to this poor honest fellow, ingratitude is so natural to the heart of man, that I began to be tired of his acquaint-

ance. . . ."* He has no more interest in religion as such than does the Ca-
puchin cocksman Balthazar, but is glibly anti-Catholic and anti-
Semitic. His service on Uncle Tom Bowling's slave ship he finds merely
"disagreeable"—and not on moral grounds at that, but because the Ne-
groes have the bad grace to die in large numbers "of an epidemic fever,
not unlike the jail distemper," during their six weeks in the hold. The
novel's humor is mainly of the bedroom-and-chamberpot variety, running especially to more or less sadistic and unimaginative practical jokes.
Money and sex Roderick values—enough at least to fawn, bribe, intrigue,
smuggle, seduce, deceive, dissemble, and defraud to have them—but
what he really gets his kicks from is revenge. To break a sycophantic
tutor's incisors and flog the bare buttocks of a tyrant schoolmaster give
him at least as much satisfaction as his learning itself ever does (and
Roderick's, like Smollett's, is not inconsiderable); one doubts, moreover,
that his final good fortune would have been complete without the comeuppance of his old antagonists. Not enough that the "female cousins" be
sent away envious, empty-handed, and muttering in the last chapter:
Smollett must marry one to a pauper and sire a footman's bastard on the
other to perfect their ignominy.

Now, *peripeteia* in the form of sheer revenge is as old as the narrative
imagination; Routing the Pretenders is the bloody denouement-work of
Odysseus, Perseus, Aeneas, Watu Gunung, and a hundred other knock-
about heroes. And prideful ire is a standard mainspring of adventure: the
anger of Poseidon, the anger of Juno. But seldom does the wrath of the
protagonist himself link episode to episode, and in the temperament of no
other heroes that I know of does pure vindictiveness play quite so large a
role as in Smollett's. Heart, head, and hormones all have their influence
on Roderick's behavior, but his special organ is the spleen. *I form cabals
against the pedant—demolish the teeth of* [a] *tutor—form a project of re-*

---

* A sentiment altogether consonant with the one Weighty Observation of which
Smollett delivers himself in the novel: "I have found by experience that, though small
favours may be acknowledged and slight injuries atoned, there is no wretch so un-
grateful as he whom you have most generously obliged, and no enemy so implacable
as those who have done you the greatest wrong." Strap's virtues have been overrated
anyhow. He has none of the ingratiating attributes of other notable sidekicks: the
hard-knock cynicism of Sancho Panza, the man-to-man devotion of Roland's Oliver,
the ebullient roguery of Falstaff, the nick-of-time helpfulness of Tarzan's Cheetah. His
bumbling is dangerous, his cowardice not especially amusing, his fidelity self-in-
terested and feckless. A poor foil and a worse advisor, unresourceful and indifferently
diverting, he more than merits Roderick's occasional abuse—though not always at just
the time it's laid on him.

venge—concert a scheme of revenge—conceive a mortal hatred—revenge myself on my rival—In order to be revenged, learn the science of defence—resent their disdain—long to be revenged on Melinda—resolve to revenge myself on Strutwell—thus run the headings, chapter after chapter. What hunger is to Lazarillo de Tormes and lust to Don Juan Tenorio, resentment is to Roderick Random: more than a drive; almost an organizing principle. Odysseus wants to get home; Jason, to get the Fleece; Roderick, to get even.

In this respect as in some others the creature is the image of his maker, a pugnacious and unforgiving soul in whose disposition, as in Roderick's, "pride and resentment . . . were two chief ingredients. . . ." Smollett's father, like "Don Rodrigo," married against *his* father's will, and while old Sir James Smollett stopped short of disowning young Archibald, he limited his bounty to the tenancy of Dalquhurn, the little farm where Tobias was born and where Archibald died two years after siring him. Biographers remind us that there's no factual evidence either to support or to refute the common assumption that Smollett's childhood was as bitter as Roderick's; the ferocious tone of those first five chapters rings awfully true, though, and Smollett hadn't that gift of Hamlet's player, so useful to any fictionist, "in a dream of passion, [to] force his soul . . . to his own conceit. . . ." As Lewis Melville remarks, "He could not invent: he could only exaggerate." We do know that the hard-luck story of Mr. Melopoyn, that tedious, ill-placed diversion near the end of *Roderick Random,* reflects young Tobias's experience with his first literary effort, a play called *The Regicide*—more a catastrophe than a tragedy—as well as his own opinion of its merits and his imputation of stupidity or malice to any who disagreed. He lampooned and caricatured its critics at every opportunity, and as soon as he had funds enough—from *Roderick Random*—published *The Regicide* at his own expense, with a spiteful preface against its detractors.*

The incident is typical: Excepting possibly his youthful stint in the Royal Navy (of which the nautical portion of *Roderick Random* may be taken as a fair exaggeration) and the death at fifteen of his poetry-writing daughter Elizabeth, whom he adored, the external events of Smollett's life seem not arduous enough to account for his sustained outrage. Senti-

---

* "Earl Sheerwit," in Melopoyn's chronicle, corresponds to Lord Chesterfield, whose patronage Smollett sought unsuccessfully; "Supple" to Charles Fleetwood, manager of the Drury Lane Theatre; "Bellower" to John Rich of Covent Garden; "Brayer" to Willoughby Lacy, Garrick's manager; and "Marmozet" to Garrick himself.

mental biographers and fellow novelists like Disraeli and Walter Scott are inclined to overstate—as doubtless Smollett himself did—his vicissitudes and adversities, perhaps to justify his native bad temper; they are inclined to picture him as the impoverished artist, neglected by the public, exploited by the publishers, exhausted by obligatory hackwork, "perishing in a foreign land," and all that. This is mostly nonsense, unless Scott's own golden career is used as the standard; more artists than not have suffered greater hardship than Smollett ever did. Recognition as an author came early to him, if not early enough, and his productivity, while certainly of uneven excellence, was unimpaired to the year of his death. Both his medical practice (in Downing Street, Bath, and Chelsea) and his editorial ventures (with the *Critical Review* and *The Briton*) were for the most part moderately successful; his potboiling *Travels, History of England, Compendium of Voyages,* translations, and the rest, are no longer read, but seem after all to have boiled a pot which would have simmered even without them. His Creole wife, Anne Lascelles, evidently shared Narcissa's "divinity": the affectionate docility, the substantial dowry, the "angelic charms" above all. Not every man's cup of tea, maybe, but, as some critic has observed, it is a type that many novelists are inclined to marry, even without the Jamaican estate, and one bets they have their reasons. Smollett, we're told, was now and then bored with her, but affectionate and not unfaithful; and Anne, who had a great deal more to put up with than he did, stuck with him until his death and honored his memory until hers: better than par for the course, I'd say. His health, if less than robust, rarely cramped his style or otherwise much burdened him until his last year, when it gave out altogether. Most interesting, perhaps, his esteem for himself and his work never flagged; his critics remained invariably fools and knaves, and to anguish of the spirit he was a stranger. Finally, if he died in Italy it was because, always an ardent traveler, he happened to be living there at the time, and he had stopped there because he liked the place, not because of any enforced or voluntary exile. There are lots of worse places than Tuscany to die in. Much of what misfortune he did suffer was directly or indirectly his own doing, not that *that* ever made anything easier to take; the perennial chip on his shoulder led him into lawsuits, feuds, and fisticuffs—in one case actually into jail, for calling Vice Admiral Charles Knowles in effect and in print an ignorant, irresolute liar. Yet whether the conviction of libel was just or not, even his three months in the Kings Bench prison, as Saintsbury comments, "in the case of persons who could pay, merely meant confinement to a rather expensive and inconvenient lodging, with no other hardship or interference with business or pleasure." Oliver Goldsmith, among other luminaries, dropped in to pay his respects, and John Newbery offered the prisoner the editorship of *The British Magazine.* Some season in hell!

So if, as his physician in Livorno attests, Smollett died "without trying to help himself . . . suffering from the outrages of human life, almost a misanthrope," it wasn't that his own life was particularly misfortunate. He'd be a less interesting fellow if it were. The doctor's diagnosis is good enough: "Was of a very choleric disposition," he notes farther on, "but reflective." It was the outrages of *human* life that Smollett's "passionate and fiery temperament" could not reflect upon without resentment—outrages of which his own ordinary hardships were only, so to speak, illustrations—and this fact elevates the mood of his work beyond irascible self-pity or *mere* bad temper to a level of general pertinence. For I think that while Smollett's epical resentment may be a less profound reaction to the human condition than Sophoclean pity-and-terror, say, and less inspiring than Dostoevskian compassion, it is as legitimate as either. "To what end was this world formed?" Candide inquires; as a translator of Voltaire, Smollett surely knew and concurred with Martin's reply: "To infuriate us." That being as likely a premise as another, to demolish your infuriator's teeth may be as reasonable (and therapeutic!) a mode of coping as to cultivate your garden, not to mention turning your other cheek to the blackguard. However true it may be, in our time at least, that we must love our fellow man or perish, that fact in itself doesn't make the wretch a bit more lovable; indeed, one failing of the Love-boys in our current literature is that they're inclined to understand the phrase *Love or perish* as an ultimatum instead of a fair statement of alternatives. If Smollett chose to perish, he's not the first or greatest man who ever did. If he found life mainly exasperating even when comfortable, and his neighbor generally tiresome even when pacific, we're not likely to hug him for telling us so, or give him the Nobel Prize, but we might be impressed by his antisentimental candor. In fact, if one has had a bellyful of Erich Fromm and J. D. Salinger, one may find Roderick Random's orneriness downright bracing, like the Rhine-wine cordial Smollett ordered on his deathbed and never got to drink.

That's one good reason for keeping *Roderick Random* in print: as a healthy, hard-nosed counteragent to the cult of love. A librarian acquaintance of mine grimaced when he saw the novel under my arm and allowed as how he'd never quite cottoned to Smollett: "All that cruelty! No warmth at all!" But how invigorating the cold Scotch air is in those opening pages, the exchange between Roderick's father and grand-father—how mean and quick and counter to every sentimental expecta-tion! How satisfying too (and more than justified, in this case) Roderick's youthful ferocity, his settling of scores with bully and pedant. No wonder young David Copperfield, suffering the tyranny of the Murdstones, was able "[to sustain his] own idea of Roderick Random for a month at a stretch": Smollett surely helped him not only by "[keeping] alive [his] fancy, and [his] hope of something beyond that place and time," but also by providing for his vicarious relief a splendid paradigm of revenge. If only the tormentors of all our tender years had had such comeuppance at our hands!

And what refreshment, for an age when self-knowledge seems always bad news and self-despisal perforce a staple of our fiction, to holiday briefly in a world free from the curse of insight: where the wickedness lies for a change in all those *other* rascals instead of in oneself (hadn't we sus-pected it all along, but dared not say so?), and the heads of malefactors get knocked instead of examined; where no one (except ourselves the hero) has to be loved unless he pleases us; where the hero regards himself and is by others regarded—unabashedly, unironically, and unselfcon-sciously—as the devil of a good chap, "some [of whose] situations . . . had been low, but none of them infamous . . . the crime not of [him], but of [his] fortune," and who at the end wholeheartedly rejoices in a shower of blessings which he has done nothing whatever to deserve, except to be heedlessly, selfishly, exuberantly himself. The book is a tonic, a psychic energizer, and we whose self-esteem is suffering from overmuch aware-ness and responsibility may excuse its deficiencies as one puts up with the side-effects of amphetamine.

There are of course literary as well as therapeutic rewards for the reader of *Roderick Random:* quite a few, above and beyond whatever "picture-of-an-age" interest it might have, or importance to university courses in the history of the novel.* Its merits are, like Roderick's own,

---

* Richardson's *Pamela* and Fielding's *Joseph Andrews* and *Jonathan Wild,* are its only English predecessors, by eight, five, and four years respectively. Their authors—Field-ing at least—are more talented than Smollett, everyone agrees, but not necessarily in these earliest productions. When *Roderick Random* appeared, anonymously, in 1748, a number of people took it to be Fielding's work—including Lady Mary Montagu, Fielding's cousin. But Smollett's gratuitous, malicious, half-hysterical lampoons of

for the most part the virtues of its vices: the energy, robustness, and in-domitable extroversion which are the blessings of unsubtlety and insensi-tivity; the guileless candor and directness associated with artlessness, for better as well as worse—in a word, the animal, heathen *innocence* which graces the scapegrace even when he's bribing or seducing, and which isn't to be confused with either optimism or naïveté. What's more, deep waters as often run still as conversely, and at least some of what Smollett lacks in depth he gains in bedazzling speed: not the economical, strategic velocity of *Candide,* but the tumbling, ad libitum exuberance of a Mack Sennett comedy. It's inconsistent (Mr. Melopoyn's two-chapter complaint and some of the tiresome hanky-panky at Bath are barely sufferable), and it's not always effective (witness the blurred introduction of Miss Williams in the last sentences of Chapter XX—an inept, overhasty plant for her reap-pearance two chapters later), but when it goes it's a dizzy ride, in the hands of a tough-minded, thin-skinned, ebullient twenty-six-year-old with an uncommon store of experience and energy.

The ride is more exciting for the amplitude and pitch of its ups and downs. Smollett's criticism of *Gil Blas* for too-quick transitions of fortune is as inappropriate as is the rest of that silly Preface; what we prize in a roller coaster is not plausibility but precipitateness. And it is the more di-verting for the splendid variety of the passing scene. Smollett may lack breadth of vision, but width he has aplenty, in all directions, more than Richardson and Fielding combined. Sailors, soldiers, fine gentlemen and ladies, whores, homosexuals, cardsharpers, fortune hunters, tradesmen of all description, clerics, fops, scholars, lunatics, highwaymen, peasants, and poets both male and female—they crowd a stage that extends from Glasgow to Guinea, from Paris to Paraguay, and among themselves per-petrate battles, debaucheries, swindles, shanghais, duels, seductions, res-cues, pranks, poems, shipwrecks, heroisms, murders, and marriages. They wail and guffaw, curse and sing, make love and foul their breeches: In short, they *live,* at a clip and with a brute *joie de vivre* that our modern spirits can scarcely comprehend. Having allowed as much as possible for exaggeration, we are still astonished, appalled, at the way they live—and maybe a little envious, even if we wouldn't swap our anxious comfort . . .

Fielding seem to have been inspired more by resentment of Fielding's patron Lyttelton (who had committed the unpardonable sin of neglecting to read *The Regicide* when Smollett sent it to him years earlier) than by envy of Fielding's talent or popularity. Fielding's counter-lampoons are better-humored.

for the world. "Don Rodrigo" summed up the *esprit* of the action when, after hearing his son's hard history, he "blessed God for the adversity [Roderick] had undergone, which . . . enlarged the understanding, improved the heart, steeled the constitution, and qualified a young man for all the duties and enjoyments of life, much better than any education which affluence could bestow." For the enjoyments as well as the duties: That's the pregnant article in this manifesto of the literature of hard knocks.

Adventure and adversity—hazarding forth and overcoming—are what the enduring attractiveness of *Roderick Random* comes to. Those ancient, most profoundly lifelike human sports, the obstacle race and the scavenger hunt, are also the oldest, appealingest matter for the storyteller. Of painful searching and futile running around, our literature is unavoidably full, as of despair in all its Kierkegaardian varieties, including the comic; but not of proper adversity, for the obstacle race implies obstacles not regarded as insurmountable, and the scavenger hunt presumes an ultimately findable treasure. They also imply a racer, a hunter—that is, a hero, scapegrace or otherwise, not an antihero; and heroes, for good and obvious reasons, are hard come by in the age of antimatter and the antinovel. Finally, both adversity and adventure imply a certain attitude toward the obstacles and settings-out, and this attitude, the spirit of adventurousness, has also been regrettably absent in modern fiction, for the same good reasons. I say "has been" because there is evidence, in some *really* recent novels, of a renaissance of this same spirit: hints of the possibility of a post-naturalistic, post-existentialist, post-psychological, post-antinovel novel in which the astonishing, the extravagant ("outwandering"), the heroical—in sum, the adventurous—will come again and welcomely into its own. For those among us who have sustained our own idea of Roderick Random (never mind Smollet's idea of him!) not for months but for years at a stretch, it can't happen too soon.

Mystery and Tragedy

THE TWIN MOTIONS OF RITUAL HEROISM

LITERARY public-lecture-writing is not my cup of tea; it is an occasional temptation, like changing jobs or writing literary essays, to which occasionally I succumb. After "How To Make a Universe" at Hiram College, I fell into that once-a-month habit of reading publicly from my fiction, but I didn't venture another public essay-lecture until this one, four Decembers later.

By then I was in the home stretch of the novel *Giles Goat-Boy* and about to decide to change jobs, though not professions, after a dozen agreeable years at Penn State. This lecture was first delivered on December 10, 1964, at the State University of New York at Geneseo, in handsome Finger Lakes country, from where I went over to Buffalo to be interviewed for a professorship at the state university center there. It makes plain, for better or worse, some preoccupations of the *Goat-Boy* novel: preoccupations carried over from *The Sot-Weed Factor* and on into the goat-boy's successor, *Lost in the Funhouse*. It was to have been one of a series of guest lectures at Geneseo by writers on writers; for the reason explained in its opening sentence, I prayed for and was granted absolution from the series theme.

The difficulty of this visiting-lecture series for your present visitor is that although I enjoy reading pieces of my own and others' work aloud in public places, I don't know anybody else's works well enough to hold forth upon them except in the privacy of my classroom, and I don't much enjoy analyzing my own. It's sobering enough to see what curious things my novels say to other people; never mind what they say to me.

So I've decided to speak about a topic instead of a particular writer: the ritual of mythic heroism as I understand it, and some relevance of this ritual to two famous general ways of thinking about life and the world. It is a topic I would never essay if I knew very much about it; but fools rush in, and I've banked my soul anyhow on the reality of the *Limbus Fa-*

tuorum, that apartment in Hell reserved by medieval eschatologists for chaps too invincibly crankish to fit the usual categories. The fact is that the novelist, whose trade is the manufacture of universes, needs ideally to know everything, or he's liable to do an even odder job than God did. On the other hand, he doesn't need to know anything until he needs to know it, and at times it can be important for him to preserve a saving ignorance if he's to get his work done. I shall advert to this matter.

My interest in the pattern of mythical heroic adventure dates from a weekend in 1961, after my novel *The Sot-Weed Factor* had been published. That weekend, in preparation for a lecture on Virgil's *Aenead* in an undergraduate course in the humanities, I happened to read Lord Raglan's famous treatise called *The Hero* (1936). The truth or falsehood of Raglan's thesis—that myths are not derived from historical facts, but from the dramatic features of traditional rites—doesn't particularly interest me; but I was interested indeed in the remarkable generalizations he makes, at one point in the book, about the *pattern* of mythic heroism as it seems to occur in virtually every culture on the planet: a list of twenty-two prerequisites, as it were, for admission into the heroic fraternity. Some of you may be familiar with Raglan's curriculum (if you think there's a connection between this Lord Raglan and the Raglan sleeve, you're right):

1. The hero's mother is a royal virgin;
2. His father is a king and
3. Often a near relative of his mother, but
4. The circumstances of his conception are unusual, and
5. He is also reputed to be the son of a god.
6. At birth an attempt is made on his life, usually by his father or his maternal grandfather, but
7. He is spirited away, and
8. Reared by foster parents in a far country.
9. We are told nothing of his childhood, but
10. On reaching manhood he returns or goes to his future kingdom.
11. After a victory over the king and/or a giant, dragon, or wild beast,
12. He marries a princess, often the daughter of his predecessor, and (at about age 34 or 35)
13. Becomes king.
14. For a time he reigns uneventfully, and

15. Prescribes laws, but
16. He later loses favor with the gods and/or his subjects and
17. Is driven from the throne or city, after which
18. He meets with a mysterious death,
19. Often at the top of a hill.
20. His children, if any, do not succeed him.
21. His body is not buried, but nevertheless
22. He has one or more holy sepulchres.

Raglan proceeds to apply these criteria to mythical heroes, Eastern and Western, and rank them by scores, a fascinating procedure: Oedipus gets an *A,* with 21 out of 22 (he wasn't a famous legislator, though he *did* run Thebes); Moses an *A—*, with 20; Watu Gunung, of Java, checks in with a solid *B* (18 points); Nyikang of the Upper-Nile Shiluks manages a *C—* (14 points), and so forth. The temptation to play the game yourself is irresistible; if we allow the criteria to be read more or less metaphorically, Jesus and General MacArthur both come off respectably well, for example. But what struck me was that without my even having registered them for the course, my *Sot-Weed Factor* hero Ebenezer Cooke and his tutor Henry Burlingame each made fair scores, and taken together (as properly they might be, opposite sides of the same coin) they did almost as well as Oedipus—there's always one smart fellow in the class who ups the curve. Ironically, the *real* Ebenezer Cooke might have done even better: No one knows where he's buried, though the Cook's Point estate, his Holy Sepulchre on the Eastern Shore of Maryland, is presently owned and tended by a respectful New Jersey dentist. I made up a grave for my Ebenezer because I wanted to compose his epitaph, and thus inadvertently did him out of a point.

Needless to say, my curiosity was provoked, the more so when a critic remarked that my novel had been influenced by Otto Rank's *Myth of the Birth of the Hero.* I borrowed that book from the Penn State Library; I peeked into it; sure enough, the critic was right. Well now, I thought, one of two things is true: Either it's very hard to invent *any* extravagant hero who won't at least metaphorically fit that pattern, or else, without quite knowing it, I had "got aholt of something big," as John Steinbeck's parson says. Too late to go back with Raglan's crib and set Ebenezer up for an *A+,* but I decided to poke a little further into this hero business while I was making notes for a new story, and perhaps learn a bit more about where I'd been before going on to the next place.

I hadn't poked far before I ran across an even more remarkable actuarial model of heroic adventure, this one the fruit of the synthesizing imagination of Professor Joseph Campbell of Sarah Lawrence College, a mythologist and comparative-religionist who also knows his way around Freud and Jung, the history of philosophy, and philosophies of history. Campbell even draws us a diagram, and when I knitted into it a little Raglan, a little Jung, and a few odds and ends I had up my own sleeve, it came out a fascinating pattern indeed:

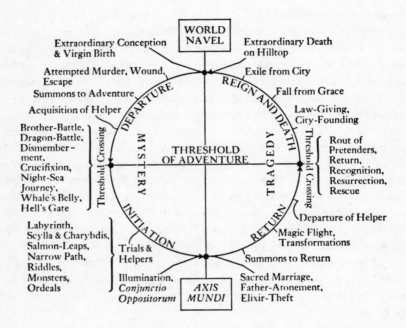

Try running Odysseus or Aeneas around this track, or the aforementioned son of Mary and Joseph, or for that matter Lewis Carroll's Alice or D. H. Lawrence's Paul Morel in *Sons and Lovers,* and you'll appreciate how ubiquitous the pattern is. Much more might be said in the way of detailing and illustrating it; but I commend you to the more learned hands of Raglan, Rank, Jung, Campbell, and company if you're interested (the basic diagram itself comes from Campbell's book *The Hero With a Thousand Faces;* New York: Bollingen Series XVII, 1949).

Two distinctions ought to be made at this point. The first is between whatever meanings one might attribute to the pattern itself and the signif-

icance of its uses, conscious or unconscious, by particular artists in particular works of literature. The *myth* of Aeneas's descent into Hades may be
said to have allegorical correspondences—a number of them—but its rendering in Book VI of Virgil's poem is largely religious and political propaganda. The author of "Bre'r Rabbit and the Tarbaby" probably wasn't
much interested in mysticism, and while a Zen Buddhist's interest in *him*
would be entirely legitimate, we needn't make an adept out of Joel Chan-
dler Harris. Substantial elements of the Master Plan appear in Dante,
Lewis Carroll, D. H. Lawrence, E. M. Forster, Steinbeck, Joyce, and
heaven knows how many other writers, ancient and modern, some of
whom can be supposed to have been aware of using it, some not, and it
goes without saying that its particular literary point is likely to be different in every case, perhaps sometimes absent altogether.

As to the significance of the pattern itself, apart from its literary ad-
aptations, a good thing about Campbell is that he seems to keep clear a
second distinction, between the kind of meaning conscious symbols have
and the kind that myths have. To explain a symbol—cultural, literary,
whatever—you look for its referent; but you don't explain a myth these
days at all, my mythological colleagues tell me: What you do is look for
correspondences, merely, between it and other things, and correspondences of course may be manifold, coexistent, and equally "legitimate,"
though of unequal interest and heuristic value. My point about the general ritual of adventure will be that it doesn't "mean" anything; but it has
been held to correspond notably to at least seven things—a nice mythic
number—six of which I'll merely note in passing and the seventh enter
into, like that last door at the end of the passageway which you aren't
supposed to open.

The first two correspondences exemplify what could be called the
class of "natural" hypotheses, and I gather that they don't cut as much ice
with students of myth as they used to: the "solar" hypothesis and the
"seasonal" hypothesis. Obviously the westward movement of the hero,
his contest with the forces of darkness, and his descent into and resurrec-
tion from subterranean realms, as well as the generally cyclic path of his
biography, correspond both to the daily apparent motion of the sun and
to the succession of the seasons in temperate zones of the earth; this correspondence led some nineteenth-century investigators to maintain that
the myths were fanciful primitive accounts of such natural phenomena. It
is an extremely complicated way to explain the astronomical facts of
life—a way perhaps more suggestive of nineteenth-century German

scholarship than of "primitive" science—and nowadays, I understand, we're more inclined to go at it the other way around, regarding the daily motion of the sun and the annual sequence of the seasons as metaphors for the myth instead of vice versa. This is a much likelier state of affairs, it seems to me. No one who makes up stories can be much perplexed by the relative paucity of equatorial and polar literature, for example: Aside from the fact that there aren't many readers and writers at the poles and the equator, where on earth will you find your basic metaphors for life and death if the seasons don't change? The myth and the natural facts are surely analogous (*isomorphic* is the fashionable term) and throw reciprocal metaphorical light on each other; no need to see one as symbol and the other as referent.

A second class of correspondences can be called *experiential.* I'll mention three; very likely there are others, and very likely too each has been argued to be the "explanation" of the ritual of adventure. But let's ignore from now on the empirical question of what the originators of the myths may in fact have consciously intended them to express; except as a historical datum, that question doesn't seem especially important, and to take it too seriously may be a large-scale equivalent of the Intentional Fallacy in art criticism. The fact is that the Diurnal, Maturational, and Psychoanalytic "hypotheses" aren't mutually exclusive, once we stop regarding them as hypotheses and think of them as correspondences—isomorphies—instead. They have in common their view of the heroic pattern as a dramatic emblem of ordinary human experience.

Thus, to take the first of them, what happens to the hero in his lifetime figures the daily adventure of all our psychic lives. Our rational consciousness cognizes, in common with other people's rational consciousnesses, the sunlit, rigid, discrete forms of waking experience. In the individual subconscious these forms become, as in dreaming, self-luminous and fluid: We "wake" from the "unreality" of our conscious perceptions to dream through the twilit imagings of subconsciousness toward the province of deep, dreamless sleep—the place of dark, formless, unconscious, immediate knowledge. Day, twilight, night; consciousness, subconsciousness, unconsciousness; waking, dreaming, sleeping deeply; cognition, assimilation, immediate knowledge; being, becoming, notbeing; life, half-life, death; discrete form, fluid form, formlessness—there are lots of ways to slice it. In each case, the geography is the geography of the psyche, and the adventure is our daily round.

The maturational and the psychoanalytic or individuational hypotheses compare to the diurnal somewhat as the seasonal hypothesis to the solar. Whether or not, as Raglan claims, the myths literally originate from the dramatic ceremonies of the rites of passage—circumcision, Bar Mitzvah, marriage, funeral, what have you—the pattern certainly does exemplify in heroic scale the passage itself, from any number of viewpoints. We're *all* God's children, speaking literally or figuratively. Our mommies and daddies are all kings and queens whom we shall have to displace, and our conceptions were extraordinary because they engendered the uniqueness of each of us. We all bear the scars of infant traumas. What kid hasn't suspected, or hoped, that his parents might be really the President and First Lady instead of that impossible couple downstairs minding the store? And of course, whether in professional psychoanalysis or the normal process of maturation and self-discovery, we all must come to terms with sibling, "shadow," *alter ego;* undergo the ordeals and humiliations of adolescence, lose our innocence, prove our manhood or womanhood, slough off the vestments of our former or egoistic selves; rebel, question, despair, and drive to the best of our capacity down to the bottom of the womb of things; discover there our deepest identity, perhaps by losing it in another. We make final terms with father, self, past time, and the world: the alignment that must carry us through the years of our maturity. We found our little dynasties, do our little work, pass our climacterics, and become ourselves the ogres whom our children must depose. Then naked we return whence naked we came, to the bosom of God or of nothingness—and what can any man tell his children, finally, or leave behind for them? Et cetera—you get the idea, and can work out your own details with appropriate rhetoric: Christian, Freudian, Jungian, what you will. It may be questionable practice in literature classes, but in civilian life a very great many of us find the most intense relevance of Homer's *Odyssey,* for example, in our own prolonged endeavor to get Back Home.

The third class of correspondences is philosophical. According to the cosmogony of many cultures, the primal void originally gave rise to space, and space to life (in the form of "uncreated creators," those androgynous protodeities); life gives rise to polarity, and polarity to profusion (as the sexual Olympians, or other "created creators," give rise to giants and heroes and ultimately to men). This proliferation is followed, or will be, by decadence and deterioration: Nation eventually destroys nation, kin takes arms against kin, and the whole show culminates in a splendid *Götterdämmerung,* the gods expiring and the universe relapsing cataclysmically into nothingness—whence it may or may not in time re-generate, depending on what paper you take. The mythic hero who oper-ates in this sort of cosmology may be thought of as backtracking through the history of creation, reversing as it were the first law of embryology; the hero-work consists in going to the source as well as to the bottom of things, playing the tape of time backwards in order to acquire the means—the literal or symbolical equipage—to carry history and/or the culture forward. This interpretation is more interesting and pertinent than I have time enough to make it appear; again I refer you to Campbell and company if you're curious. I shall remark, though, that the Cosmo-gonic hypothesis, too, seems to me to lend itself to experiential corre-spondence, in this case to the lives not of the commonalty but of the intellectual, spiritual, and artistic elite: the masters in any field who drive to the origins and first principles of their discipline in order to turn it around a corner—often, in the case of visionaries and others with deep vocation, at great personal cost.

Stripping the Cosmogonic hypothesis in this way of its grand chro-nology and its metaphorical personages, we come near to the Mystical interpretation of the hero-work, and the point of this lecture. It was here, I ought to add, that I stopped researching, in order not to overburden imagination with information. My notes for a new novel had by this time got copious, almost out of hand, and so inextricably mixed up with cer-tain possibilities of the hero business that it was necessary, like Gustave Aschenbach in Thomas Mann's *Death in Venice,* to turn my back on knowledge lest it paralyze action. The storyteller's stock in trade, after all, is fabrications, not facts, and though he may require a few seeds of truth from which to sprout his lies, there's nothing in his contract obliging him to spill those beans, and too many of them will only clutter up his plot.

Any variety of unitive mysticism would serve to illustrate this last in-terpretation of the hero pattern and lead us to the relationship between mystery and tragedy. Since we Westerners perceive mysticism as a char-acteristically Eastern reaction to the world, I'll use Buddhist terminol-ogy—and compare it by the way with Plato's famous metaphysical myth in *The Republic* for the sake of his interesting inversion of the usual meta-phors.

The Buddhist term for things as we commonly perceive them is *sam-sara:* the world of birth and death. Through the Veil of Maya (the screen of conscious analytical perception), we see reality as differentiated into this and that: the polar contradictions of male and female, subject and object, life and death, space and time, truth and falsehood, being and not-being—in short, the problematical daylight realm from which the hero sets out, and to which he returns. In analogous but obverse wise, Plato figures the common consciousness as chained in a dark cave, and compares our normal perceptions of reality to shadows projected from outside onto the cave's back wall. The mystic then is like the hero: Summoned by whatever voice, he comes to grips with the contradictions and self-defeating nature of differentiated reality (in the case of the Buddhists) or material reality (in the case of the Platonists); he leaves analytical consciousness behind him like Bre'r Rabbit's clothes on the Tarbaby, and after the very trying—and in the case of young Zen novices, often humiliating—ordeals of logical binds, despair, riddling *koans,* insults to "common sense," perhaps even physical mortifications, he is if he is fortunate vouchsafed a *satori*—an enlightenment as to the "true" (which is to say, undifferentiated) nature of reality: *prajna.* He sees that seamless nature knows nothing of the concepts and distinctions by which the "waking" consciousness apprehends her; that, in the paradoxical language of the mystics, I and thou, male and female, subject and object, good and evil, self and Buddha-self, are all aspects of the same thing, of the One. Thus the paradoxical metaphors of rebirth in death, enlightenment in darkness, associated with the hero's arrival at the *Axis Mundi:* They become symbols of the mystical transcension of category.

Up to a point, Plato's allegory of the cave proceeds similarly, though with the symbols always reversed. The philosopher-king is the man who ventures *out* of the cave (by means of a ladder of abstraction and generalization which he may borrow from *The Symposium*): He ascends from the apprehension of beauty, for example, in a particular material thing to its apprehension in classes of material things and then in classes of nonmaterial things and abstractions, until—but only if he is of the elect—he transcends the cave altogether and with his mind's eye looks on Beauty Bare and the other Platonic Ideas, which in turn derive their reality from the Form of the Good, just as the objects whose shadows are cast into the cave derive their luminosity from a single sun.

Obviously there are differences between pure mysticism and Plato's logical realism. For one thing, the mystics don't leave material reality behind; they merely transcend its categories to see it in a different way. For another, they press their supralogical logic further: Plato maintains such distinctions as perceiver and perceived, objects and essences, and, presumably, the Form of the Good and the Form of the Bad; but your out-

and-out mystic, when he arrives at the *Axis Mundi,* transcends among the
other polarities the differentiation between Differentiated Reality and
Undifferentiated Reality. He understands (that's a falsification, of course,
since he is not then different from his understanding or the thing his understanding is of) that *nirvana* and *samsara* are not different (though not
the same either, it must go without saying) and therefore that the undif-
ference of things, the realization whereof constitutes his enlightenment,
makes no *difference,* strictly speaking, though at the same time of course it
makes all the difference in the world, exactly.

William James lists the four famous hallmarks of this experience in
his chapter on mysticism in *The Varieties of Religious Experience;* we'll
see that they apply equally to the hero at the *Axis Mundi,* the mystic
united with the All, and the philosopher-king outside the cave.

1. *Passivity.* The hero may slay dragons and answer riddles, but his
reward comes giftlike. "And hast thou slain the Jabberwock? Come to my
arms, my Beamish boy!" The Zens in particular insist that Truth is like
those dim stars that can be seen only when you stop looking straight at
them, and Diotima warns Socrates that only the elect may ascend to that
top rung of the ladder, where logic ends and mystery commences. To be a
saint takes more than mere effort and ambition: "Many a one," Kafka
tells us in "The Country Doctor," "proffers his side and can scarcely hear
the ax in the forest, far less that it is coming nearer to him" to give him
the Christ-like wound he yearns for.

2. *Noumenality.* The hero, the mystic, and the philosopher-king no
longer believe; they *know.* After his interlude with Dido and his descent
into Hades, Aeneas is never again diverted or detained from his destiny.

3. *Transience.* Alas, the trouble with transports, visions, and other
ecstasies is that they end—in half an hour or so, William James remarks,
perhaps optimistically. The messenger summons the hero back from his
honeymoon to run the store; *karuna* or some such thing fetches the
Boddhisatva back into *samsara,* full of compassionate detachment; civic
responsibility leads the philosopher-king, with tears in his eyes, back to
his fellow men in the cave of shadows.

4. *Ineffability,* the unhappiest quality of the mystical experience.
Odysseus is the king, but he looks like the pig-man; there are jewels
stitched up in Marco Polo's hems, but he's ragged as a tramp. The mystic
One can't be described, because language is analytical. It can't be drawn,
because it has no attributes: Very Beauty is not like any beautiful thing.

So they all come back and do their best, and their best can never quite work out: A pox will come upon Thebes; the disciples will misconstrue the master's gospel; even the model republic, Plato acknowledges, must ultimately degenerate and fall. And at last the philosopher-king retires, with emeritus rank, to publish before he perishes; depending upon how seriously you take Plato's Myth of Er, he may or may not be reincarnated to recommence the cycle. The Buddha, likewise, under his Bo tree at the end of his ministry, and the hero on his foreordained exurban hilltop, prefigure the winding down of the cosmos.

Let's leave the diagram for a minute to review the contrast between mysticism—the most profound and characteristic Eastern reaction to the human condition—and tragicism, or the tragic view, which I regard as the noblest Western reaction to the same state of affairs, though perhaps not the most characteristic or popular. Confronted with the proposition "I am dying of cancer," for example, your mysterious East might address its energies to the syntax: *Death, self,* and *cancer* are all transcendable concepts imposed arbitrarily upon reality by the Veil of Maya and the nature of language; anyhow, if I'm dying of cancer, then cancer is living of me: *Sub specie aeternitatis,* what the hell. Your Westerner more typically will attack the cancer with one hand and the finality of the verb with the other: If I'm dying of cancer, then we'd better find a cure for the damned thing fast—that there *is* a cure somewhere, there can of course be no doubt— but if we find it too late, it'll be only this particular Package that I leave behind anyhow; the Goods will get through Customs intact to Beulah Land.

But the *tragic* response to this proposition, and to the human situation in general, is different from all of these. It's notable that while the Greek philosophers, various as they were, pretty much agreed that Truth is a fine thing to have, and made up future university mottoes like *Know thyself* and *The unexamined life is not worth living,* the Greek tragic poets—Sophocles especially—had a quite different opinion. Imagine what King Oedipus at Colonus would say to those mottoes! The postulates of the tragic view of life, as I understand it, are principally four, and constitute a kind of existentialist reading of Sophocles:

1. *The world is morally ambiguous and brutally compensatory.* Virtues have their vices, and conversely: If you want this, you've got to take that; the pans remain more or less balanced, but always ultimately for the worse. Readers who say "If only Oedipus hadn't been so *rash*" are like

people who wish their children to be high-spirited but not troublesome. If Oedipus hadn't rashly insisted on knowing who he was, he wouldn't have *been* who he was.

2. Consequently, *there are only different ways to lose;* no "victories," in the sentimental sense, are possible. Greatness is punished; mediocrity is not rewarded. You can "not go gently to that last goodnight," or you can go gently: Either way you go, and it *is* goodnight. Oedipus's choice, if he had any, was to take it on the chin in Thebes or in the back in Corinth, where presumably his fate would have sought him out: in other words, to be a tragic hero or a member of the chorus. Endowed with his temperament, he hadn't really any option. The pity and terror in our response to the tragic hero's fall, then, come not from our feeling "There but for the grace of Zeus go I," but, more grimly, "There but for my petty-spiritedness go I."

3. *The self is not transcendable.* The tragic view imagines no dualism of ego-self and Buddha-self, or corruptible body and immortal soul, but only the ambivalence of a self whose noblest assertions of its individual dignity against the non- or suprahuman are precisely what bring it to catastrophe. King Oedipus's *hubris* is antimystical: It is Aristotelian rationality inspired by the moral virtue of *megalopsychia,* "greatsouledness"—but operating in a Sophoclean rather than an Aristotelian universe.

4. Therefore *the human condition is essentially ironic and technically absurd.* Understanding "Fate" and "the Gods" simply as Sophoclean metaphors for The Way Things Are, there's no lesson in Oedipus's suffering except the metaphysical one; no divine meaning or plan (as it's argued there is in Job's), only a meaningless Olympian plot. For the tragic hero there's no redemption, only understanding; no joyous affirmation, only dignified acceptance of suffering. The tragical universe is nihilistic in the sense that this suffering doesn't "add up": Nobody's keeping score upstairs against ultimate redress; there's no discernible justice, only an awful compensation. Those who say of Oedipus, after the catastrophe, "But at least he *knows* himself now, and is ready for the condition of prophethood"—as if to say Truth is expensive, sure, but so are RollsRoyces; you gotta pay for class—are being sentimental: Oedipus certainly doesn't feel that way; neither does the chorus, and neither does Sophocles. Yet the alternative, of course—persisting in ignorance of the awful truth—is equally unacceptable (though it's touching that Jocasta at one point seems willing to give it a try; there's a mother for you). "Affirma-

tion of the human spirit . . ." all very well, as long as it's clearly understood that the affirmation doesn't *get* you anywhere: It is meaningless beyond itself, and people outside the drama too readily get sentimental about its terminal value. Be it repeated: On the tragic view there is not any way to win; there are only more or less noble and spectacular ways to go down.

The effect, however, of the tragic denouement is certainly different from that of Sartre's *Nausea* or Camus's *The Stranger,* for example, and the source of the difference—aside from the relative powers of poetry and prose—I believe to be less in the respective theaters of action than in the natures of the actors. Specifically, it is that quality of *megalopsychia,* other things being approximately equal, that makes the difference between *Angst* and catharsis through pity and terror. But *megalopsychia* is a heroic attribute, precisely—and so we come back to our diagram. (It is also, by the way, not a quality one ups and decides to have; Aristotle makes more sense to me than Sartre on the matter of moral dispositions.)

The *myth* of Oedipus involves the entire cycle, as Raglan demonstrates; the Tragedy of Oedipus the King involves only the last quadrant. But elements of the tragic situation as I've outlined it run through the whole second half of the pattern, beginning with the hero's summons to return; the tragic irony is in our foreknowledge (and/or the hero's, depending on the story) of the ultimate futility of his "reign," and of his destined end. It is an insight which, if the hero has it, he acquires exactly at the *Axis Mundi,* as a feature of his general illumination. The hero voyages westward, but it's the East he reaches, as Magellan did: the realm of selflessness and mystical transcension. The truly Westward motion, at least potentially, is the long voyage home to the country of waking consciousness: of the analytical, reasoning self bound by the paradoxes of its necessary concepts and doomed to misunderstanding, failure of its enterprises, and, in a sense, self-destruction. Literarily, to date, these have been very different voyages, because of the contradictions between the mystical and the tragical *cosmoi:* There is nothing tragic in the *Divina Commedia* or the *Aenead* (though in the Dido story Virgil comes so teasingly close to the tragic view of Herohood that you can almost feel his relief when he gets Aeneas out of Dido's Carthage and back to epical slam-bangery), and there's no mystery in *Oedipus the King,* that quintessential Western drama. East has so far been East; West West.

But, as the mythic model demonstrates, it is one voyage after all, and its philosophical hemispheres impinge at two interesting places. One is down there at the *Axis Mundi,* where, as Odysseus tells his shipmates, "East and West mean nothing"—nor does any other distinction, including the one between mystery and tragedy. The bottom of things—difficult enough to get to, much more so to return from, in any age—seems to me a place worth the closest attention of any author or civilian concerned with the possibility of rapprochement between the two profoundest motions of the human spirit. The other conjunction is up there at the end of the road, in that dark hilltop grove where even Sophocles, as he drew near it in *Oedipus at Colonus,* could imagine or hope that mystery might begin where tragedy ends.

That latter is a place I leave to ninety-year-old playwrights and people with inside information not vouchsafed to me. But even a thirty-four-year-old concocter of comic novels (going on thirty-five) might have a word to say, or to try in vain to say, about that *Axis Mundi* place—once he has left there, and if he can find the other half of his round-trip ticket.

Muse, Spare Me

IN 1965 the term *postmodernist* was not yet current, though the American fiction it would come to describe was being written. The term *Black Humorist,* on the other hand, left over from the Fifties, was still in vogue, though the literary phenomenon *it* described had pretty much run its course. The little Friday-piece below was commissioned that year by *Book Week,* at that time the book-review supplement of the New York *World Journal Tribune.* The editors asked for a few hundred words upon the Black Humorists, of whom I was supposed to be one. As I had never tried my hand at a newspaper piece, I agreed to give it a go on condition I be allowed to say almost nothing about Black Humor, of which I had almost nothing to say, and to speak instead mostly of Scheherazade, about whom I seem frequently to have things to say. They said Okay.

For the posturing in my first paragraph—"I'm not impressed by the apocalyptic character of the present age . . ."—I apologize. If I ever wasn't, I have certainly become so.

I beseech the Muse to keep me from ever becoming a Black Humorist. Mind, I don't object to Black Humorists, in their place; but to be numbered with them inspires me to a kind of spiritual White Backlash. For one thing, they are in their way *responsible,* like more conventional social satirists: They dramatize—and good for them!—the Madness of Contemporary Society, of Modern Warfare, of Life With the Bomb, of What Have We Nowadays. But I say, Muse, spare me (at the desk, I mean) from social-historical responsibility, and in the last analysis from every other kind as well, except artistic. Your teller of stories will likely be responsive to his time; he needn't be responsible to it. I'm not impressed by the apocalyptic character of the present age—nor is the age to my indifference—though I note the fact, and shall return to it. Joyce figured the writer as Dedalus, Mann as Faust; the best of the Black Humorists are good comical Amoses and Isaiahs.

My own favorite image in this line used to be Cassandra—a madly *laughing* Cassandra, of course—the darling of many another young writer convinced that he has unhappy truth by the tail, or on his back, and that no one's getting the message. Later, shorn of such vanity, I preferred an image out of Dante: the Florentine assassins alluded to in Canto XIX of the *Inferno*. Head-downwards in a hole and sentenced to be buried alive, the murderer postpones his fate by drawing out his confession to the attendant priest. The beauties of this image are its two nice paradoxes: The more sins he has to confess, the longer retribution is delayed, and since he has nothing to lose anyhow, he may well invent a few good ones to hold the priest's attention.

But as soon as his audience grants absolution, the wretch's mouth is stopped with earth: "Nothing fails like success," as Leslie Fiedler says of our popular novelists. Less satisfactory are the details that his audience is also captive, duty-bound to hear him out whether entertained or not; respite is granted for as long as he talks, not merely for as long as he amuses, and there's no real stay of execution, only a hold in the countdown. Moreover, though the fact that the assassin's tale consists of his own misdemeanors (a perverse kind of authorial self-aggrandizement) may make the image apter yet for some novelists we know—assassins indeed of the characters they "draw from life," as one draws a man to the gallows—it does not, I hope, apply to my own concoctions.

In any case, the image I'm lately fonder of—the aptest, sweetest, hauntingest, hopefullest I know for the storyteller—is Scheherazade. The whole frame of those thousand nights and a night speaks to my heart, directly and intimately—and in many ways at once, personal and technical. The sultan Shahryar, you remember, is so disenchanted with life in general and love in particular that he "marries" a virgin every night and has her killed in the morning. Scheherazade, who has "perused the books, annals, and legends of preceding kings, and the stories, examples, and instances of by-gone men . . . antique races and departed rulers," volunteers herself. The King "abates her virginity" (as if it were an intense condition), whereafter, with the prearranged assistance of her younger sister, Dunyazade—about whose role much might be said—Scheherazade beguiles her deflowerer with a tale, artfully continued, involuted, compounded, and complicated through a thousand and one nocturnal installments, during the invention of which she also bears three sons by her imperious audience. It is on behalf of these offspring that, her in-spiration spent at last, she begs for her life; and the king grants her—in honor of her stories, not her children—the relative tenure of formal mar-riage. Scheherazade's tales are published (in 30 volumes), and their au-thor lives happily with her hard-earned family. But not *ever* after; only until they all are taken by the Destroyer of Delights, whereafter, we're specifically told, "their houses fell waste and their palaces lay in ruins . . . and [other] kings inherited their riches"—including *The Thousand and One Nights.*

My love affair with Scheherazade is an old and continuing one. As an illiterate undergraduate, I worked off part of my tuition filing books in the Classics Library at Johns Hopkins, which included the stacks of the Oriental Seminary. One was tacitly permitted to get lost for hours in that splendrous labyrinth and to intoxicate, engorge oneself with *story.* Espe-cially I became enamored of the great tale-cycles and collections: Soma-deva's *Ocean of Story* in ten huge volumes, Burton's *Thousand Nights and a Night* in seventeen, the *Panchatantra,* the *Gesta Romanorum,* the *Novel-lini,* and the *Pent- Hept-* and *Decameron.* If anything ever makes a writer out of me, it will be the digestion of that enormous, slightly surreptitious feast of narrative.

Most of those spellbinding liars I have forgotten, but never Sche-herazade. Though the tales she tells aren't my favorites, she remains my favorite teller, and it is a heady paradox that this persistence, being the figure of her literal aim, thereby generates itself, and becomes the em-blem as well of my figurative aspiration. When I think of my condition and my hope, musewise, in the time between now and when I shall run out of ink or otherwise expire, it is Scheherazade who comes to mind, for many reasons—not least of which is a technical interest in the ancient device of the framing-story, used more beautifully in the *Nights* than any-where else I know. Chaucer's frame, for example, the pilgrimage to Can-terbury, is an excellent if venerable ground-metaphor—life as a redemptive journey—but, having established it, he does nothing with it. Boccaccio's frame—ten wealthy young ladies and gentlemen amusing themselves with clever stories while the great post-Easter plague of 1348 lays waste the countryside—is more arresting for its apocalyptic nature, for the pretty rules with which the company replaces those of their liter-ally dying society, for the hints of growing relationships between the *ra-conteurs* and *raconteuses* themselves, and for the occasional relevance of the tales to the tellers and to the general situation. On the other hand, the very complex serial frames of the *Ocean of Story,* for example, are full-fledged stories in themselves, but except for the marvelous (and surely fictitious) "history of the text" and the haunting title, they have no apparent meaningfulness beyond their immediate narrative interest.

The story of Scheherazade excels these others in all respects. For one thing, her tales are told at night: an inestimable advantage, for the whole conception, despite its humor, is darker, more magical and dreamish than Boccaccio's or Chaucer's. Consider too the prerequisites for her taletellerhood: not only native endowment and mastery of the tradition, but the sacrifice of her present personal maidenhead to her auditor and absolute critic—whose pleasure, by the way, fertilizes as well as spares her, and who finally rewards her (for what they have in a manner of speaking created together) with official distinctions which *he* will not take away (though her productivity, it seems, ends with the award of tenure), but time will.

Consider finally that in the years of her flourishing, her talent is always on the line: not enough to have satisfied the old cynic once, or twice; she's only as good as her next piece, Scheherazade; night by night it's publish or perish. Thus her situation is no less apocalyptic in its way than the *Decameron*'s, and perhaps more pointed, even without regard to the interesting "public" state of affairs: the King's epical despair and the ruin it's bringing his kingdom to. For though the death of one person is not the death of a people, even mankind's demise will have to consist of each of our dyings. In this respect, all apocalypses are ultimately personal—an important fact, since it validates apocalyptic visions age after age despite the otherwise awkward circumstance that the world has, so far, persisted.

Even the detail that Scheherazade's stories are drawn from the literal and legendary foretime, I find arresting. It reminds me that the eschewing of contemporaneous, "original" material is a basic literary notion, by comparison to which its use is but an occasional anomaly and fad of the last couple of centuries. Not only classical epic and tragedy, and Elizabethan and neoclassical drama, but virtually all folk and heroic narrative, both Eastern and Western, follows Horace's advice: *". . . safer shall the bard his pen employ / With yore, to dramatize the Tale of Troy, / Than, venturing trackless regions to explore, / Delineate characters untouched before."*

Joyce's Dedalus calls history a nightmare from which he's trying to wake; some other writers have found it more a wet-dream (and their readers, perhaps, a soporific). For me, also, the past is a dream—but I laugh in my sleep. The use of historical or legendary material, especially in a farcical, even a comic, spirit, has a number of virtues, among which are esthetic distance and the opportunity for counterrealism. Attacked with a long face, the historical muse is likely to give birth to costume romances, adult Westerns, tiresome allegories, and ponderous mythologizings; but she responds to a lighthearted approach. *Magic* is what chiefly saves Scheherazade's tales from these poor categories—a device we may hardly use today, for the realistic tradition and its accompanying cultural history are under our belts, for better or worse, and may not be ignored. They may, however, be come to terms with and got beyond, not by the use of farce alone, surely, but by farce inspired with passion—and with mystery, which, older than magic, still enwraps our lives as it does the whole queer universe. In passionate, mysterious farce, I think, lies also the possibility of transcending categories more profound than Tragedy and Comedy: I mean the distinction between Tragedy and Mystery—or, if you like, tragicism and mysticism, the finest expressions respectively of the Western and Eastern spirits. No matter that the achievement of such a synthesis would want the talents of Scheherazade, Shakespeare, and Schopenhauer combined; it is a pole star that even a middling comic novelist may steer by, without mistaking it for his destination.

Like a parable of Kafka's or a great myth, the story of deflowered Scheherazade, yarning tirelessly through the dark hours to save her neck, corresponds to a number of things at once, and flashes meaning from all its facets. For me its rich dark circumstances, mixing the subtle and the coarse, the comic and the grim, the realistic and the fantastic, the apocalyptic and the hopeful, figure, among other things, both the estate of the fictioner in general and the particular endeavors and aspirations of this one, at least, who can wish nothing better than to spin like that vizier's excellent daughter, through what nights remain to him, tales within tales within tales, full-stored with "description and discourse and rare traits and anecdotes and moral instances and reminiscences . . . proverbs and parables, chronicles and pleasantries, quips and jests, stories and . . . dialogues and histories and elegies and other verses . . ." until he and his scribblings are fetched low by the Destroyer of Delights.

The Tragic View of Recognition

(BRANDEIS AWARD STATEMENT, 1966)

LITERARY PRIZES: another innocence to lose.

In 1966, the year *Giles Goat-Boy* appeared, I was given what the Brandeis University Arts Award Commission called a "citation in fiction." The term suggests a legal summons; for the reasons set forth below, I decided not to defy it. Besides, the main award of the evening was being presented to Eudora Welty, a writer I admired but had never met. Therefore I hired the requisite black-tie regalia and went to New York City for the awards ceremony. En route I composed my maiden acceptance statement: the statement, it will be seen, of a writer attempting for the first time in his career to write short stories.

In the event, I was disabused of yet a further innocence: *Big*-prize winners are expected to speak, but those who are merely cited merely stand and get cited and then sit down and then go home and return their rented costumes. I take the present occasion to clear my throat and thank the Brandeis people, belatedly, for citing me.

Not counting Cracker Jacks, this is the first prize of any sort I've won.

It is tempting therefore to decline it at once, like Jean-Paul Sartre the Nobel, especially if one has rather enjoyed being what they call underground. Late or soon, that is whither we must all repair; take it from me, it is not so bad down there. My aspiration was to become a giant truffle, or one of those stones I used to strike with my spade in my salad garden in the Alleghenies: stones that seem like nothing much until you set about to dig them and find that they go to the bottom of the world. Indeed, that they *are* the bottom of the world.

Bedrock.

I happen to believe, though, what Goethe remarked to the Duke of Weimar: that refusing a distinction can be as immodest as chasing after it. Speaking as a Master of Arts in the field of Innocence, I suspect that when it is artificially preserved it sours into arrested development, and that what began as healthy privacy congeals into reclusive crankhood. This is the Tragic View of Recognition.

For these reasons, it is especially pleasing to share literary honors with Eudora Welty, who has preserved her balance nicely on the line between public and private property, and whose fiction I have often taught and been taught by. My own preference from the first has been the novel—

> O, the novel,
> With its great galumphing grace,
> Amazing as a whale.

But the number of whales required to constitute a surfeit is perhaps not vast. When we read the beautiful brief writings of Franz Kafka, of Jorge Luis Borges, of Eudora Welty, we realize the continuing viability and appeal of small narratives that delight the ear and can be held whole in the mind's eye like poems. Miss Welty has made some of the best in our American literature. I thank you kindly for honoring me; I congratulate you heartily for honoring her.

The Literature of Exhaustion

YES, WELL.

"Every man is not only himself," says Sir Thomas Browne: "Men are lived over again." At one point during my tenure at Penn State, a fellow with the same name as mine in that big-university small town was arrested on charges of molesting a young woman. His interesting defense was that he was a Stanislavsky Method actor rehearsing for the role of rapist in an upcoming student-theater piece. For some while after, his fans occasionally rang me up by mistake. One of them, when enough conversation had revealed his error, said "Sorry: You're the wrong John Barth."

Not for that reason, in 1965 I moved my family from Pine Grove Mills—an Allegheny mountain village not far from State College, Pennsylvania—up and over the Appalachians to Buffalo, where for the next seven years I taught in the new and prosperous State University of New York's operation at the old University of Buffalo. In time I was appointed to that university's Edward S. Butler Professorship, endowed by and named for a late local philanthropist. Thus it came to be declared, on the jackets of some editions of the books I published in those years, that their author "is currently Edward S. Butler Professor of Literature at the State University of New York at Buffalo." And sure enough (O world out there, what innocents you harbor!), mail began coming in addressed to "Edward S. Butler, Professor of Literature," and author—under that *nom de plume du jour,* I presume the authors of those letters to have presumed—of *Giles Goat-Boy, Lost in the Funhouse,* and *Chimera.*

Those years—1965–1973—were the American High Sixties. The Vietnam War was in overdrive through most of the period; the U.S. economy was fat and bloody; academic imperialism was as popular as the political kind. Among Governor Nelson Rockefeller's ambitions was to establish major university centers at each end and the middle of the Thomas E. Dewey Thruway (Stony Brook, Albany, Buffalo) as a tiara for the Empire State's 57-campus university system. SUNY/Buffalo therefore was given virtual *carte blanche* to pirate professors away from other universities and build buildings for them to teach in: At one dizzy point in its planning, Gordon Bunshaft's proposed new campus complex for the school was reported to be the largest single architectural project in the world, after Brasilia. Eighty percent of the populous English department I joined had been hired within the preceding two years, as additions to the original staff; so numerous were our illustrious immigrants from raided faculties, troubled marriages, and more straitlaced life-styles, we came to call ourselves proudly the Ellis Island of Academia. The somewhat shabby older buildings and hastily built new ones, all jam-packed and about to be abandoned, reinforced that image.

The politically active among our faculty and students had their own ambitions for the place: the Berkeley of the East. They wanted no part of Mr. Bunshaft's suburban New Jerusalem rising from filled-in marshland north of the city ("All great cultures," my new colleague Leslie Fiedler remarked, "are built on marshes"). In some humors, as when our government lied with more than usual egregiousness about its war, they wanted little enough of the *old* campus, either. They struck and trashed; then the police and National Guard struck and trashed *them*. Mace and peppergas wafted through the academic groves; the red flag of communism and the black flag of anarchism were literally waved at English Department faculty-student meetings, which—a sight as astonishing to me as those flags—were attended by *hundreds*, like an Allen Ginsberg poetry reading with harmonium and Tibetan finger-cymbals.

Altogether a stimulating place to work through those troubled years: Pop Art popping at the Albright-Knox Museum; strange new music from Lukas Foss, Lejaren Hiller, and their electronic colleagues; dope as ubiquitous as martinis at faculty dinner parties; polluted Lake Erie flushing over Niagara Falls ("the toilet bowl of America," our Ontario friends called it); and, across the Peace Bridge, endless Canada, to which hosts of our young men fled as their counterparts had done in other of our national convulsions, and from which Professor McLuhan expounded the limitations, indeed the obsolescence, of the printed word in our electronic culture.

The long novel *Giles Goat-Boy* done, I took sabbatical leave from novel-writing and, inspired by those lively new surroundings and by the remarkable short fiction of the Argentine Jorge Luis Borges, which I'd recently come to know, I spent two years happily fiddling with short narrative: never my long suit. In the salad of a writer's motives, trifling ingredients are tossed with more serious. Among my ambitions in writing *The Sot-Weed Factor* was to perpetrate a novel so thick that its title could be printed horizontally across its spine; among my reasons for writing *Lost in the Funhouse*—a series of short fictions for print, tape, and live voice—was that novelists aren't easily included in anthologies of fiction.

But I was interested also in exploring the oral narrative tradition from which printed fiction evolved. Poetry readings became popular in the Sixties, but except in the areas of folktales and oral history there was not much interest in "live" narrative, in fiction as a performing art. For several weeks one summer, the university's English Department leased the Music Department's electronics studio, complete with its audio engineers, for the use of any students or staff interested in experimenting with electronic means in verse or fiction. I took the opportunity to record (for use in my once-a-month lecture visits) the taped portions of several tape-and-live-voice pieces from *Lost in the Funhouse.*

In that time and place, *experimental* was not yet an adjective of dismissal. On the contrary: As in the European Nineteen Teens, artistic experiment was in the Buffalo air. Even our less sophisticated undergraduates, many from the New York City area, seemed to breathe it in with the other hydrocarbons, the perfumes of Lake Erie and the Love Canal. Unaware in many cases of the *history* of, say, edible or self-destructing art, they had nevertheless a kind of media street-smarts; if their experiments (which, sure enough, included edible and self-destructing narratives) most often failed, they failed no more often than non-"experimental" apprentice work. For apprentices, *all* work is experimental, as in another sense it is even for seasoned professionals. In my own literary temperament, the mix of romantic and neoclassical is so mutable that I hold no particular brief either for or against programmatic experimentalism. Passion and virtuosity are what matter; where they are, they will shine through any aesthetics. But I confess to missing, in apprentice seminars in the later 1970s and the 1980s, that lively Make-It-New spirit of the Buffalo Sixties. A roomful of young traditionalists can be as depressing as a roomful of young Republicans.

In 1967 I set down my mixed feelings about the avant-gardism of the time in the following essay, first delivered as a Peters Rushton Seminars Lecture at the University of Virginia and subsequently published in the *Atlantic.* It has been frequently reprinted and as frequently misread as one more Death of the Novel or Swan-Song of Literature piece. It isn't. Rereading it now, I sniff traces of tear gas in its margins; I hear an echo of disruption between its lines. Its urgencies are dated; there are thin notes in it of quackery and wisecrackery that displease me now. But the main line of its argument I stand by: that virtuosity is a virtue, and that what artists feel about the state of the world and the state of their art is less important than what they do with that feeling.

I want to discuss three things more or less together: first, some old questions raised by the new "intermedia" arts; second, some aspects of the Argentine writer Jorge Luis Borges, whose fiction I greatly admire; third, some professional concerns of my own, related to these other matters and having to do with what I'm calling "the literature of exhausted possibility"—or, more chicly, "the literature of exhaustion."

By "exhaustion" I don't mean anything so tired as the subject of physical, moral, or intellectual decadence, only the used-upness of certain forms or the felt exhaustion of certain possibilities—by no means necessarily a cause for despair. That a great many Western artists for a great many years have quarreled with received definitions of artistic media, genres, and forms goes without saying: Pop Art, dramatic and musical "happenings," the whole range of "intermedia" or "mixed-means" art bear recentest witness to the romantic tradition of rebelling against Tradition.

A catalogue I received some time ago in the mail, for example, advertises such items as Robert Filliou's *Ample Food for Stupid Thought,* a box full of postcards on which are inscribed "apparently meaningless questions," to be mailed to whomever the purchaser judges them suited for; also Ray Johnson's *Paper Snake,* a collection of whimsical writings, "often pointed," the catalogue assures us, and once mailed to various friends (what the catalogue describes as The New York Correspondence School of Literature); likewise Daniel Spoerri's *Anecdoted Typography of Chance,* "on the surface" a description of all the objects that happen to be on the author's parlor table—"in fact, however . . . a cosmology of Spoerri's existence."

The document listing these items is—"on the surface," at least—the catalogue of The Something Else Press, a swinging outfit. "In fact, however," it may be one of their offerings, for all I know: The New York Direct-Mail-Advertising School of Literature. In any case, their wares are lively to read about, and make for interesting conversation in fiction-writing classes, for example, where we discuss Somebody-or-other's unbound, unpaginated, randomly assembled novel-in-a-box and the desirability of printing *Finnegans Wake* on a very long roller-towel. It is easier and more sociable to talk technique than it is to make art, and the area of "happenings" and their kin is mainly a way of discussing aesthetics, really; of illustrating more or less valid and interesting points about the nature of art and the definition of its terms and genres.

One conspicuous thing, for example, about the "intermedia" arts is their tendency to eliminate not only the traditional audience—those who apprehend the artist's art (in "happenings" the audience is often the "cast," as in "environments," and some of the new music isn't intended to be performed at all)—but also the most traditional notion of the artist: the Aristotelian conscious agent who achieves with technique and cunning the artistic effect; in other words, one endowed with uncommon talent, who has moreover developed and disciplined that endowment into virtuosity. It is an aristocratic notion on the face of it, which the democratic West seems eager to have done with; not only the "omniscient" author of older fiction, but the very idea of the controlling artist, has been condemned as politically reactionary, authoritarian, even fascist.

Personally, being of the temper that chooses to rebel along traditional lines, I'm inclined to prefer the kind of art that not many people can *do:*

the kind that requires expertise and artistry as well as bright aesthetic ideas and/or inspiration. I enjoy the Pop Art in the famous Albright-Knox collection, a few blocks from my house in Buffalo, like a lively conversation; but I was on the whole more impressed by the jugglers and acrobats at Baltimore's old Hippodrome, where I used to go every time they changed shows: not artists, perhaps, but genuine *virtuosi,* doing things that anyone can dream up and discuss but almost no one can do.

I suppose the distinction is between things worth remarking and things worth doing. "Somebody ought to make a novel with scenes that pop up, like the old children's books," one says, with the implication that one isn't going to bother doing it oneself.

However, art and its forms and techniques live in history and certainly do change. I sympathize with a remark attributed to Saul Bellow, that to be technically up-to-date is the least important attribute of a writer—though I would add that this least important attribute may be nevertheless essential. In any case, to be technically *out* of date is likely to be a genuine defect: Beethoven's Sixth Symphony or the Chartres cathedral, if executed today, might be simply embarrassing (in fact, they *couldn't* be executed today, unless in the Borgesian spirit discussed below). A good many current novelists write turn-of-the-century-type novels, only in more or less mid-twentieth-century language and about contemporary people and topics; this makes them less interesting (to me) than excellent writers who are also technically contemporary: Joyce and Kafka, for instance, in their time, and in ours, Samuel Beckett and Jorge Luis Borges. The intermedia arts, I'd say, tend to be intermediary, too, between the traditional realms of aesthetics on the one hand and artistic creation on the other. I think the wise artist and civilian will regard them with quite the kind and degree of seriousness with which he regards good shoptalk: He'll listen carefully, if noncommittally, and keep an eye on his intermedia colleagues, if only the corner of his eye. Whether or not they themselves produce memorable and lasting works of contemporary art, they may very possibly suggest something usable in the making or understanding of such works.

Jorge Luis Borges will serve to illustrate the difference between a technically old-fashioned artist, a technically up-to-date non-artist, and a technically up-to-date artist. In the first category I'd locate all those novelists who for better or worse write not as if the twentieth century didn't exist, but as if the great writers of the last sixty years or so hadn't existed.

Our century is more than two-thirds done; it is dismaying to see so many of our writers following Dostoevsky or Tolstoy or Balzac, when the question seems to me to be how to succeed not even Joyce and Kafka, but those who *succeeded* Joyce and Kafka and are now in the evenings of their own careers.* In the second category—technically up-to-date non-artists—are such folk as a neighbor of mine in Buffalo who fashions dead Winnies-the-Pooh in sometimes monumental scale out of oilcloth stuffed with sand and impales them on stakes or hangs them by the neck. In the third category belong the few people whose artistic thinking is as *au courant* as any French New Novelist's, but who manage nonetheless to speak eloquently and memorably to our human hearts and conditions, as the great artists have always done. Of these, two of the finest living specimens that I know of are Samuel Beckett and Jorge Luis Borges—with Vladimir Nabokov, just about the only contemporaries of my reading acquaintance mentionable with the "old masters" of twentieth-century fiction. In the unexciting history of literary awards, the 1961 International Publishers' Prize, shared by Beckett and Borges, is a happy exception indeed.

One of the modern things about these two writers is that in an age of ultimacies and "final solutions"—at least *felt* ultimacies, in everything from weaponry to theology, the celebrated dehumanization of society, and the history of the novel—their work in separate ways reflects and deals with ultimacy, both technically and thematically, as for example *Finnegans Wake* does in its different manner. One notices, for whatever its symptomatic worth, that Joyce was virtually blind at the end, Borges is literally so, and Beckett has become virtually mute, musewise, having progressed from marvelously constructed English sentences through terser and terser French ones to the unsyntactical, unpunctuated prose of *Comment C'est* and "ultimately" to wordless mimes. One might extrapolate a theoretical course for Beckett: Language after all consists of silence as well as sound, and mime is still communication ("that nineteenth-century idea," a Yale student once snarled at me), but by the language of action. But the language of action consists of rest as well as movement, and so in the context of Beckett's progress, immobile, silent figures still aren't altogether ultimate. How about an empty, silent stage, then, or blank

---

* Author's note, 1984: Did I really say this remarkably silly thing back in '67? Yup, and I believed it, too. What I hope are more reasonable formulations of the idea may be found in the Friday-pieces "The Spirit of Place" and "The Literature of Replenishment," farther on.

pages*—a "happening" where nothing happens, like Cage's *4'33"* performed in an empty hall? But dramatic communication consists of the absence as well as the presence of the actors; "we have our exits and our entrances"; and so even that would be imperfectly ultimate in Beckett's case. Nothing at all, then, I suppose; but Nothingness is necessarily and inextricably the background against which Being, et cetera. For Beckett, at this point in his career, to cease to create altogether would be fairly meaningful: his crowning work; his "last word." What a convenient corner to paint yourself into! "And now I shall finish," the valet Arsene says in *Watt*, "and you will hear my voice no more." Only the silence *Molloy* speaks of, "of which the universe is made."

After which, I add on behalf of the rest of us, it might be conceivable to rediscover validly the artifices of language and literature—such far-out notions as grammar, punctuation . . . even characterization! Even *plot!*—if one goes about it the right way, aware of what one's predecessors have been up to.

Now, J. L. Borges is perfectly aware of all these things. Back in the great decades of literary experimentalism he was associated with *Prisma*, a "muralist" magazine that published its pages on walls and billboards; his later *Labyrinths* and *Ficciones* not only anticipate the farthest-out ideas of The Something Else Press crowd—not a difficult thing to do—but, being excellent works of art as well, they illustrate in a simple way the difference between the *fact* of aesthetic ultimacies and their artistic *use*. What it comes to is that an artist doesn't merely exemplify an ultimacy; he employs it.

Consider Borges's story "Pierre Menard, Author of the Quixote": The hero, an utterly sophisticated turn-of-the-century French Symbolist, by an astounding effort of imagination, produces—not *copies* or *imitates*, but *composes*—several chapters of Cervantes's novel.

> It is a revelation [Borges's narrator tells us] to compare Menard's *Don Quixote* with Cervantes's. The latter, for example, wrote (part one, chapter nine):
>
> > . . . truth, whose mother is history, rival of time, depository of deeds, witness of the past, exemplar and adviser to the present, the future's counselor.

---

* An ultimacy already attained in the nineteenth century by that *avant-gardiste* of East Aurora, N.Y., Elbert Hubbard, in his *Essay on Silence*, and much repeated to the present day in such empty "novelties" as *The Wit and Wisdom of Lyndon Johnson*, etc.

Written in the seventeenth century, written by the "lay genius" Cervantes, this enumeration is a mere rhetorical praise of history. Menard, on the other hand, writes:

> ... truth, whose mother is history, rival of time, depository of deeds, witness of the past, exemplar and adviser to the present, the future's counselor.

History, the *mother* of truth: the idea is astounding. Menard, a contemporary of William James, does not define history as an inquiry into reality but as its origin.

Et cetera. Borges's story is of course a satire, but the idea has considerable intellectual validity. I declared earlier that if Beethoven's Sixth were composed today, it might be an embarrassment; but clearly it wouldn't be, necessarily, if done with ironic intent by a composer quite aware of where we've been and where we are. It would have then potentially, for better or worse, the kind of significance of Warhol's Campbell's Soup cans, the difference being that in the former case a work of art is being reproduced instead of a work of non-art, and the ironic comment would therefore be more directly on the genre and history of the art than on the state of the culture. In fact, of course, to make the valid intellectual point one needn't even recompose the Sixth Symphony, any more than Menard really needed to re-create the *Quixote*. It would have been sufficient for Menard to attribute the novel to himself in order to have a new work of art, from the intellectual point of view. Indeed, in several stories Borges plays with this very idea, and I can readily imagine Beckett's next novel, for example, as *Tom Jones,* just as Nabokov's recentest was his multivolume annotated translation of Pushkin. I myself have always aspired to write Burton's version of *The 1001 Nights,* complete with appendices and the like, in ten volumes, and for intellectual purposes I needn't even write it. What evenings we might spend discussing Saarinen's Parthenon, D. H. Lawrence's *Wuthering Heights,* or the Johnson Administration by Robert Rauschenberg!

The idea, I say, is intellectually serious, as are Borges's other characteristic ideas, most of a metaphysical rather than an aesthetic nature. But the important thing to observe is that Borges *doesn't* attribute the *Quixote* to himself, much less recompose it like Pierre Menard; instead, he writes a remarkable and original work of literature, the implicit theme of which is the difficulty, perhaps the unnecessity, of writing original works of literature. His artistic victory, if you like, is that he confronts an intellectual dead end and employs it against itself to accomplish new human work. If this corresponds to what mystics do—"every moment leaping into the infinite," Kierkegaard says, "and every moment falling surely back into the finite"—it's only one more aspect of that old analogy. In homelier terms, it's a matter of every moment throwing out the bath water without for a moment losing the baby.

Another way of describing Borges's accomplishment is with a pair of his own terms, *algebra* and *fire*. In one of his most often anthologized stories, *Tlön, Uqbar, Orbis Tertius*, he imagines an entirely hypothetical world, the invention of a secret society of scholars who elaborate its every aspect in a surreptitious encyclopedia. This *First Encyclopedia of Tlön* (what fictionist would not wish to have dreamed up the *Britannica?*) describes a coherent alternative to this world complete in every respect from its algebra to its fire, Borges tells us, and of such imaginative power that, once conceived, it begins to obtrude itself into and eventually to supplant our prior reality. My point is that neither the algebra nor the fire, metaphorically speaking, could achieve this result without the other. Borges's algebra is what I'm considering here—algebra is easier to talk about than fire—but any smart cookie could equal it. The imaginary authors of the *First Encyclopedia of Tlön* itself are not artists, though their work is in a manner of speaking fictional and would find a ready publisher in The Something Else Press. The author of the story *Tlön, Uqbar, Orbis Tertius*, who merely *alludes* to the fascinating *Encyclopedia, is* an artist; what makes him one, of the first rank, like Kafka, is the combination of that intellectually serious vision with great human insight, poetic power, and consummate mastery of his means—a definition which would have gone without saying, I suppose, in any century but ours.

Not long ago, incidentally, in a footnote to a scholarly edition of Sir Thomas Browne, I came upon a perfect Borges datum, reminiscent of Tlön's self-realization: the actual case of a book called *The Three Impostors,* alluded to in Browne's *Religio Medici* among other places. *The Three Impostors* is a nonexistent blasphemous treatise against Moses, Christ, and Mohammed, which in the seventeenth century was widely held to exist, or to have once existed. Commentators attributed it variously to Boccaccio, Pietro Aretino, Giordano Bruno, and Tommaso Campanella, and though no one, Browne included, had ever seen a copy of it, it was frequently cited, refuted, railed against, and generally discussed as if everyone had read it—until, sure enough, in the *eighteenth* century a spurious work appeared with a forged date of 1598 and the title *De Tribus*

Impostoribus. It's a wonder that Borges doesn't mention this work, as he seems to have read absolutely everything, including all the books that don't exist, and Browne is a particular favorite of his. In fact, the narrator of *Tlön, Uqbar, Orbis Tertius* declares at the end:

> ... English and French and mere Spanish will disappear from the globe. The world will be Tlön. I pay no attention to all this and go on revising, in the still days at the Adrogue Hotel, an uncertain Queve-dian translation (which I do not intend to publish) of Browne's *Urn-Burial.* *

This "contamination of reality by dream," as Borges calls it, is one of his pet themes, and commenting upon such contaminations is one of his favorite fictional devices. Like many of the best such devices, it turns the artist's mode or form into a metaphor for his concerns, as does the diary-ending of *Portrait of the Artist as a Young Man* or the cyclical construction of *Finnegans Wake.* In Borges's case, the story *Tlön,* etc., for example, is a real piece of imagined reality in our world, analogous to those Tlönian artifacts called *hrönir,* which imagine themselves into existence. In short, it's a paradigm of or metaphor for itself; not just the *form* of the story but the *fact* of the story is symbolic; the medium is (part of) the message.

Moreover, like all of Borges's work, it illustrates in other of its aspects my subject: how an artist may paradoxically turn the felt ultimacies of our time into material and means for his work—*paradoxically,* because by doing so he transcends what had appeared to be his refutation, in the same way that the mystic who transcends finitude is said to be enabled to live, spiritually and physically, in the finite world. Suppose you're a writer by vocation—a "print-oriented bastard," as the McLuhanites call us—and you feel, for example, that the novel, if not narrative literature generally, if not the printed word altogether, has by this hour of the world just about shot its bolt, as Leslie Fiedler and others maintain. (I'm inclined to agree, with reservations and hedges. Literary forms certainly have histories and historical contingencies, and it may well be that the novel's time as a major art form is up, as the "times" of classical tragedy, Italian and German grand opera, or the sonnet-sequence came to be. No necessary cause for alarm in this at all, except perhaps to certain novel-

---

* Moreover, on rereading *Tlön,* etc., I find now a remark I'd swear wasn't in it last year: that the eccentric American millionaire who endows the *Encyclopedia* does so on condition that "The work will make no pact with the impostor Jesus Christ."

ists, and one way to handle such a feeling might be to write a novel about
it. Whether historically the novel expires or persists as a major art form
seems immaterial to me; if enough writers and critics *feel* apocalyptical
about it, their feeling becomes a considerable cultural fact, like the *feeling*
that Western civilization, or the world, is going to end rather soon. If you
took a bunch of people out into the desert and the world didn't end, you'd
come home shamefaced, I imagine; but the persistence of an art form
doesn't invalidate work created in the comparable apocalyptic ambience.
That is one of the fringe benefits of being an artist instead of a prophet.
There are others.) If you happened to be Vladimir Nabokov, you might
address that felt ultimacy by writing *Pale Fire:* a fine novel by a learned
pedant, in the form of a pedantic commentary on a poem invented for the
purpose. If you were Borges you might write *Labyrinths:* fictions by a
learned librarian in the form of footnotes, as he describes them, to imaginary or hypothetical books. And I'll add that if you were the author of
this paper, you'd have written something like *The Sot-Weed Factor* or
Giles Goat-Boy: novels which imitate the form of the Novel, by an author
who imitates the role of Author.

   If this sort of thing sounds unpleasantly decadent, nevertheless it's
about where the genre began, with *Quixote* imitating *Amadis of Gaul,*
Cervantes pretending to be the Cid Hamete Benengeli (and Alonso Qui-
jano pretending to be Don Quixote), or Fielding parodying Richardson.
"History repeats itself as farce"—meaning, of course, in the form or mode
of farce, not that history is farcical. The imitation, like the Dadaist echoes
in the work of the "intermedia" types, is something new and *may be* quite
serious and passionate despite its farcical aspect.

   This is the difference between a proper, "naïve" novel and a deliber-
ate imitation of a novel, or a novel imitative of other kinds of documents.
The first sort attempts (has been historically inclined to attempt) to imitate actions more or less directly, and its conventional devices—cause
and effect, linear anecdote, characterization, authorial selection, arrangement, and interpretation—have been objected to as obsolete notions, or
metaphors for obsolete notions: Alain Robbe-Grillet's essays *For a New
Novel* come to mind. There are replies to these objections, not to the point
here, but one can see that in any case they're obviated by imitations-of-
novels, for instance, which attempt to represent not life directly but a representation of life. In fact such works are no more removed from "life"
than Richardson's or Goethe's epistolary novels are; both imitate "real"
documents, and the subject of both, ultimately, is life, not the documents.

A novel is as much a piece of the real world as a letter, and the letters in *The Sorrows of Young Werther* are, after all, fictitious.

One might imaginably compound this imitation, and though Borges doesn't, he's fascinated with the idea. One of his more frequent literary allusions is to the 602nd night in a certain edition of *The 1001 Nights,* when, owing to a copyist's error, Scheherazade begins to tell the King the story of the 1001 nights, from the beginning. Happily, the King interrupts; if he didn't, there'd be no 603rd night ever, and while this would solve Scheherazade's problem, it would put the "outside" author in a bind. (I suspect that Borges dreamed this whole thing up; the business he mentions isn't in any edition of *The 1001 Nights* I've been able to consult. Not *yet,* anyhow: After reading *Tlön, Uqbar, Orbis Tertius,* one is inclined to recheck every semester or so.)

Borges is interested in the 602nd night because it's an instance of the story-within-the-story turned back upon itself, and his interest in such instances is threefold. First, as he himself declares, they disturb us metaphysically: When the characters in a work of fiction become readers or authors of the fiction they're in, we're reminded of the fictitious aspect of our own existence—one of Borges's cardinal themes, as it was of Shakespeare, Calderón, Unamuno, and other folk. Second, the 602nd night is a literary illustration of the *regressus in infinitum,* as are many other of Borges's principal images and motifs. Third, Scheherazade's accidental gambit, like Borges's other versions of the *regressus in infinitum,* is an image of the exhaustion, or attempted exhaustion, of possibilities—in this case literary possibilities—and so we return to our main subject.

What makes Borges's stance, if you like, more interesting to me even than, say, Nabokov's or Beckett's, is the premise with which he approaches literature. In the words of one of his editors: "For [Borges] no one has claim to originality in literature; all writers are more or less faithful amanuenses of the spirit, translators and annotators of pre-existing archetypes." Thus his inclination to write brief comments on imaginary books: For one to attempt to add overtly to the sum of "original" literature by even so much as a conventional short story, not to mention a novel, would be too presumptuous, too naïve; literature has been done long since. A librarian's point of view! And it would itself be too presumptuous if it weren't part of a lively, relevant metaphysical vision, slyly employed against itself precisely to make new and original literature. Borges defines the Baroque as "that style which deliberately exhausts (or tries to exhaust) its possibilities and borders upon its own caricature."

While his own work is *not* Baroque, except intellectually (the Baroque was never so terse, laconic, economical), it suggests the view that intellectual and literary history has been Baroque, and has pretty well exhausted the possibilities of novelty. His *ficciones* are not only footnotes to imaginary texts, but postscripts to the real corpus of literature.*

This premise gives resonance and relation to all his principal images. The facing mirrors that recur in his stories are a dual *regressus.* The doubles that his characters, like Nabokov's, run afoul of suggest dizzying multiples and remind one of Browne's remark that "every man is not only himself . . . men are lived over again." (It would please Borges, and illustrate Browne's point, to call Browne a precursor of Borges. "Every writer," Borges says in his essay on Kafka, "creates his own precursors.") Borges's favorite third-century heretical sect is the Histriones—I think and hope he invented them—who believe that repetition is impossible in history and who therefore live viciously in order to purge the future of the vices they commit; to exhaust the possibilities of the world in order to bring its end nearer. The writer he most often mentions, after Cervantes, is Shakespeare; in one piece he imagines the playwright on his deathbed asking God to permit him to be one and himself, having been everyone and no one; God replies from the whirlwind that He is no one either: He has dreamed the world like Shakespeare, and including Shakespeare. Homer's story in Book IV of the *Odyssey,* of Menelaus on the beach at Pharos, tackling Proteus, appeals profoundly to Borges: Proteus is he who "exhausts the guises of reality" while Menelaus—who, one recalls, disguised his own identity in order to ambush him—holds fast. Zeno's paradox of Achilles and the Tortoise embodies a *regressus in infinitum* which Borges carries through philosophical history, pointing out that Aristotle uses it to refute Plato's theory of forms, Hume to refute the possibility of cause and effect, Lewis Carroll to refute syllogistic deduction, William James to refute the notion of temporal passage, and Bradley to refute the general possibility of logical relations. Borges himself uses it, citing Schopenhauer, as evidence that the world is our dream, our idea, in which "tenuous and eternal crevices of unreason" can be found to remind us

---

* It is true that he asserts in another place that the possibilities of literature can never be exhausted, since it is impossible to exhaust even a single book. However, his remark about the Baroque includes the *attempt* to exhaust as well as the hypothetical achievement of exhaustion. What's more, his cardinal themes and images rather contradict that passing optimism—a state of affairs reminiscent of the aesthetics of Tlön, where no book is regarded as complete which doesn't contain its counterbook, or refutation.

that our creation is false, or at least fictive. The infinite library of one of his most popular stories is an image particularly pertinent to the literature of exhaustion: The "Library of Babel" houses every possible combination of alphabetical characters and spaces, and thus every possible book and statement, including your and my refutations and vindications, the history of the actual future, the history of every possible future, and, though he doesn't mention it, the encyclopedia not only of Tlön but of every imaginable other world—since, as in Lucretius's universe, the number of elements and so of combinations is finite (though very large), and the number of instances of each element and combination of elements is infinite, like the library itself.

That brings us to his favorite image of all, the labyrinth, and to my point. *Labyrinths* is the name of his most substantial translated volume, and the only current full-length study of Borges in English, by Ana María Barrenechea, is called *Borges the Labyrinth-Maker*. A labyrinth, after all, is a place in which, ideally, all the possibilities of choice (of direction, in this case) are embodied, and—barring special dispensation like Theseus's—must be exhausted before one reaches the heart. Where, mind, the Minotaur waits with two final possibilities: defeat and death or victory and freedom. The legendary Theseus is non-Baroque; thanks to Ariadne's thread he can take a shortcut through the labyrinth at Knossos. But Menelaus on the beach at Pharos, for example, is genuinely Baroque in the Borgesian spirit, and illustrates a positive artistic morality in the literature of exhaustion. He is not there, after all, for kicks; Menelaus is *lost*, in the larger labyrinth of the world, and has got to hold fast while the Old Man of the Sea exhausts reality's frightening guises so that he may extort direction from him when Proteus returns to his "true" self. It is a heroic enterprise, with salvation as its object—one recalls that the aim of the Histriones is to get history done with so that Jesus may come again the sooner, and that Shakespeare's heroic metamorphoses culminate not merely in a theophany but in an apotheosis.

Now, not just any old body is equipped for this labor; Theseus in the Cretan labyrinth becomes in the end the aptest image for Borges after all. Distressing as the fact is to us liberal democrats, the commonalty, alas, will *always* lose their way and their soul; it is the chosen remnant, the virtuoso, the Thesean *hero*, who, confronted with Baroque reality, Baroque history, the Baroque state of his art, need *not* rehearse its possibilities to exhaustion, any more than Borges needs actually to *write* the *Encyclopedia of Tlön* or the books in the Library of Babel. He need only be aware of

their existence or possibility, acknowledge them, and with the aid of very
special gifts—as extraordinary as saint- or herohood and not likely to be
found in The New York Correspondence School of Literature—go
straight through the maze to the accomplishment of his work.

More Troll Than Cabbage

INTRODUCTION FOR
TAPE-AND-LIVE-VOICE PERFORMANCES
FROM THE SERIES *LOST IN THE FUNHOUSE*

AS A BOY experimenting with sin, I once hollowed out a book—it was called *365 Bedtime Stories*—to hide a pack of Chesterfield cigarettes in, the way Renaissance princes sometimes packed pistols in eviscerated prayer-books. It had been my thought while writing the series *Lost in the Funhouse* to publish the finished book with a tape cassette enclosed in that same fashion. I have however a *daimon* like Socrates's, who seldom tells me what to do, but (less dependably than Socrates's) sometimes whispers ''For pity's sake, don't do *that*.'' Distinctly, when the time came, it announced that the tape-in-a-book idea was an egregious gimmick; that even to print the tape-and-live-voice pieces in reading-script format would be tiresome, unbecoming. In 1968 the book appeared therefore by my own decision in ordinary left-to-right roman type as if composed for print alone like any other book, at cost of part of the sense and most of the entertainment of the tape pieces, which to the eye alone may be wearisomely self-reflexive exercises in hyperselfconsciousness. That's show business; and for writers as writers, show business is no business.

As show business, on the other hand, those little experiments worked well for a season or two on the campus circuit, until my nay-saying *daimon* whispered that it was time to close a run that began at the Library of Congress on Mayday, 1967.

Why should a mere introduction to a program of readings be here collected and printed? Because this Friday Book is also a resumé of my Stories Thus Far and an account of what I believe myself to have been up to in writing them.

I have a program of readings from my novels that I've given here and there on university campuses in the last year. It's called "The Heroical Curriculum"; what it consists of is a series of excerpts from *The Floating Opera, The End of the Road, The Sot-Weed Factor,* and *Giles Goat-Boy,* selected ostensibly to illustrate some of their common themes—that self-knowledge is generally bad news, for example; or that if you don't look out, you may get pinched between two of the great axioms of Western civilization: Socrates's lesson that the unexamined life is not worth living, and Sophocles's lesson that the well-examined life may turn out to be unlivable. But the real motivating principle behind the selections was that they all read well out loud and lead one to suppose that my fiction has been getting better over the years.

If we can only accept that last as granted, I'd like to skip the demonstration today and do a thing more risky from the show-biz point of view: I want to lay on you a sample of the short pieces I've been up to since my goat-boy book was finished in 1966. They are what used to be called "experimental" pieces: Most haven't been published yet; some won't ever be. A few don't make much ordinary sense out of the context of their neighbors; others were composed specifically for tape and would lose part of their point in print. At least one was composed exclusively for public readings like this one—but I didn't bring it to Washington with me.

If a writer is not simply going to repeat himself (which isn't always a bad thing to do), he has to keep changing, more or less reinventing himself. He hopes that the changes are "developments"; that his "stages," like a rocket's, are all pushing the same payload toward heaven, in their different ways. He hopes too—since some legs of the trip are liable to be rougher than others—that his audience will stay with him across the troll-bridges and that they'll reach the sweet cabbage fields together. It may be that there is more troll than cabbage in these pieces; I hope not.

I don't think it's a good idea, as a rule, for artists to explain their art, even if they can. Jorge Luis Borges puts it arrogantly: God shouldn't stoop to theology. A modern painter put it more politely and poetically: Birds have no need of ornithology. But since you'll be hearing these pieces aloud and for the first time, I'll say one or two things about them and about the series-in-progress from which they're taken.

One advantage of electronic tape as a narrative medium is that it has some of the virtues of the oral tradition, where literature started—I mean the immediacy of the human voice and the intimacy of story*telling,* which can only be echoed on the printed page—and some of the virtues of print, such as referability and repeatability. You can replay a tough or delightful passage on tape, or pause to let it sink in, as you can when you're reading but can't when you're watching a film or a stage play.

These pieces share some preoccupations with my novels. They're meant to be serious enough to be taken seriously, but they're not longfaced. They're pessimistic, but I hope they're entertaining. In all of them, for better or worse, the process of narration becomes the content of the narrative, to some degree and in various ways; or the form or medium has metaphorical value and dramatical relevance. The medium really is part of the message. Second, most of them exploit, one way or another, ambiguities of language and narrative viewpoint—especially narrative viewpoint—to make their particular sense. Neither of these is a new idea. Third, one objective of most of these stories—the most important to me—is to try whether different kinds of artistical felt ultimacies and cul-de-sacs can be employed against themselves to do valid new work: whether disabling contradictions, for example, can be escalated or exacerbated into enabling paradoxes. This objective represents to me in its little way a general task of civilized people nowadays.

Finally, if the pieces are successful by my personal standards, they have to be more than just tricky. If I believed my writing were no more than the formal fun-and-games that *Time* magazine makes it out to be, I'd take up some other line of work. The subject of literature, says Aristotle, is "human life, its happiness and its misery." I agree with Aristotle.

That's why we object to the word *experimental*. It suggests cold exercises in technique, and technique in art, we all know, has the same importance as technique in love: Heartless skill has its appeal; so does heartfelt ineptitude; but what we want is passionate virtuosity. If these pieces aren't also *moving*, then the experiment is unsuccessful, and their author is lost in the funhouse indeed.

The Role of the Prosaic in Fiction

THE BEST symposium was Plato's; all symposia since have been anticlimactic. My *daimon,* in his absolute way, says "Say *no* to all symposia," but I don't always listen.

I cannot imagine why Canisius College, a small Catholic school downtown from SUNY/Buffalo, sponsored a symposium on so curious a topic as "The Role of the Prosaic in Fiction": a far cry indeed from the topic of Plato's *Symposium.* I cannot imagine either why I agreed to sit on it: The honorarium was modest, and I had no a priori interest in the subject. Perhaps it was out of respect for my fellow symposiasts: the late crusted reactionary George P. Elliott, some of whose fiction I admired but whose literary opinions—an anticipation of the later John Gardner's—I found disagreeable; and my friend and colleague the erudite, unpredictable, iconoclastic, large-spirited troublemaker Leslie Fiedler, from whose outrageous statements I have seldom failed to learn. Or perhaps it was that in April 1970 I was as aforementioned between lives, living alone for the moment in a cottage on Lake Chautauqua, writing a triad of novellas called *Chimera,* commuting up the Thruway to my classes, and more disposed than normally to the prospect of an extra evening in town, even for a symposium that would not likely be a love-feast.

I have no recollection of what Elliott and Fiedler said about the role of the prosaic in fiction—what a topic!—or why they were symposing on a subject that cannot in itself have much interested *them,* either. I know that my own opinions were invented ad hoc, but that—as sometimes happens—having set them forth, I discovered that I believed them. Reviewing them now, I discover that I still do.

The three meanings of *prosaic* are (1) of or like prose; not poetic; (2) matter-of-fact, straightforward; and (3) lacking in imagination, dull. Discarding most of the third sense—since unimaginativeness has no legitimate role in literature—I think that these definitions correspond to three functions of the prosaic in fiction, having to do with three aspects of the art itself: its matter, its manner, and its medium.

1. With regard to the first aspect (and the last definition), I take "the prosaic" to mean humble facts, specification, homely particulars. Their justification in fiction is mainly self-evident: Objects in literature aren't really objects, but only the names of objects, and readers and writers share the human pleasure in naming things. We start like Adam, saying "This is a tree; this is a helpmeet; this is a pomegranate"; and we go on, in life and in literature, through Homer's catalogue of ships, Virgil's Carthaginian frescoes, the passage on horse's harness in *Don Quixote* which I remember having to look up every noun of in my Spanish-English dictionary only to find that I didn't know what the English equivalents meant either, Henry James's celebrated "solidity of specification," Nabokov's urging his Cornell students to "caress the details" (*Q:* What kind of meat was in the butchers' barrels in those flaring streets wherealong the young narrator of James Joyce's story "Araby" carries the secret burden of his love? *A:* Pigs' cheeks), and John Updike's credo that "Details are the giant's fingers." At forty and sixty and eighty, God willing, the old Adam in us is still pleased to remark: "This is a plinth; this is a paraboloid; this is a Pouilly-Fuissé 1966."

Paul Valéry declared that the reason why he could never write a novel is that he couldn't bring himself to set down such prosaic particulars as "The Marquis went out at five"; Claude Mauriac, a French New Novelist, uses that line as the title of one of his novels. In realistic fiction, from Petronius through Proust to Pinget, such prosaic detail is the very substance. In satiric fantasy it is commonly the ground and foil for its contrary, Sancho Panza to Don Quixote: Rabelais's giant pisses real piss in unreal quantity; Gulliver in Lilliput besmirches his drawers; real brand-names and place names make Donald Barthelme's world at once less and more strange. In "irreal" fictions generally, convincing prosaic detail mediates between our waking world and the dreamed ones of, say, Kafka or John Hawkes—as it does routinely in science fiction, pornographic fantasy, and various kinds of allegory. Finally, in the "minimal," "algebraical," or otherwise stripped-down fictions of Beckett, Borges, Robbe-Grillet, or Calvino, prosaic detail, when we come upon it, is the source of the fire for which the algebra exists. Such fictions remind us of Gertrude Stein's remark about the Spanish landscape: It has few things in it, and so each stands out with a peculiar substantiveness. Our relief, when we come upon the homely chair in Ted Hughes's story "Snow," is as great as the narrator's; that chair is the only object in sight besides himself, and from it he infers a world.

2. Second, we can take *prosaic* to mean a "straightforward" or "naïve" as opposed to an oblique or self-reflexive manner of storytelling. Not much modern fiction is prosaic in this sense. Innocent story—the "naïve anecdote," Robbe-Grillet calls it—has pretty much gone the way of innocently representational painting and sculpture. It survives in non-"straightforward" forms such as parody and some fantasy, in nonfiction such as Capote's, Mailer's, and Tom Wolfe's, and in programmatically traditional writers like Styron, Updike, and Bellow, where even so it tends to a freight of symbolism, even allegory, or, at its most heavyfooted (as in Updike's otherwise admirable *The Centaur*), mythography-in-reverse.

More usually, what prosaic "straightforwardness" there is in contemporary fiction is either a sly disguise, as in Kafka or Nabokov, a momentary relief, as in Beckett's occasional terse anecdotes, or, as with the cases of homely detail I spoke of before, a kind of simplicity at which one arrives by way of irony and complexity. Fools, children, sentimentalists, pet dogs, and false-naïfs may wear their hearts on their sleeves; the rest of us can't be got to so easily. Artistic good faith is one thing, aesthetic simplism another.

To sum up this point: The role of prosaic *straightforwardness* in modern fiction is characteristically duplicitous.

3. The third sense of *prosaic* and the first of its definitions—prose versus verse as a narrative medium—seems to me the most interesting aspect of our subject. Printed prose is historically a most peculiar, almost an aberrant, way of telling stories, and by far the most inherently anesthetic: It is the only medium of art I can think of which appeals directly to none of our five senses. The oral and folk tradition in narrative made use of verse or of live-voice dynamics, embellished by gesture and expression—a kind of rudimentary theater—as do the best raconteurs of all times and places. Commonly there was musical accompaniment as well: a one-man theater-of-mixed-means. Early written fiction—the Sanskrit tale-cycles, the *Thousand and One Nights,* and so forth—reflects this; while it typically and sometimes elaborately acknowledges its condition as *writing* (see for example the wonderful *Kathapitha,* or "Story of the Story," which opens Somadeva's enormous *Katha Sarit Sagara,* or "Ocean of Streams of Story"), such fiction is usually about people *telling* one another stories, interspersed with poems, songs, and dances.

Verse especially, as a narrative medium, has served purposes more subtle than merely heightening the sensory appeal of language. Jaromir Hladik, the playwright in Borges's story "The Secret Miracle," chooses metrical verse as the essential medium for his drama because "it makes it impossible for the spectators to lose sight of irreality, one of art's requisites"—in other words, it prevents our mucking up the useful distinction between art and life. In the eighteenth and particularly the nineteenth century, as verse-drama and narrative poetry were more and more supplanted by the novel and by realistic prose drama, one observes that grand opera and classical ballet—those least prosaic, most irreal of narrative media—flowered, almost as if in compensation, as the inheritors of the older narrative tradition. It passes in our century to the cinema, whose camera effects and musical soundtrack can redeem any scene from being prosaic in the pejorative sense and heighten, if not always save, the prose of the spoken dialogue—always adding, even in the most realistic films, Borges's "essential element of irreality."

But novels and stories in printed verse—Philip Toynbee's, for example—simply seem seldom to work, except in rare cases where the medium is employed with some ironical covering of tracks, as in Nabokov's *Pale Fire.* In most post-realistic prose fiction, the essential element in the transmutation of the prosaic into art is provided either by *irreality in the conceit,* as in Borges himself (and Kafka, Beckett, late Joyce, middle Malamud, Ionesco, Calvino, Landolfi, Gombrowicz, Grass, Brautigan, Barthelme, Vonnegut, and who have you), or by a *radical unprosaicizing of the prose,* as in late Joyce, Faulkner, Hawkes, some Nabokov, etc., or by *radical manipulations of narrative viewpoint, dramatic form, or format,* as in most of the aforementioned plus the French New Novelists, William H. Gass, Robert Coover, and The Something Else Press writers—or by combinations of all of these.

In short, the role of the prosaic in prose fiction comes first to something akin to the role of "flat" lines in poetry as described by Yeats when he remarked that a mountain is mountainous because it has valley on either side; and, second, to something akin to the role of ordinary reality in dreams: to supply the bones to be transformed by the writer's imagination into something rich and strange. To the extent that this transformation doesn't occur, one has prosaic fiction in the unhappy sense: dull and tedious writing.

The Ocean of Story

THE ELEVENTH-CENTURY Sanskrit *Ocean of Story* got mentioned in that foregoing symposium statement because, between writing the *Chimera* novellas, I was reading through that huge, peculiar work and registering my reactions to it in a demi-essay. When Henry Sams, chairman of the immense Department of English at Penn State during most of my stay there, retired from that office, his colleagues published the somewhat presumptuously titled *Directions in Literary Criticism: Essays in Honor of Henry A. Sams.** My grateful contribution to that *Festschrift* follows: no Direction in Literary Criticism, merely a bemusement I knew Henry would share.

The road to India is a long road, but it is the only way to India. One can't expect to get through *The Thousand and One Nights* in one night. When I worry that one of my stories is growing overlong, I tell myself the story of a *really* long story: *Katha Sarit Sagara,* or *The Ocean of Streams of Story,* more or less by the eleventh-century Indian poet Somadeva.

Its title haunted me for a dozen years (as did Calderón's *La Vida Es Sueño*) before I ever read beyond it. As an undergraduate book-filer in the classics and Oriental Seminary stacks of Johns Hopkins's Gilman Hall Library, I would push daily past the ten huge sea-green volumes of Penzer's edition (privately printed in London in 1924 and still the only English-language edition one sees) of Tawney's nineteenth-century prose translation of Somadeva's Sanskrit redaction of King Satavahana's third-century publication of his minister Gunadhya's Paisachi versification of the demigod Kanabhuti's retelling of the demigod Pushpadanta's version of the Great Tale first told by the god Siva to his consort Parvati.

---

* Eds. Weintraub and Young. University Park, PA: Pennsylvania State University Press, 1973.

Inevitably, semester after semester, that golden title, *The Ocean of Story,* took my eye and fancy. But waiting on the book cart to be reshelved (and read, surreptitiously, on company time) were more-navigated ways of narrative: *The Thousand and One Nights, The Panchatantra,* the *Pent-, Hept-,* and *Decamerons.* One never found allusions to *The Ocean of Story* in other literature or heard it mentioned by one's professors and better-read friends; indeed, one never saw Somadeva off the shelf—where I filed beside his *mare incognitum* my resolve one day to embark upon its endless reaches. For the present there were those more famous works to be read, more of them than one ever would find time for, and from the springs of literature issued unceasingly a torrent of new writing as well, to be breasted if possible. Presently one's own outpourings were added to the general flood. There was no time.

Until one arrived, enough years later, at the free port of understanding that, like Magellan, one will never accomplish the whole voyage. One will not likely *ever* get around now to Camöens's *Lusiad,* I came to realize, or the rest of Hardy, or the end of *Eugene Onegin,* or the beginning of *Jerusalem Delivered;* and even a second lifetime would not suffice to get said the whole of what oneself had aspired to say. This recognition, when not traumatic, grants an extravagant liberty: The voyage being incompletable, one may take side trips of any length in any number, at one's pleasure! In connection, therefore, with a casual research of some years' standing through the whole corpus of frame-tale literature, I lately made at last my leisure-cruise from end to end of *The Ocean of Story.*

Was it that too long deferral of the journey staled its charm? Or that no merely actual fiction could realize the long work of my imagination upon that title? In any case, I must report that:

1. In the main, alas, the tales rehearsed by Somadeva (whose noble ambition was to tell them *all*) are less memorable than Scheherazade's, say, or Boccaccio's or Chaucer's—or less memorably recounted, in the several instances where the plots are analogous. In keeping with Somadeva's (and his precursors') conceit of an ultimate narrative ocean into which all the streams of fancy flow at last, entire Gangeses of pre-existing fiction are tapped and incorporated, such as the *Panchatantra* and the *Vetalapanchavimsati,* or *25 Tales by a Vampire.* It is principally through the numerous redactions, recensions, and meanders of these tributaries—*Siddhi-Kur, The Seven Sages, Kalilah and Dimnah, Syntipas the Philosopher, The Fables of Bidpai, Sindibad's Parables*—and later reworkings of these reworkings—Johannes de Alta Silva's *Dolopathos,* John of Capua's

Directorium Vitae Humanae, Firenzuola's *Discorsi degli Animali,* and
Doni's *Novelle,* for example—that waters from *The Ocean of Story* finally
enter the mainstream of Western literature, and in most instances they
gain flavor from their circuitous journey. To put the figure more accurately: Several of the springs that fed *The Ocean of Story* trickled westward also and separately, with the consequence that Somadeva's vast
poem strikes one less as a source of Western narrative motifs than as a
kind of anthology or compendium of such sources. Hence, in part, its
persisting obscurity, except among Orientalists, despite its being, in
Penzer's odd phrase, "for its size, the earliest collection of stories extant in
the world."

   2. The frame-structure, too, is less arresting or fecund than that of
The Thousand and One Nights, The Decameron, or, for that matter, the
anonymous seventeenth-century English delight entitled *Westward for
Smelts.* Nothing in the circumstantial history of Prince Naravahanadatta
and the Vidyaharas captures the imagination as does the image of Scheherazade yarning through the night to save her neck, or Boccaccio's twilit
company beguiling themselves with fiction in despite of plagued fact. On
the other hand, Somadeva's structure is considerably more complex—the
most complex, I think, among the nearly 200 specimens of frame-tale literature I've thus far noted. Not only is the narrative at several points involved to the fourth degree (tales within tales within tales within tales),
but at any degree, including the first or outermost, the frame may be serial and achronological—as if, for example, the pilgrimage to Canterbury
were only one among several frame-conceits in Chaucer's poem, and
began outside Rochester at that, the departure from London being filled
in only later; as if, moreover, his *Troilus and Criseyde* were one of several
tales told by Patient Grisilde, whose tale in turn were one of several told
by Chanticleer, whose tale were one of several told by the Nun's Priest, et
cetera. The intrication is enormous (stout Penzer uses a schematic outline
in his table of contents: The story of King Brahmadatta, for instance, is
Tale 1BB in the midst of Tale 1B in the *Cont*[inuation] of Tale 1 in the
Cont[inuation] of the *M*[ain] *I*[ntroduction] in Chapter III of Book I);
but like the complexity of termite tunnels or lymphatic cancer, it is more
dismaying than delightful from the human point of view.

   3. Just as the accounts of Hakluyt's voyagers may be more fascinating than the places they voyaged to, the Burtonesque notes and appendices (by many hands) to Penzer's edition of Somadeva—disquisitions on
such heady matters as the place of collyrium in the history of cosmetic

art, or the Bitch-and-Pepper motif in the literature of the world—are frequently more engaging than the texts they illuminate. In the course of an indifferent sub-sub-sub-tale about the founding of the city of Pataliputra, for example, a poker-faced note describes two remarkable ancient customs alleged to prevail there: The first is the ancient custom of the women, annually in the rainy season, to bake cakes in the form of phalluses and offer them to any Brahman whom they judge to be (what the English field-researcher translates as) "a blockhead." The second is the equally ancient custom of the Brahmans, always to refuse those cakes because they regard the first ancient custom as disgusting. One's conviction is affirmed that it would be a more splendid destiny to have cooked up *Burton's* version of *The Thousand and One Nights*—footnotes, Terminal Essay, and all—than to have written the original.

4. These reservations notwithstanding, *The Ocean of Story* contains at least one narrative conception of the very first rank, without real analogues that I know of in any of its contemporaries or predecessors, and more gloriously elaborate by far than any of its several analogues in later fiction: I mean the *Kathapitha,* or "history of the text" of the *Katha Sarit Sagara* itself, which history comprises the primary narrative frame of Book I and the *M*[ain] *I*[ntroduction] to the entire work, and happens to be among my very favorite stories in the world:

One day the god Siva is so delighted at the way Parvati makes love to him that he offers her anything she wishes in reward. She asks for a story. Perching her on his lap, he tells her a short one on the subject of his own splendid exploits in a former life, including his romance with a beautiful woman whom he tactfully supposes to have been Parvati herself in one of *her* former incarnations.

The goddess abruptly cuts him off. She has heard that one before; so has everybody else. What she craves is an absolutely original story that no one at all has heard and, it is implied, that no one but herself will *ever* hear, unless she chooses to repeat it. Siva comes up with the *Brihat Katha,* or Great Tale—actually seven great tales of 100,000 couplets each. It takes a very long time to tell (if the *Odyssey,* as has been estimated, was sung in four evenings, the same minstrel at the same pace would by my reckoning need 509 evenings—a little under a year and a half—to do Siva's piece), but in this instance teller, tale, and told all happen to be immortal; Parvati sits silent and presumably entertained—until she learns that the tale has been overheard after all, by one of their house staff! The *Gana* (servant deity) Pushpadanta, who has hidden invisible in the divine boudoir (as the monks in Marguerite of Navarre's *Heptameron* squat behind the shrubbery of the monastery every evening to overhear the tales Marguerite's friends exchange), repeats the Great Tale to his wife, who repeats it to Parvati, who is so incensed that she condemns not only Pushpadanta but his friend Malyavan—who had merely pled on his behalf—to be born as mortal men: Pushpadanta will have to live on earth under the name of Vararuchi until he crosses paths in the woods with the hermit Kanabhuti (in fact the demigod Supratika, also currently doing time) and repeats to him the entire Great Tale; Malyavan will be obliged to mortality under the name Gunadhya until *he* happens to cross paths with this same Kanabhuti/Supratika, hears the Great Tale from him, and writes it down—whereupon, like the others who have been delivered of it, he'll enter heaven.

Got that?

The first of these redemptions comes to pass with comparative ease in the space of a mere four chapters properly laced with narrative digression; the second with more difficulty and corresponding interest and structural extravagance. Malyavan is reborn as Gunadhya and works his mortal way to a ministership in the court of King Satavahana, an adequate monarch in every particular except that he makes mistakes in his grammar. Satavahana himself could perhaps live with this failing, were it not that one of his favorite harem girls is an intellectual who teases him with his solecisms. Humiliated, he demands that his ministers educate him. Gunadhya volunteers to teach him Sanskrit grammar in six years flat; his rival for the King's favor, Sarvavarman, rashly declares *he'll* do the job in six months or else wear Gunadhya's shoes on his head for a dozen years. Gunadhya counters that if Sarvavarman makes good his boast, he, Gunadhya, will renounce forever the three languages he knows: Sanskrit, Prakrit, and the vernacular dialect. Inasmuch as Sanskrit grammar could not in fact be taught in six months at that time, Gunadhya is full of confidence. But Sarvavarman, alarmed at his own impulsiveness, petitions the gods for help, and for reasons never disclosed they reveal to him a revolutionary new concise Sanskrit grammar, the *Katantra,* which wins him the bet and reforms subsequent education.

Reduced to silence, Gunadhya takes to the woods with a pair of his favorite students. After an unspecified wordless interval, he comes across Kanabhuti/Supratika, who has in the meanwhile been told the Great Tale by Vararuchi/Pushpadanta and is anxious to pass it along so that he too can return to heaven. But what to do about the language problem?

Kanabhuti solves it by teaching Gunadhya a new tongue—Paisacha, or "goblin-language"—and reciting the Great Tale in *that*. It takes Gunadhya seven more years in the woods to throw the thing into written couplets, owing to its length; no doubt also to the Nabokovian difficulty of versifying in an adopted goblin-language; and perhaps to the nature of his medium: He writes literally with his own blood. But he finally sets down the 700,000th distich, and his two faithful students rush off with the masterpiece to King Satavahana—who takes one look at it and says, presumably in perfect Sanskrit: "Away with this barbaric Paisacha!"

Back to the woods it goes, where its rejected author, as a last resort, commences reading it aloud to himself. All the animals of the forest gather motionless to listen, moved to tears not only by the beauty of the composition but by the spectacle of Gunadhya's burning each page of manuscript in a hole in the rock as he finishes reading it, rather like Rodolfo in Act One of *La Bohème*.

Presently King Satavahana, though eating regally, falls ill of malnutrition. Medical research discloses that the cause of his malaise is a deficiency of nutritive value in the meat fetched in by the palace huntsmen, and still further investigation reveals the cause of this deficiency to be a certain mad poet out in the bush, whose narration so spellbinds the beasts of the country that they forget to ruminate. The king hurries to the forest, recognizes his minister Gunadhya, and snatches from the fire what's left of the Great Tale: alas, a mere 100,000 distichs, the other six-sevenths of the magnum opus having gone up in smoke. Anyhow vindicated, Gunadhya/Malyavan proceeds to heaven; the students are promoted to administrators; and Satavahana, to redeem himself, prefaces the truncated masterwork with a book called *Kathapitha*, the History of the Tale or Story of the Story, which I've just rehearsed, and publishes the whole (in ordinary ink) under the title *Brihat Katha*, or Great Tale. Eight centuries later, the Kashmirian court-poet Somadeva, to amuse another royal lady, pares down this *Brihat Katha*, including Satavahana's prefatory *Kathapitha*, to a radically terse 22,000 couplets—the mere ten folio volumes of Penzer's edition, scarcely twice the length of the *Iliad* and the *Odyssey* combined.

Whether Queen Suryavati was as pleased with this revised and abbreviated version as the goddess Parvati was with the original is not recorded. But we may assume that in order to recite to her from memory such a short short story, Somadeva—Mr. Soma—wouldn't even have needed to make use of a certain great secret recipe for epical recall, from the chief constituent of which he takes his name. Since it may be that this pharmacological formula, rather than the narrative ones analyzed by Professors Milman Parry and Albert Lord,* is the *real* key to epical composition, I offer it here from my own memory of the *Samavidhana Brahmana* as quoted in a footnote from the unfrequented deeps of *The Ocean of Story:*

1. Fast for three nights.
2. Recite a certain incantation and then eat of the soma plant one thousand times.
3. Or bruise the soma plant in water and drink that water for a year.
4. Or ferment the soma plant and drink that liquor for a month.
5. Or drink it forever.

---

* In *The Singer of Tales* (Cambridge: Harvard Univ. Press, 1971).

A Poet to the Rescue

FOR REASONS of temperament more than of philosophy, during the period of our war in Vietnam I remained apart from, though sympathetic to, the great antiwar demonstrations in our cities. To the less great ones on our campuses I was less sympathetic, especially to the sit-ins, takeovers, trashings, and disruptions: Whatever their dealings with the federal government, American universities are not federal institutions to be treated as symbols of our sometimes wrongheaded foreign policies. Academic freedom is a rare and precious thing; riot police, tear gas, and armed National Guardsmen are to be kept off university campuses at almost any cost except the constraint of that freedom. In confrontations between antiwar marchers and federal officials, my heart was with the marchers; in confrontations between campus demonstrators and beleaguered university administrators, my sympathies were often with the administrators. If I had been of draftable age, perhaps I'd have felt otherwise. I hope not. The war was wrong; the choices it forced upon American men just a touch older than my own sons were abhorrent; *its* disruption of the proper function of universities was deplorable—but the universities were neither the enemy nor a fit symbol of the enemy.

That said, I hasten to add that my politically activist students and colleagues in Buffalo certainly taught me, and many another, more than we'd known before about the political ramifications of the academic enterprise. My general innocence is perhaps invincible, but I remain grateful for their disabusing me of some of its particulars.

Three scenes are particularly fixed in my memory as talismans of the political-academic High Sixties. The first is eerily tranquil. We have invited Ralph Ellison to preside over an informal writing seminar and to deliver a public lecture. His fee is high, but our speakers' budget is fat. When he arrives in Buffalo, however, the campus is in a volatile mood, on the verge of another political rumble. Mr. Ellison chats amiably with a contingent of my apprentice writers that afternoon, but it is decided (not by him) that his evening appearance had better be canceled. A veteran of the Old Left who has little admiration for the New, our visitor is understood to be hawkish on Vietnam; it is feared, not without reason, that his celebrated presence in a well-filled auditorium will be a red flag, so to speak, to militant black students in particular, who might seize the occasion for a demonstration that will once more bring armed force upon the university. Four or five of us, therefore, at great expense to the State of New York, spend a quiet evening with our visitor at the nearby apartment of Lionel Abel, another Old Leftist and friend of Ellison's from early *Partisan Review* days. The dinner conversation, as the campus rumbles, is of Jean-Paul Sartre, of Herman Melville, of old times on the *Partisan Review*. I have been warned that one is not supposed to ask our guest of honor how his very-long-awaited successor to *The Invisible Man* is coming along, but I forget and ask. "Okay," I believe he answers. And he does in fact, if I am not mistaken, speak favorably of preventive bombing—I cannot recall exactly of whom, or apropos of what. Literary critics, maybe.

In Scene Two, at the turn of the decade, the campus is semi-struck again; 400 riot police and National Guardsmen surround it on a pleasant spring morning with tear-gas grenades at the ready. But we are all seasoned hands at this sort of thing now, and as in a city long under siege we carry on as normally as possible. I am sitting with Leslie Fiedler and others on a Ph.D. oral examination committee and have arranged for my youngest child, then about sixteen, to meet me for lunch afterward. The examination goes badly: The candidate, himself a product of the times, has written a programmatically ahistorical dissertation we've come to call Groovy American Fiction From Last Semester; its perspective sweeps as far back as the day Bob Dylan introduced the Beatles to dope. We all like the young man personally, but none of us is quite responsible for him; his original doctoral committee have dispersed to other universities or are on leave. He has no particular wish to be an academic anyhow; what he really wants to do is make movies. He cannot answer many of our routine literary-historical questions satisfactorily. To encourage him, I invite him to discourse upon the history of the idea that history is unimportant. Alas, he has no idea that that idea has a history.

At examination's end, he waits in the corridor while we confer. Only half joking, we propose a new degree, the Terminal Ph.D.: We will give him the doctorate if he will swear a solemn oath never to profess literature. We adjourn. My then-longhaired son, in the hallway now with the candidate, casually reports that the shit hit the fan just as he was crossing campus: Some demonstratorial last straw has provoked the firing of those gas grenades. Sure enough, the stuff is now all around us; my first whiff of it, and I have no idea what to do. Nor am I alone in my ignorance: Suddenly students and teachers find their roles reversed. While I worry about our maybe getting truncheoned by indiscriminating, fed-up cops, veteran graduate students sniff the air as connoisseurs sniff wine and say things like "Peppergas. Berkeley. Sixty-seven." The fellow lately floundering under our mild examination is now all knowledgeable assurance: If we get gassed, we are *not* to rub our eyes, but bathe them in the drinking fountain. If push comes to shove, double up on the floor to protect gut, kidneys, and testicles; clasp head in hands to protect ears and skull. My son knows these things, too, though he hasn't been through them; he's cool as a cucumber. As it turns out, we don't get really gassed, much less kicked and clubbed. Lunch ensues; life, including academic life, goes on. But I do not forget my feeling of helplessness and that dramatic peripeteia.

By Scene Three, the 1960s have worn into the 1970s like a too-long movie. Everybody knows the jig is up in Vietnam, but we are bombing the bejesus out of Cambodia anyhow. I fly in from my monthly off-campus reading to find home base once again astir with a combined antiwar demonstration and literary vaudeville show. Allen Ginsberg is onstage; also Leslie Fiedler, George Plimpton, and many another, including the composer and then-conductor of the Buffalo Philharmonic, Lukas Foss. But the poet Walter Lowenfels (''We are all poets, really'') has preceded them, and the idea has caught on that virtuoso performance is a variety of fascism. *Ginsberg himself is disrupted,* in mid-act, by a tom-tom-beating commune called Up Against the Wall You Motherfuckers. He is denounced as a media sellout and fascist virtuoso. We are all poets, really; what right has any one of us to stand up there being talented and famous while the rest of us sit passively in audience? One pictures Ginsberg aging visibly before the microphones. The Motherfuckers will not stop for him and his Tibetan finger-cymbals; they will not stop for Fiedler, who had been among the first to prophesy that America was changing from a whiskey culture into a drug culture. They will of course not stop for the likes of Lukas Foss, a bona fide virtuoso performer, not to mention the urbane Mr. Plimpton.

Only Archie Shepp—a black jazz saxophonist from New York City lately appointed Professor of Music at SUNY/Buffalo and in residence between gigs—can deal with them. I had reservations about Shepp's appointment to the faculty, much as I respected his musical prowess. Artists who accept academic appointments should be dedicated to teaching and to the university's general enterprise as well as being considerable artists; students had complained that Shepp's professoring was a rip-off: that he was cynically ad-libbing his class meetings and taunting his white students with the hopelessness of their ever understanding the black art of jazz. Whatever the justice or injustice of these complaints (Shepp was not long on the faculty), the man earned his keep that night. A crowd who would have pilloried Ralph Ellison—unless he nailed them with a preemptive strike—did not dare disrupt a lean and street-looking black jazzman: Snapping his fingers and improvising scat vocals over the rhythm of the tom-toms as Lukas Foss worked out a chord progression on the celeste (!), Shepp soon had the Motherfuckers and then the whole hall clapping along.

Freeze frame and fade—to the Yom Kippur War of '73, the Arab oil embargo, another decade, another world.

Well. We *are* all poets, really; otherwise we couldn't understand one another at all, much less enjoy poetry. But if we are all poets really, I'd really rather read or listen to some of us more than to some others of us. While our government was doing its thing in southeast Asia and we teachers and students were doing ours on campus, one poet-friend of mine was doing something different, which I wrote about in 1972 for Norman Cousins's short-lived *World* magazine.

In the *Odyssey,* speaking of the ten-year Greek expedition against Troy by which almost nobody on either side gained more than he lost, and most lost everything, Homer casually remarks that wars are fought so that poets will have something to sing about. The remark is ironic: Homer isn't saying that his or anyone's poetry justifies the Trojan War, any more than the flood of antiwar verse turned out by our poets in the past ten years justifies our government's war against the Vietnamese. It's just a poet's way of saying that all the official justifications are likely to be delusions or lies; that there's no real justification at all for destroying those people and their country, for example, and in the process leading moderate Americans to emotional treason: the positive *hope* that the Pentagon and the White House will lose their wretched war.

When poets address an abomination almost too enormous to imagine, they're likely to focus not on the spectacular features of it, but on some relative detail, to bring the larger horror home. So W. S. Merwin, in a poem written a dozen years ago about the threat of thermonuclear war, doesn't speak of the incineration of millions of people, great libraries and museums of art, cities drenched in history and beauty. He talks instead of innocent things atomized quite by the way: migrating birds, delicate deer, wildflowers. In that same spirit, a major effort is being made by a friend of mine, himself a poet, to save one small and delicate thing from the general destruction of Vietnamese civilization.

The young man's name is John Balaban; he studied fiction-writing with me at Penn State some years ago and poetry-writing with Robert Lowell at Harvard. But instead of merely writing anguished poems about Vietnam with his right hand while pursuing a literary career with his left, John Balaban has made three separate rescue trips, each about a year long, to the country itself.

The first two times, under the auspices of the Committee of Responsibility, it was children that he and his co-workers rescued: specifically, children burned so badly by American napalm that only high-tech American hospital care could aid them. Balaban's work kept him close enough to the action to get him wounded in the 1969 Tet offensive, and close enough to the people to learn not only the Vietnamese language but also something of the country's literary life and history, in particular its extraordinarily rich and complex tradition of oral poetry.

Like Chinese, but even more so than Chinese, Vietnamese is a tonal language: that is, the same word, pronounced at various pitches, may take on various meanings, perhaps quite unrelated to one another. This is what gives some Asiatic languages their peculiar sound in occidental ears; it also gives the poets, as well as the ordinary speakers of those languages, a whole extra dimension of verbal associations to work and play with, in addition to the puns and wordplays that speakers of every language regularly make use of. For this reason, oral poetry—poetry composed to be performed out loud, for the ear—has always played a much more prominent role in Vietnamese cultural life, Mr. Balaban informs me, than it plays in Russian or American cultural life, even in the age of Yevgeny Yevtushenko and Allen Ginsberg. And it's an art practiced not only by the bright young poets of Saigon and Hué and Hanoi, but also on the folk level, by illiterate farmers in the Mekong Delta and Montagnard peasant women, who perform from memory traditional poems of great age and wit, and of a complexity that one can only call *oriental.*

In English, for example, we have a number of "palindromic" words—words like Madam or deified, which read the same backwards as forwards—and a few very short palindrome sentences, such as *Madam, I'm Adam,* or *Able was I ere I saw Elba;* we even have a few palindromic verses, unrhymed and bordering on nonsense, the longest of which (that I know of) is only two short lines:

> Dog as a devil deified,
> Diefied lived as a God*

Contrast this with one of several amazing specimens of Vietnamese oral poetry that John Balaban came across between burned children: a sort of bilingual syllabic palindrome, strictly metrical, which reads frontwards as a poem in Chinese, and backwards—tonalities and all—as a poem in demotic Vietnamese, both of them perfectly coherent! Or another, a "children's" palindrome (word for word, not letter for letter) eighteen lines long!

But of course, like everything else in South Vietnam, from rain forests to family relationships, this splendid oral poetic tradition is rapidly disappearing, depending as it does on "live" performers in both senses of the word. And so my young poet-friend's third and current year in Viet-

---

* Since writing this in 1972 I have seen much longer (and proportionately more tortured) English language palindromes in *The Journal of Recreational Linguistics,* among other places. A reader of this article even sent me a photocopied typescript of a 50-page novella of his authoring, perfectly palindromic letter for letter, and almost perfectly unintelligible.

nam, which he has just concluded and rather narrowly survived, has been a rescue mission of a different sort: Armed with a tape recorder, a diplomat's tact, a poet's sensibility, and a hero's courage, John Balaban has gone into the rice paddies and the literary cafés, the hill villages and university halls of South Vietnam, has sought out and won the trust of such oral poets as he could reach, and has preserved on tape at least some fragments of this fine and shattered art, which we may hope he will publish with appropriate commentary.*

As with engravings of the passenger pigeon or photographs of the great American Indian chiefs, one must be grateful that an artist got there in time to preserve the image, even though he couldn't save the subject. John Balaban's poetical rescue work absolves us of nothing, any more than the rescue of those burned children does—but thank heaven he did it.

---

* He did. See *Ca Dao Viet Nam: A Bilingual Anthology of Vietnamese Folk Poetry* (Greensboro, NC: Unicorn Press, 1980), from which I borrowed heavily for the Vietnamese-poetry passages of my 1982 novel *Sabbatical: A Romance.*

Aspiration, Inspiration, Respiration, Expiration

INTRODUCTION TO A READING FROM *CHIMERA*

WHILE Allen Ginsberg was being disrupted by the Buffalo Motherfuckers and John Balaban was rescuing oral poetry and burned children in Vietnam, Yours Truly was finishing the successor to *Lost in the Funhouse:* the book *Chimera,* which, like its predecessor, has nothing to do with politics at all. Through the season before its publication, I read from it on the campuses with some variation upon the following introduction, which I include here mainly to keep the chronicle complete and by way of transition to the Friday-piece after it. It would have been from one such reading that I returned to the Buffalo disruption aforedescribed.

Good evening.

In classical Greek myth, the Chimera is a fire-breathing she-monster with a lion's head, a goat's body (the word *chimera* means "nanny-goat"), and a serpent's tail. The term has three other definitions. 1. It is a creature of the imagination, any impossible or monstrous fancy. 2. It is an organism composed of genetically distinct tissues, such as one partly male and partly female. 3. It is a novel written by Yours Truly, to come out from Random House this fall (1972). This so-called novel—so called because novels sell better than collections of short stories, not to mention series of novellas—is in fact a series of three novellas, as different in appearance as a lion from a goat, et cetera, but built upon a single skeleton, warmed by the same blood, and in turn, I hope, all fueling equally the beast's internal-external combustion.

You may remember that the original Chimera was done to death by the hero Bellerophon, an ambitious cousin of the hero Perseus. Bellerophon flew over her on the winged horse Pegasus (who was born when Perseus beheaded Medusa) and stuck a lead-pointed spear, like a great big pencil, down her throat, so that the lead was melted by her flaming breath and seared her vitals. In a sense, Chimera cooperated in her own demise, at the hands of a fellow who subsequently (and vainly) attempted to join the company of immortals by flying directly to Olympus aboard Pegasus, his horsefeathered half-brother. Such presumption does not please the gods, who call it *hubris* and punish it with bolts of lightning.

As you see, the Chimera story is a complicated myth of aspiration, inspiration, respiration, and expiration. I myself take it to be also a story about story-writing, but never mind that.

My version of it, the largest third of my so-called *Chimera* novel, is a longish novella entitled "Bellerophoniad." "Perseid," a novella about Bellerophon's more authentic cousin, is the middle-sized shaggy center of the beast. Her tail (which however leads off the book) is a shortish novella as apparently different from Perseus's and Bellerophon's stories as is a pretty garter snake from a goat or a lion. It is not about myths at all, Greek or barbarian, this last one: It's about an endless love affair of mine with one of the most splendid women and storytellers ever, Scheherazade.

To be sure, like most autobiographical fiction—a genre I have no use for—my love story pretends to be about something else: Scheherazade's kid sister, Dunyazade, who in my version as in the original sits at the foot of the royal bed for 1001 nights, watching Scheherazade and the king make love and listening to all those stories. The four characters in this novella are Shahryar, "King of the Islands of India and China"; his younger brother, Shah Zaman, King of Samarkand; Scheherazade, the daughter of Shahryar's Grand Vizier (I cannot speak her name without hearing the solo violin of her voice in Rimsky-Korsakov's *Scheherazade Suite*); and little Dunyazade herself. The story, "Dunyazadiad," is in three parts, like the Chimera: the first is told by Dunyazade to Shah Zaman, in circumstances not revealed until the end of her narrative; the second part, shorter, is a dialogue between Dunyazade and Shah Zaman, narrated by the author; the very short conclusion is an address by the author to the reader, or listener.

The story is really meant more for telling than for reading—but as it takes two hours to tell it all, I shall stop halfway through, in the manner of Scheherazade. You can read the rest, if you care to, in the May issue of *Esquire* magazine—and you are not forbidden to buy the whole beast when she appears, breathing fire and algebra, in the fall.*

---

* More upon the subjects of fire, algebra, the novella form, and the *Chimera* book in the Friday-piece "Algebra and Fire: A Chat With the Doctors," farther on.

The Tragic View of Literary Prizes

(NATIONAL BOOK AWARD
ACCEPTANCE STATEMENT, 1973)

LITERARY PRIZES: yes, well.

Chimera won half of the late lamented National Book Award in Fiction for 1972, from a half-hung jury with whose assorted literary tastes I was familiar from their own writings: Evan Connell, Leslie Fiedler, William Gass, Walker Percy, Jonathan Yardley. That the book was even among the nominees was gratifying, as had been the nominations of *The Floating Opera* in 1956 and *Lost in the Funhouse* in 1968. In those days, the NBA was the only U.S. fiction prize one took with some seriousness—to the growing dissatisfaction of publishers and booksellers, who after 1979 withdrew their support from that award and replaced it with the less reputable American Book Awards. I did not for a moment expect *Chimera* to win.

That it did, sort of, was therefore all the more fun. Shelly and I went down to New York from Boston University, where I was visiting-professoring that year, and having this time inquired in advance whether half-winners were expected to make half-statements, whole statements, or no statements,* I was able to pronounce in the Alice Tully Hall of Lincoln Center my sentiments on the matter of literary prizes and to use at last that dandy remark of Goethe's which I'd dug up for the Brandeis Award festivities seven years earlier and still remembered.

The only three really negative reviews of my *Chimera* novellas were in *The New York Times Book Review, The New York Review of Books,* and *The New Yorker.* Can this city be trying to tell me something?

I shall not listen.

Instead of thanking the fiction judges for discharging their unenviable task as responsibly as they could, I'm going to thank a number of fellow storytellers whose art has given me delight this year, whether or

---

* See my undelivered statement "The Tragic View of Recognition," earlier on in this book.

not their books were among the nominees. Most especially I thank the old magician of Montreux, Vladimir Nabokov, who should long since have won the Nobel Prize, and Donald Barthelme, who was good to begin with and gets better with each new book. Also the elder masters Eudora Welty and I. B. Singer, whose stories I've read and taught with pleasure over the years; and Ishmael Reed and John Gardner, truly formidable imaginations.

Then there is my former Penn State office-mate Thomas Rogers, whose novel *Confessions of a Child of the Century* was among this year's distinguished nominees. Tom and I thought it amusing back in 1968 to be the first deskmates in literary history ever to be co-nominees for the same award: His *Pursuit of Happiness* and my *Lost in the Funhouse* both lost the NBA that year, to Jerzy Kosinski's *Steps*. That we were co-nominees again this year, we regard as pretty spooky. If it happens a third time, we're going to collaborate on a Pennsylvania-Dutch gothic thriller called *The Verhexed* and sweep the field together.

Well. In a letter to the Duke of Weimar, Goethe wrote: "I am convinced that it is almost as immodest to refuse high distinction as stubbornly to pursue it." I agree, despite the famous capriciousness and ephemerality of such distinctions. We all share the Tragic View of Literary Prizes; yet it would be boring if there were none, and it is more agreeable to shrug them off having won them. A worthwhile literary prize, in my estimation, is one that on occasion will be awarded to a writer despite the fact that he or she deserves it. By this definition, the National Book Award in Fiction is a worthwhile literary prize; I'm pleased to accept it on behalf of Scheherazade, Pegasus, & Company, and the Chimera they still pursue.

Praying for Everybody

THAT SAME YEAR, 1973, the Barths decided neither to remain in lively Boston nor to return to scrappy Buffalo, where by then I had lived and worked for seven years, but to move to Baltimore instead: Shelly to teach at the St.Timothy's School, me to join the Johns Hopkins University Writing Seminars in which I'd served my own apprenticeship twenty years earlier.

Though I had in that interim presided over many and many a writing workshop, this would be my first experience of teaching in an autonomous, degree-granting "creative writing" department, entirely distinct from the university's department of English. The happy prospect of returning to Johns Hopkins and the Chesapeake Bay country notwithstanding, my feelings about such programs were as mixed as were the university's. A small but historically rigorous school——the first American university patterned after German rather than English or Scottish models——Hopkins had never gone in for practicum courses in the arts: Those were the proper bailiwick of institutes and conservatories, not of universities. Yet it was recognized that writing was more akin to the general intellectual enterprise than were painting and singing, for example, and so——in keeping with the university's traditions of pedagogical experiment and original research——the Hopkins writing program was among the first to be established, after Harvard's and Iowa's.

By 1973, however, its fortunes had fallen far from the days when the romance philologist Leo Spitzer and the aesthetician and historian of ideas George Boas had joined the poet and founder of the program, Elliott Coleman, in administering a first-rate interdepartmental doctorate in literary aesthetics, designed for writers with an academic string to their bow who wanted a serious Ph.D. Spitzer was now dead, Boas emeritus, Coleman ill and verging upon retirement, and the Writing Seminars attenuated and amateurish, no longer a credit to the school. The appropriate deans and I agreed in interview that the university should either gently retire the program when its founder retired or else thoroughly and expensively renovate it. The options struck me as about equally sensible; if they chose the latter and hired me, I wanted authority to hire a new

chairman——preferably a literary critic or theorist who also wrote fiction or poetry——with authority in turn to hire a whole new staff, from poets to secretaries.

That is what came to pass, and I found myself thinking more attentively
than I'd done before about the justification for such programs, which were prolif-
erating like rabbits (there are now well above 200 degree-granting creative writing programs in our republic).* Early in the year, therefore, I went down from
Boston to Washington, D.C., to join a symposium at the Library of Congress
upon a subject not thitherto much to my taste——The Teaching of Creative Writing——as well as to check out the real-estate scene in Baltimore. My particular
panel of symposiasts included Wallace Stegner, who compared the training of
writers to the training of horses: The writing teacher, Stegner declared, can be
an authoritarian who breaks his colts with a two-by-four; or he can be a rebel
who by his unorthodoxy tries to stimulate originality in his charges (I've forgotten
how this applies to horses); or he can abdicate responsibility and let go the reins
entirely, admiring everything his students do and being correspondingly loved
by them; or he can really teach, declaring his principles and stating his standards and obliging his students to demonstrate that any innovation they make is
better than what they give up to make it.

By some arrangement of the panelists' presentations which I cannot recall,
mine was drafted in response to his.

There is no disagreeing with Wallace Stegner's wise and plain account of the possibility of helping talented novices along in their literary
apprenticeships. I concur as well, warmly, with his pedagogical-eques-
trian typology; having had the advantage, as a student at Johns Hopkins,
of two writing teachers in his good fourth category, I've striven since in
several universities to measure up to that ideal.

There are a couple of things that Wallace didn't say because they go
without saying. I shall now say them.

First, we acknowledge that while a fair amount of current published
fiction of the literary sort in the United States is written by people who've
had some experience in college fiction-writing courses, the fact remains
that the great majority of students in college fiction-writing courses—
even Creative Writing diplomates—never achieve professional publication, for the reason that their work never gets to be good enough to be
competitive. This majority is no doubt vaster in some writing operations
than in others, but it is always very large. Elliott Coleman's list of his
published former students over the past quarter-century is impressive; if
he kept a list of his unpublished ones, it would be even more so. And a
friend of mine who taught fiction-writing at Penn State for at least twenty

---

* *Now* means 1973. By 1984 there were above 300.

years and kept in close touch with his former students confessed to me, upon his retirement, that except for Vance Packard and James Dugan, whose writings were nonfiction, not *one* of his alumni had ever published a word, to his knowledge. So it goes.

But—second—there is nothing to be inferred from this state of affairs, beyond the gospel truth that many are called but few are chosen, and that, as Cardinal Newman remarked, in effect, no matter how you slice it, the few can never mean the many. Surely that circumstance doesn't make our enterprise futile, any more than the odds against grace invalidate the practice of religion. If anything, it validates us; we can say (again with Newman) that since we've no way of knowing which of our parishioners God has elected, we pray for all of them. In fact, at the end of each semester's work I like to pass on to my apprentice writers Samuel Beckett's favorite quotation from St. Augustine. Referring to the thieves who were crucified along with Jesus, Augustine writes, "Do not despair; one thief was saved. Do not presume; one thief was damned." The advice applies both to our students vis-à-vis their literary aspirations and to us vis-à-vis our students—though in neither case are the odds anything like as good as fifty-fifty.

Having acknowledged this state of affairs, I find myself believing that the right response to it—on the part of those who preside over even our "advanced" studio courses, not to mention the less advanced ones—is a particular concern to appraise the manuscripts in hand in terms of the existing corpus of literature; to analyze imperfect solutions of particular "executive problems," as Cleanth Brooks calls them, by comparison to perfect, or at least successful, solutions of similar problems. This is one of the obvious ways to turn a practicum course in fiction-writing into an adjunct to general literary study; it might be small consolation to students with more ambition than ability, but it's some justification for our ministering to them, if it's done right.

Clearly it is not very helpful to say to a student "Kafka did this same sort of thing, but a lot more brilliantly." The student *knows* that already.* And comparison to the great can be a put-down even in its more generous forms: Wilfred Sheed reports Edmund Wilson's habit, in conversation, of prefacing a criticism with something like "Now see here, Sheed, this is

---

* Leslie Fiedler told me once that whenever a student asks him "How can I become a much better writer?" he's tempted to answer, "Be born again." Setting aside the fact that now and then a person truly *is* reborn, such candid advisement is not very useful advice.

where you and Tolstoy go wrong. . . ." On the other hand, it can surely be illuminating, and may even be consoling, to be reminded that the problems of narrative strategy we wrestle with as apprentices have been famously wrestled with by our distinguished predecessors, and not always perfectly successfully.

I believe this kind of historical perspective is especially enlightening when brought to bear on very innovative work. It is not to put a young writer down that we show him that his edible or self-destructing or do-it-yourself narrative has venerable antecedents in the history of avant-gardism. It is to give him spiritual ancestors and comrades on the one hand, and on the other to conserve his imaginative energy; to spare him from forever reinventing the wheel.

So much for what goes without saying. As for what doesn't, perhaps it could be left unsaid. But I'll lay on the table two unrelated observations that I'm regularly put in mind of in the classroom.

One has to do with the meretriciousness of most radical formal innovation in fiction—in all the arts, I'm sure. My observation is that most of the "traditionalist" fiction I read in typescript is fairly forgettable too, compared to real literary accomplishment. The most gifted seminar I've presided over to date at Buffalo, with neither encouragement nor discouragement from me, turned itself into a seminar in Alternatives to the Line and Page: action fiction, three-dimensional fiction, fiction for tape and live voice, wordless fiction. Most of what its members produced I have forgotten, but several of the experiments were extraordinarily successful. Though sometimes unmarketable for technical reasons, they were in fact genuine alternatives to the line and the page. The best ones managed even to be moving. A year later, virtually the same group was back to pages, lines, sentences, even characters and linear plots, with about the same percentage of hits and misses—but, I observed, with a livelier sense of their medium than they had before their excursion to its perimeters. A roomful of determined young traditionalists, on the other hand, who neither know nor care about those perimeters, can be depressing to preside over. Youth should be more adventurous. I had rather apply snaffle and bit than spur and crop.

The other observation—picking up on Wallace Stegner's Third Truth, that teaching any art becomes progressively more difficult as one moves on from the rudiments—has to do with the hierarchy of problems in fiction-writing workshops. My experience has been that the first gifts a gifted novice shows are usually a way with the language, as if it were his ally instead of his adversary, or at worst a *friendly* adversary; a flair for observing and rendering detail; and (less regularly) a sense of the fictive potential in people and situations. To put it another way, he has an inchoate authenticity of eye and voice; real steam in the boilers; real monkeys on the back; a *Weltanschauung in utero,* which those who've been there, students and teachers alike, usually recognize right off. On the other hand, the *last* thing we usually learn is the Aristotelian business of what constitutes a whole dramatic action and the most strategic ordering of its parts. I find that the good apprentice writers in my own advanced seminars will themselves make most of the critical points I'll have noted to make about one another's diction, detail, management of narrative viewpoint, characterization, and the manipulation of images. What I find myself addressing, perhaps more and more as I move through my own apprenticeship, are such things as the motivation and foreshadowing and pacing of main actions; the dramatical-moral voltages of characters—all that goes by the name of *dramaturgy,* a way with story as distinguished from a way with words, whether in relatively traditionalist fiction like John Updike's or William Styron's, or in less traditionalist fiction like Italo Calvino's or Gabriel García Márquez's. Because I myself am in love with stories at least as much as with language, it is in this area, dramaturgy, that I find myself most often in the role of adversary, coach, and instructor with my students past the novice level. And, other things equal, it is the writers who begin with or arrive at good dramaturgical sense whom I'm most optimistic about when their schooldays are done. Among them, I'd bet that the statistics of eventual publication are considerably less chastening.

Doing the Numbers

A FOOTNOTE TO THE FOREGOING

"THE STATISTICS of eventual publication. . . ." Ten years of presiding over the Johns Hopkins fictioneers prompt this 1983 footnote to the foregoing.

At the State University of New York at Buffalo, our graduate-student apprentice writers were regular English Department Ph.D. candidates who happened to write fiction as well, but were admitted to the graduate program primarily on their academic qualifications. In consequence, the level of critical articulateness in the room was generally higher than the level of raw fictive talent. Most of those students are now professors. A few have published the odd short story; none has yet become an established professional writer.

The same applies to the alumni of that excellent Aesthetics of Literature doctoral program aforementioned, presided over at Johns Hopkins in the 1950s by a poet, a philosopher, and a philologist: Elliott Coleman, George Boas, and Leo Spitzer, respectively. Its intellectual standards were so high, and literary scholarship was made so appealing by those three excellent gentlemen and their colleagues, that with but a few exceptions all the graduates of that program are now scholar-critics whose occasional fiction or verse is a graceful second string to their bow. Those of us who wound up being writers who also teach, more than teachers who also write, were either never admitted to that program or, like myself, dropped out of it because we felt ourselves distinctly in the wrong métier and out of our intellectual depth.

For me it was a familiar feeling, the same I'd experienced years before at Juilliard. As I'd recognized then that my musical ability was real but small, I recognized later (with some disappointment, but not much) that my ability for abstract thinking and rigorous critical analysis was likewise not of pre-professional caliber. I shrugged my shoulders and got on with novelizing, writing the odd essay or lecture in the same spirit as I played jazz, for serious diversion.

Among our graduate-student apprentices at Hopkins, as among those at Iowa, Stanford, and other writing programs both good and competitive, the statistics of eventual, substantial literary publication are by no means so discouraging as those aforecited, for the obvious reason that the writers are selected in the first place mainly for their apparent promise as writers. Their academic qualifications we take seriously, even unto their scores on the Graduate Record Examination: My opinion is that writers who elect to serve a part of their apprenticeship in a good university rather than elsewhere should be not seriously out of place in that university. But such bonuses as through-the-roof GRE scores, glowing testimonials from well-known professors, and impressive academic transcripts from good colleges serve mainly as tie-breakers and recommendations for teaching assistantships. The Ivy League has sent us a number of our best TAs, but most of our strongest writers have come to us from colleges not famous for their academic excellence. A powerful writing sample sweeps nearly everything else aside, and a few of our subsequently most successful fiction alumni (Frederick Barthelme and Mary Robison, for example) we accepted into the program more despite their academic backgrounds than on their account. Such applicants are obviously artists-in-the-making, who will be at least as good for the university as the university will be for them.

But even with our ablest apprentices, I like early on to Do the Numbers. There exist currently in our republic, I tell them, worse than 300 degree-granting programs in creative writing, according to the bulletin of an organization called Associated Writing Programs. Let us suppose that, on the average, each of these turns out twenty certified, diplomatized Writers every year (the Hopkins program, a small one, turns out nearly twice that number if one counts both BAs and MAs, but since many of our MAs hold BAs in creative writing from elsewhere—indeed, some hold MAs or MFAs from elsewhere, a circumstance we elect to ignore—I adjust the average downwards to compensate). That comes conservatively to 5,000 officially anointed new U.S. writers per annum. Let us suppose that half of these are poets, playwrights, or screenwriters by chief election and half are fiction-writers—my rough impression from having visited a good many such operations. We now have 2,500 newly ordained fictionists each spring.

Next we shall estimate the productive lifetime of American professional writers of fiction—those who join the Authors Guild or PEN, for example—to average . . . three decades, would you say? From about age 30 to about age 60, balancing against each other the many curtailed and the not a few extended careers? Such a writer may then expect that during his professional lifetime his national culture will be the richer for 75,000 newly consecrated competitors in his medium—and that only on the assumption that the popularity of writing programs in America unaccountably levels off this year from its enormous growth since 1945, though the fact is that the shrunken academic job market since 1973 in the traditional liberal arts has boosted rather than dampened the demand for creative-writing degrees. In paradoxical truth, an MFA in Writing may find academic employment more readily than a Ph.D. in English. Not economic recession, not declining literacy, failing bookstores, the usurpation of the kingdom of narrative by movies and television—nothing quenches the American thirst for courses in creative writing. In day school, night school, high school, college, graduate school, correspondence school, summer school, prison school; in writers' colonies and conferences and camps and cruises, it is scribble scribble scribble scribble scribble scribble scribble.

So, my friends: 74,999 new certified American writers of fiction in your productive lifetime, plus yourself. It will not do to point out, correctly, that most of these diplomates will never publish a word of their art outside of their campus literary magazines, and therefore will never compete with you for the by no means infinite attention of readers of fiction. All that that circumstance tells us is that the 41,000-odd new titles published by the 13,000-odd book-publishers in America counted by the R. R. Bowker Company in 1982 (to take one year as representative), of which the largest single category is fiction, were written mainly by authors not authorized to do so by our degree-granting writing programs. The numbers still stand: The ten or fifteen novels or story-collections published by our average American professional fiction-writer in his/her 30-year productive lifetime must compete for shelf space, review space, and readerly mind-space with maybe a quarter-million other new titles offered by American publishers alone over that period.

If, after all, the chief real product of all those writing programs is more readers rather than more writers, what a service they perform!

Well, but what is an aspiring young writer to do with these formidable, not to say appalling, numbers? My advice to my students is twofold.

First, be duly impressed. There is an enormous lot of competition for readerly attention out there, not only from those 74,999 (or however-many) other certified living American writers, but also from the thousands of non-American living writers and the tens and tens of thousands of your predecessors in the art of fiction. Why should anyone who owes you nothing (unlike your classmates in this room) read even a single page of yours, when there are so many other things to enjoy in the fiction way from the world's authors living and dead, so many other things yet to read besides fiction, and so many other agreeable things to do besides read at all? "The writer's first obligation," said Henry James, "is to be interesting." *Very* interesting.

Second, having been duly impressed by the numbers, forget them. Talent tends to cut through odds. Many are called and few are chosen, but those few *are* chosen, usually. Inasmuch as the few can never mean the many, you had as well relax and trust your muse, for there's little you can do towards that final election except read everything and practice your ass off.

Just a touch of cockiness might come in handy, too. I confess to you, worthy apprentices, that if at your age the muse had not only revealed to me the depressing numbers I have just reviewed with you, but warned me further that my particular American literary generation was fated to produce, say, only three writers of merit, I would have said to myself (I would not now), Who needs the other two?

Intelligent Despisal

AN ADDRESS TO THE GRADUATING CLASS
OF WESTERN MARYLAND COLLEGE, JUNE 1973

BY THE SPRING of 1973, Lyndon Johnson was out, Richard Nixon was in, and the economic buzzards of our Vietnam war, like its veterans, were coming home to roost. The new phenomenon of ''stagflation'' was challenging economists and exasperating the rest of us; government social programs and aid to universities were cut back; the job market for American college graduates was much shrunk—and my oldest child was graduating from college, with two younger ones not far behind her.

As academic parents tend to do during pregnancy and at graduation time, I caught myself that spring thinking in commencement-speech terms: What sort of world, et cetera? I should have liked to be invited to address my daughter's graduating class at Connecticut College that year. As I wasn't (Senator Lowell Weicker of Connecticut was), and as we were moving to Maryland anyhow, I was pleased to accept President Ralph John's invitation to speak at the commencement ceremonies at Western Maryland College instead, a small liberal-arts college in Westminster. It was my maiden and I think final such address; my maiden and no doubt final venture also onto the thin ice of political-economic indignation. My impression was that it was generally well received by the students and faculty and politely so by the trustees; but it got me denounced in the Eastern Shore press as a flaming socialist whose return to the Free State of Maryland was to be regretted.

None of us knew that a few months later the Yom Kippur War and the Arab oil embargo would deliver the *coup de grace* to the 1960s and render quaint my perturbation at 6 percent inflation and 7½ percent home mortgages, not to mention my invocation of that standard liberal bugaboo, rich and powerful General Motors. . . . If most of the numbers and some of the stock-liberal sentiments are decidedly dated ten years later, Reaganomics has made the main line of my harangue more to the point in 1983 than it was in 1973. And to the tragic view of political institutions, I wholeheartedly renew my subscription.

Hello.

To those of you about to receive degrees, my congratulations on having completed your courses of study. We now pronounce you intellectually and culturally sophisticated, technically equipped, morally enlarged, spiritually matured, critically honed, politically subtled, and socioeconomically upward-mobile. You are now perfectly prepared to commence your graduate professional training or your vocational life, as the case may be: I assume that all of you in the former category have already won admission to first-rank graduate and professional schools, with lucrative fellowships to support you, and that all in the latter category have chosen from among the exciting and rewarding pursuits that our society holds out to the college-educated. In short, you've all found groovy jobs that pay a lot of money, and we can quit worrying about you.

My congratulations next to those of you in the audience whose privilege and delight it has been to finance this happy enterprise. Where I teach, and at the colleges my various children attend, that privilege and delight comes to about $20,000 per kid for the baccalaureate, counting tuition, support, materials, and transportation, and the bill goes up about ten percent per year. That's a lot of delight. One of my Boston University students (who was paying his own way) informed me once, just before a lecture, that given the usual four-course load for eight semesters, the $20,000 figure comes to $625 a course; now that the classical fifteen-week semester has shrunk to more like thirteen weeks, for a course meeting three times a week it comes to $15.63 per lecture, or 31¢ a minute unless the professor talks overtime, in which case the rate goes down a bit.

You who paid for those minutes are entitled now to a summer in the Mediterranean or a winter in the Caribbean, your choice, or both if you're a student who paid your own way. But financial reality being what it is, I imagine most of you will settle cheerfully—as I shall in the case of my own graduating daughter—for a certain amount of undying gratitude from your now-splendidly-educated kid.

It would be agreeable if we could give them a world no worse than the one our parents signed over to us a generation ago, but they can't have everything. Anyhow, it's not a *whole lot* worse, just steadily worse, and steadiness counts for something. We're anyhow comforted to know that they all intend to follow the careers we parents had in mind for them. Now that they have those dandy jobs and fellowships I mentioned before, tomorrow they'll put on nice clothes, quit doing dope, and buckle down in proper careerist fashion; soon after that they'll marry the right mates instead of living in sin with the wrong ones; rapidly thereafter they'll incur promotions, children, and a 7½ percent mortgage loan, two-thirds of which (with any luck at all) should be amortized in time for them to borrow it back again at 10 percent to send their *own* kids off to college. By that time, at the present rate of inflation, a bachelor's degree will run about $44,000—but no doubt the quality of higher education in America will have improved correspondingly, as it's been doing right along.

That fetches me to my final congratulations, to those of you whose trust it has been to perfect the intellectual and cultural sophistication, technical equipment, moral enlargement, et cetera, of these young people. Reckoning in a manner similar to my student's, I might have pointed out to him that that 31¢ a minute he paid to hear me and the others lecture wasn't the half of it: It's more like a tenth. Assuming an average $20,000-a-year salary for professors, a two-course-per-semester teaching load for upper ranks, and paid sabbatical leaves, and forgetting about fringe benefits and overhead, the cost to the college (or the state, or somebody) for our services comes to $145.83 a lecture, or $2.92 per classroom minute.

These congratulations themselves, if delivered at the rate just established, would have cost Western Maryland College some $40 or $50 by now. I shall therefore refrain, in the interest of economy, from extending them to President John, the rest of the administrative staff, and the Board of Trustees. Administrators aren't used to congratulation anyhow, and I don't want to set a disorienting precedent.

Well. I seem to be talking economics, and economics—more specifically, alas, economizing—is necessarily a main concern of college and university administrators these days. The fifteen relatively fat years on U.S. campuses since the good old Sputnik scare of 1957 appear to be over with a vengeance. One could live more gracefully with the Biblical lean years now in progress—as with the dried-up job market for new graduates, the dismantling of social welfare programs, the cutbacks and cutoffs of federal support for practically everything that matters in a humane society—one could accept it more cheerfully if it were the effect of an out-and-out depression, 1930s-style, affecting every aspect of the national life and the community of nations as well. What rankles, to put it mildly, is that the malaise, while widespread and far-reaching, is *not* all that general; it is egregiously selective and, in my view, reprehensible, though I'm not optimistic that we can do anything about it.

Since I'm going to set forth my view as responsibly (and briefly) as I can, I'll declare the limits of my authority at the outset: I'm not an economist or a political scientist or a historian, though I read now and then in those disciplines, especially in recent years. But like many of you, I've lived forty-some years in the world, trying to pay attention to it and understand it; for twenty-one of those years I've been a parent, and for the same period I've taught in American universities. At the same time I've practiced as earnestly as I can my other profession and truest passion: writing fiction. The novelist J. P. Donleavy has defined fiction-writing as "the fine art of turning one's worst experiences into money." But whether or not one anguishes all the way to the bank, or anguishes at all (or gets to the bank at all), the vocation of writing seriously involves the continuous and deep examination of one's own experience of life and the world, and of the language and literary conventions we use to register that experience and make it meaningful. Any authority I have to speak here comes from that "professional" examination, as the word *authority* itself comes from *author*.

Now: As this author sees it, the prospects for my daughter and for you other new graduates are not quite as happy as I described them a while ago in my congratulations—which however still stand. The fact is, as many of you have divined already, outside of a few technical professions there aren't many good jobs open for this year's graduates—by which I mean jobs that are reasonably well-paying, reasonably satisfying, and reasonably relevant to your major course of study. In numerous areas there are very few jobs even *remotely* rewarding and relevant to your education. Obviously an AB in anthropology or economics can't expect to begin work tomorrow as a professional anthropologist or economist; that was never possible. But it *was* possible—more possible—in past years for him or her to find work in federal or state government service, or with newspapers, magazines, ad agencies, even business firms. I know it was, even for poor old ABs in English, because that's what any number of my classmates and former students did who chose not to go on to graduate school. Derek Bok, the president of Harvard, reported in February that whereas about 10 percent of Harvard's graduating class of 1967 were undecided about their vocational plans as late as their final semester, more than *30* percent of the Class of '73 have no idea where they're going from Harvard Yard. He didn't say how many of that 30 percent are undecided because they can't find anything to do commensurate with their education; my guess is that it's a large number, and that the number of seniors who *knew* in February what they wanted to do but don't know now how or where they're going to do it is even higher; even at Harvard.

In the past, of course, especially between 1955 and 1970, if one had the ability and the inclination, one could usually go on to graduate school, in reasonable expectation of supporting one's advanced studies with fellowships and teaching assistantships, and every expectation of a decent job, in or out of academia, with the Ph.D., often even with the MA. Very few 22- and 23-year-olds can afford to pay graduate-school expenses out of their own pockets, and very few of their parents can afford to finance even more years of higher education for them beyond the baccalaureate. Until recently, in most areas of study, neither was generally necessary. The sciences had ample research-contract money to support their graduate students, and even in English very few of our doctoral candidates at SUNY/Buffalo, for example, were paying their own freight in cash: They taught the freshman English program, or assisted their professors' research, or graded our examinations in large lecture courses. Those few who were supporting themselves could do it by education loans, if necessary, with no great fear of being unable to commence repayment of the loan immediately after graduation.

No more. We get about as many applications to graduate school as ever, but there are considerably fewer admissions in most good departments now, because of budget cuts, and even fewer fellowships and assistantships, percentagewise. Many of you have found that out already. If you do get in, you'll find that there's considerably less money to support your research projects; if you're lucky enough to get a teaching assistantship, you're likely to find your work load heavier than it would have been even last year; in any case, your professors' loads are likely to be heavier, and there'll probably be fewer course-offerings for you to choose from, less flexibility in planning your curriculum, fewer class meetings per semester, and more students per class. None of these can be construed as good news for your education.

Those of you who get your doctorates may not be in much better shape, at least in the academic marketplace, than you new baccalaureates are in the general marketplace; the Ph.D.'s lot is a fallen one compared to what it was three or four years back, and it shows every sign of falling farther, like the dollar, before it stabilizes at a relatively devalued level. (The master's degree, by the way, as you may have been told by your advisors, has become almost meaningless except for public and private schoolteachers. We don't even *offer* the MA in most good graduate departments these days, except to people who fail their doctoral studies with flying colors.) In my last year at Buffalo, an excellent graduate department, we managed eventually to place nearly all sixteen or so of our new Ph.D.s in English in *some* kind of teaching job, by heroic efforts of recommendation and string-pulling; but it wasn't easy, and this year's crop won't be that lucky. It's painful to think of a brand-new Ph.D., after maybe twenty straight years of school, obliged to *conceal* his advanced degrees in order not to price himself out of a job teaching junior high school—but one hears of it.

At *that* level, needless to say—the level of the high schools and junior high schools—the crunch is even harder. At Wayland High, in suburban Boston, where my wife used to teach, there were 280 applications this past fall for *one* position in the English Department, while teaching loads and pressures had so increased that veteran teachers in the prime of their careers were dropping out, simply unable to do that much work responsibly. The quality of education in that excellent public school is correspondingly lower—with teachers teaching five classes a day, five days a week, and upwards of thirty students in a class, it can't be anything else—and this is a privileged, mostly white upper-middle-class school in an affluent suburban community with a high tax rate, a low crime rate, and no very serious social problems. Imagine how it's come to be in the inner city, where it was awful to begin with! In good *private* schools, the education is better because the teaching loads are lighter and the kids are more or less of a cultural elite; but the schools have to charge such college-size fees to stay alive that it's an ever-smaller *financial* elite who can hack the costs. Even so, a number of good small private schools are going under. As for their teaching salaries: One woman I know of in Baltimore, an art teacher at a well-known private girls' school, is making less than $9,000 a year in her thirty-fifth year of full-time teaching!

So much for the education market. What about people without advanced degrees, like most of you all, who happen to be not interested in either graduate study or teaching? Well, one good student of mine from Penn State—a bright, lively, attractive young woman with master's degrees in two different fields—came to see me in Boston this year to get a reference for a job as a typist, not having been able to find anything better. Among the mere ABs who've dropped in to say hello in the past academic year, one was picking up nonunion manual labor where he could; one was collecting unemployment compensation; one, ineligible for that, was dealing dope. All were reduced to considering graduate school against their real inclinations, until they learned the new facts of life on *that* front. I discussed with them the possibility of careers in violent crime, that being one of the two great areas of American economic life that continue to grow bullishly even in the '70s—but being city kids who'd been mugged and ripped off themselves, they couldn't muster much enthusiasm for that line of work. What they've actually found to do for a living since, if anything, I've no idea: I look for them when I drive through Harvard Square, but the panhandlers and hawkers of underground newspapers there must be graduates of other universities.

Is there anything good at all to be said for this state of affairs (of which the review I've given is possibly a little exaggerated, but not nearly so much as I wish it were)? Well, yes: On the campus scene, I think it good to be done with the frenetic expansionism and academic empire-building of the 1950s and '60s. Growth for its own sake has lost its press in the area of education as well as in economics and population. Given a reasonably stable demand, reduced admissions means theoretically a better grade of undergraduate and graduate students, particularly in our state universities, just as the current disenchantment with higher education on the part of many young people now—a disenchantment which I half welcome—might conceivably keep off the campuses a number of people who don't really have any great love or knack for book-learning. Especially in the liberal arts, one can only rejoice at the prospect of entire roomfuls of sharp undergraduates whose chief reason for being there is simply that studying books and ideas *turns them on*.

In the same way, more competition for what few teaching jobs there are, for example, ought to lead to better teachers, and no doubt there'll be a saving for somebody somewhere if the oversupply of applicants makes it unnecessary to pay better salaries. As for the unemployed or misemployed Ph.D.s, I suppose it can be argued that, objectively, we don't *need* ever-larger crops of historians, literary scholars, and the like; perhaps we need fewer and better? I think I don't subscribe to this argument—especially in fields like history and literature, which keep getting longer as well as wider—but I understand its emotional appeal.

Next, it's pleasant to imagine that the belt-tightening now in progress in the fields of education, social services, and such will really cut out dead wood and programs of marginal value—even though we know, in education at least, that it's from these vulnerable marginal programs that the best reforms and innovations often spring; and no one ever talks about what's to be done, humanely, with the dead wood once it's cut from our payrolls. Especially from the perspective of a higher echelon, it's easy to forget that dead wood is live people. But in fact, as everybody knows who's had experience with any hierarchy at all, it's seldom just the dead wood that gets cut out; many times, indeed, it's the hand on the pruning-hook, safely tenured or politically sheltered, that's really moribund, deader than the wood it's cutting out.

Finally, it would be comforting to regard the scarcity of good employment for educated young people as poetic justice for a generation famously critical of the nine-to-five careerism of their parents, and of the Protestant work-ethic in general. "You wouldn't make your bed," one might be tempted to say; "now lie in it." If a third of the graduating class don't know yet who they are, vocationally, perhaps it's appropriate that their society in turn doesn't know what to do with *them*. But that's an attitude that won't bear much reflection; not being sure where you want to go isn't the same as not wanting to go anywhere, or as having no place to start. The ones who've really turned their backs on careers as conventionally defined; who truly have no interest in being, in Alfred Whitehead's phrase, "the competent ones of their generation"—most of those have dropped out already, for better or worse, before they got this far. My concern is for those who *are* competent, and who will find no proper exercise of their competence. There will be many of you, I fear, in that category, in the classes of '73, '74, '75, and '76, to look no farther.

Obviously I *don't* think it's a healthy situation, this state of affairs I've been depressing you with, for the ironic reason I mentioned before: precisely because it's *not* part of a general economic depression. In fact, we have many of the disadvantages of a depression—unemployment, cutbacks of community budgets and services, et cetera—with none of the advantages, if you can call them that, of an authentic depression, such as falling prices, solidarity among the disadvantaged, and *extended* government services to take up the slack, like the old Civilian Conservation Corps and the WPA, which subsidized even artists and writers to some extent. What we have instead—especially for the large class of those without organized political clout, such as the poor, the old, and the unemployed or ill-employed young—is many of the depressing features of a depression together with all the worst features of inflation. Given the prevailing inflation rate of more than 6 percent a year, you lose a fair amount of money even by saving it—lose twice, in fact, since the 4- or 5-percent interest on your savings is taxable income. Pensioners and other fixed-income people are 30 percent poorer every five years at that rate of inflation; in only sixteen years they'd be 100 percent poorer! I'm not even sure what "100 percent poorer" means, but it certainly sounds unpleasant.

Meanwhile—and here we get to it—as the poor get poorer and more numerous; as the quality of education and civil services goes down and the work load of teachers and many civil service people goes up; as price controls to protect the consumer are let go and import regulations to protect certain industries are maintained; as we make do with less of everything from weather stations to trash collection and pothole repairs, from passenger-train service to firefighting equipment; as the employment opportunities for bright young people dwindle while their cost of living escalates—those sectors of the economy with sufficient political leverage of the right sort do not participate in the general "tightening of belts," as the euphemism puts it (in some cases tightening of the tourniquet, or the garrotte, would be an apter figure). On the contrary, they get fatter: Welfare services for distressed people are cut back, while distressed corporations, especially military contractors, are bailed out; public and private education get by on austerity budgets, while General Motors, as the saying goes, could still buy the state of Delaware if DuPont would sell it. Most maddening of all, while veterans of the Pentagon's war on southeast Asia go on relief and/or turn to crime to support a drug habit picked up in service, the budget for the Department of Defense crazily *increases,* to make the world safer for no one except the military-industrial complex. Talk about addiction! The Pentagon is the most expensive habit in the world, and apparently the hardest to kick. It has turned us into deathfreaks, mugging and burgling our other priorities to pay for a dreadful militarist fix that fixes next to nothing.

In short, many of the economic ills that make your commencement a less promiseful one than mine was twenty-two years ago are apparently the result of a "stagflation" perhaps not so much uncontrollable as illcontrolled (that is to say, controlled to the benefit of interests other than yours and mine and the people's generally); and the want of effective controls seems clearly owing to our government's accession to pressures from big business and big labor, in that order; and this accession in turn, so my reading of the situation tells me, is finally not really an accession so much as a fulfillment of function on the part of a federal government that is, in Henry Steele Commager's phrase, chiefly the political arm of corporate America. And Commager doesn't mean just Republicans, either. On the part of historians and political scientists of the stature of Henry Steele

Commager and Andrew Hacker, for example, this assessment simply can't be dismissed as liberal paranoia; Hacker for one has been eloquently cognizant and critical of the liberal bias in much academic historiography. But the analyses of interlocking directorates in corporate America, and of the systematic quid pro quo between these interests and the political officials they subsidize, make conclusions like Dr. Commager's all but inescapable, even to skeptical sensibilities like my own.

What I'm saying is that the principal villain seems to be our old friend Self-Serving Corporate Capitalism, and I hope you graduates will have the good sense to despise it intelligently for its large share in the frustration of your economic and political lives, the poisoning of your air, food, and water, the famous cheapening of the quality of life in America, and the corruption of our governmental institutions and officials. That government itself is merely the accomplice to these crimes—but since political office is a *public* trust and large business corporations are merely trusts, we may properly judge the accomplice in this case more guilty than the originator of the crime. This is what I mean by despising intelligently. Large corporations aren't *really* as blameless for their actions as natural forces like fire or flood, as is sometimes said; their decisions to pollute, adulterate, despoil, defraud, and exploit the public interest for the profit of their stockholders are human decisions, morally accountable despite their limited legal liability. But they're *like* natural forces in that, they having been organized to make cars or shoes or whatever not for people, but for money, to expect them to take the public interest into account more than it is finally profitable for them to do so is as naïve as expecting the fire itself to care what or whom it burns.

The choice therefore is either to find a less dangerous substitute for fire—that is, to nationalize any corporate interests large enough to be dangerous or even deleterious to our lives, as many of the world's people have done—or else, if we want to keep the fire (and I myself certainly prefer life in this country to life in the large socialist countries), then we ought to find a much more reliable stove, and better firemen, or our goose may be cooked and our house's days numbered. To throw out the Republicans and throw in the Democrats won't help the Class of '77 as long as the same complex of corporate interests has still to be satisfied.

Then is it realistic at all to imagine so reforming our institutions that our public servants truly serve the public first instead of themselves and their subsidizers? Can we really hope to police the police, and the police who police the police? All of my reading, my experience, my reflections and intuitions, incline me to the tragic view of human institutions, including political systems. I'm not naïve enough to believe that our government is much more or less corrupt or inefficient in serving the interests of the governed than are the governments of other capitalist countries. I happen very much to wish, personally, that large areas of our manufacturing, transportation, utilities, health services, and other major industries were publically owned, as most of our educational system is, to serve their customers rather than their stockholders; but one isn't naïve either about the corruptions, inefficiencies, self-serving bureaucracies, and more or less brutal stifling of criticism in very socialist states. As for those countries which are neither capitalist democracies nor socialist republics— well, never mind. I wouldn't be permitted to make a commencement speech like this in Poland or Cuba, Algeria or Turkey, much of Latin America, most of Africa, all of Russia or China, or North or South Vietnam, for example. In North America and Western Europe (excluding Portugal, Spain, and Greece these days) I'm permitted to make it—just as I'm permitted to practice my two professions—because the interests and institutions I'm criticizing, who run these countries and govern so many aspects of our lives for their profit, are too secure in their power to take much notice of such criticism. I prefer that condition to being silenced, as a man might prefer impotency to actual emasculation, and I am impatient with radicals who equate the two. But it's irritating to be expected to be *grateful* for having been tolerated because rendered powerless.

The hopefulest thing about the classes of 1970 through '73 is that they've had the lively chance, at least, unlike most of their predecessors in America, to add to their formal education a considerable *in*formal education in political reality, from the tumultuous events on our campuses since 1967. I think I pity the campuses—and the students, professors, and administrators—who were spared all that: the takeovers and disruptions and strikes, the trashings, the tear gas, the obscenities and vulgarities and head-crackings and groin-kickings of '67, '68, '69, and '70. Thank heaven their intensity has diminished, as the more flagrant symptoms of the malaise that inspired them have passed into sore history. The best thing they accomplished, along with a few worthwhile minor academic reforms and a little extra pressure on the D.C. death-freaks, was a slight raising of the political consciousness of an unprecedented number of young people not directly involved in the fields of history, sociology, or political science: I mean our next generation of lawyers, doctors, and especially teachers. You graduating seniors have had the chance, whether you availed yourselves of it or not, to learn how many areas of our lives have a real political dimension that most of you, and many of us who've been your teachers, had been innocent of—and that's an innocence well lost.

You've also had the chance, whether you availed yourselves of it or not, to discover that while you don't have the *most* power on campus, you have a good deal more power, when you organize to use it, than either you or we had believed before the middle 1960s, and that's much more of a good lesson than not. The paradox is that in the society into which you're now graduating, you will have much *less* power over your lives in many respects than you had on campus, whereas you should have much more. Whether you—but now that *you* is *we*—whether we can do anything to change that is far from certain; what *is* certain is that in the condition of political innocence one is doubly manipulable: not only robbed, but trained to applaud and salute the robbers. If you've lost that political innocence, as I hope many of you have, you'll very likely still be robbed, but at least you won't mistake highway robbery for voluntary donation. Perhaps you'll even holler for the cops, and when you find then that cops and robbers aren't as distinguishable in fact as they are in some fiction, perhaps there'll be enough of you—of us—to commence beyond mere intelligent despisal and the delivery of liberal commencement addresses.

I hope so.

Writer's Choice

BACK to the writing desk.

Rust Hills, the off-and-on fiction editor of *Esquire* magazine, assembled in 1974 a short-story anthology called *Writer's Choice* [New York: David McKay, 1974]: one of those collections in which the authors are asked to choose which of their stories is to represent them and briefly to explain their choice. Wise readers understand that such anthologies occur more than once in a writer's career; frequently enough, in fact, that the real ground of his selection may be to recover some *not* so representative, less often anthologized piece. In this case, however, the choice was straightforward.

For my first ten years as a publishing writer, I found the short story an uncongenial, constipative genre, and did not work in it. But at about age thirty-five, having written a pair of short novels and a pair of very long ones, I commenced what was to turn out to be a seven-year investigation of alternatives to long printed narratives. The issue was another pair of books: *Lost in the Funhouse* (1968), a series of fourteen short fictions for print, tape, and live voice; and *Chimera* (1972), a triptych of novellas. My interest in electronic tape was a passing one, but my conversion to the shorter forms was so complete that I have come to find it almost impossible to read any new fiction whose pages outnumber my years. If I am in fact just now writing another full-fledged novel, it is out of a kind of perversity, so quixotic does that enterprise seem to me at this hour of the world. But *Quixote* is where we novelists came in.

The story "Lost in the Funhouse" was written for print, and occurs midway through the series of which it is the title story. I meant it to look backward—at the narrator Ambrose's earlier youth, at the earlier "Ambrose" stories in the series, and at some classical manners and concerns of the realist-illusionist short story, long may it wave—and also "forward," to some less conventional narrative manners and concerns as well as to some future, more mythic avatars of the narrator. Finally, I meant it to be accessible, entertaining, perhaps moving, for I have no use for merely formalist tours de force, and the place and time—tidewater Maryland, World War Twotime—are pungent in my memory. In short, my choice, like the story itself, is partly sentimental.

Western Wind, Eastern Shore

A FOREWORD

THAT novel-in-progress afore referred to was *LETTERS*, an enormous and intricate project that occupied most of my forties. Seven novels in one, really, it took about seven years to complete. The axis of its action corresponds to the axis of the War of 1812 (with which, among other things, it deals: my personal favorite among American wars) and, as it happens, the axis of my life: a line from tidewater Maryland through Pennsylvania to the Great Lakes and the Niagara Frontier.

The autobiographical element in my fiction is slight; more often the relation works the other way around, the fiction turning out to be banal prophecy, perhaps even a contributing cause of what its author later winds up doing. I came back to Maryland partly because my lapsed hero Bellerophon (in *Chimera*) had already fallen from Olympus into the Dorchester County marshes, and because while in Boston I had begun the novel *LETTERS*, much of which is set in the neighborhood of Chesapeake Bay.

I had taught myself how to sail on Lake Chautauqua, the thumb of New York's Finger Lakes; now we bought a small cruising sailboat, and in the spring of 1974 began exploring the literal as well as the figurative geography of the Chesapeake—an enterprise still far from finished. In connection with that enterprise I met an expert sailor-photographer, Robert de Gast, who invited me to circumnavigate the Delmarva Peninsula with him—a month's voyage—and write a text to accompany the book of photographs he had in mind. The *LETTERS* project would not permit so long a holiday, but I made the voyage with him in my imagination while Shelly and I, aboard our *Cobweb II,* improved our skills with modest weekend cruises on the Choptank River. And I was pleased to write this foreword to de Gast's book—the subtitle of which is *A Sailing Cruise Around the Eastern Shore of Maryland, Delaware, and Virginia*—when The Johns Hopkins Press published it in 1975.

Robert de Gast is a Dutch-born photographer, writer, and sailor who free-lances out of Baltimore and sails out of Annapolis, the Marblehead

of Chesapeake Bay. In May 1974, he did a simple, delightful thing which no one seems to have thought of doing before, at least for the record: Mostly alone, mostly under sail, he circumnavigated the Delmarva Peninsula, that shrimp-shaped entity (comprised of Virginia's Accomack and Northampton counties, Maryland's Eastern Shore, and nearly the entire state of Delaware) which swims north toward Pennsylvania with its feet in the Chesapeake and the Atlantic on its back. Up from the Bay Bridge, through the Chesapeake and Delaware Canal, down Delaware Bay he sailed, poking into rivers, creeks and by-ways on his way; then inside the skinny barrier islands along Delmarva's Atlantic shore (a route almost virgin to the cruising sailor), around Cape Charles, and up Pocomoke and Tangier sounds to his starting place, duly nosing into the Pocomoke River, the Little and Great Choptanks, the Tred Avon, the Wye, the Miles—most of the major estuaries and a few of the major creeks, big as rivers themselves, of the inexhaustible Eastern Shore.

Bertrand Russell observed, about coastlines generally, that their length can be measured only by ignoring enough actuality: coves, points, rocks, grains of sand. De Gast found this wistfully true of his twenty-four-day circuit of Delmarva: The whole period would not have done justice to the Choptank alone, not to mention the Wye, the Chester, the Sassafras. But he rediscovered the improbable Smyrna and the cypressed, tuckahoed, magical Pocomoke. . . .

Any competent, imaginative sailor with a shoal-draft boat and three weeks on his hands might do as much—must surely long to, once he reads this book. What Robert de Gast brought to the voyage (in addition to his delicate eye and lens, which need another paragraph) was the knowledgeability that makes his earlier photo-essays, *The Oystermen of the Chesapeake* and *The Lighthouses of the Chesapeake,* as delightful to those who know his subject intimately as to those who don't. Having mastered English *second,* he hears its tidewater dialect perhaps more accurately than we who grew up with it in our ears. He has done the requisite regional-historical homework; wears it lightly; invokes it aptly and unsentimentally. This voyager, like this voyage, is quiet, able, self-effacing.

He is seldom to be seen, for example, in the photographs which illuminate his text; neither is his shapely Olin Stephens sloop, *Slick Ca'm.* Nor are any human beings at all. These were among the first of a series of tactful artistic decisions—and surely the hardest for a sailor who loves his boat and a photographer who relishes people—following upon what I take to have been his working premise: that having essayed the oystermen and the lighthouses of the Eastern Shore, he would bring home this time, from this voyage, the place itself.

Properly therefore he works in black and white; that is, in infinite shades of gray. To the eye, the Eastern Shore is strictly, beautifully monotonous, especially those endless lowlands which, as a Netherlander himself, de Gast responds to with particular sensitivity. To Dutchmen, Eastern Shoremen, and shoal-draft sailors, the boundary between land and sea is never prominent and always negotiable; their world, as Gertrude Stein remarked of the Spanish landscape, has few things in it, and so each thing exists with peculiar substantiveness. It is a world of such ubiquitous horizontality—sand bars, mud flats, the 360° horizon itself—that any verticals in it are more or less startling, interesting, even important, *ipso facto:* a mast; a piling; a heron's legs; loblolly pine trunks; the separate reeds of spartina grass. Even the surface of the water (everywhere, everywhere!) is prevailingly "slick calm," at least in the pictures: Days One, Six, and Nineteen, when the seas got too vertical for photography, properly belong to the open-water passages of the voyage and text, not to the essence of either.

Mirrored in that calm, and in the tranquil lens and log of Robert de Gast, every low landfall is a Rorschach image: imposing nothing, evoking whatever the viewer, or voyager, brings to it. The skipper of *Slick Ca'm* brought more than most tidewater travelers, and more than any photographer so far, to his charming one-way round trip: neither a sea saga nor a soul-search nor a cruising guide nor a travelogue nor a coffee-table picture book, but a calm circumspection of the Eastern Shore.

The Spirit of Place

ANOTHER SYMPOSIUM: this one at the University of North Dakota in Grand Forks on the vernal equinox of 1975, in connection with a series of readings there by visiting poets and fictionists. I was attracted because the Dakotas were terra incognita to me; because my fellow symposiasts included at least two writers whom I enjoy listening to as well as reading: William H. Gass and Ishmael Reed; and because the topic—"The Spirit of Place"—spoke to my concerns in the *LETTERS* novel, still a-building.

While on the Chesapeake we were fitted out and ready to launch a new sailing season, grimy snowbanks still sat about the flat Dakotas. I read from *LETTERS;* Ishmael Reed read from *Flight to Canada,* his novel then in progress, and took off afterwards from Grand Forks to Manitoba to check out the territory. Most moving of all was Bill Gass's reading, on location, of the chapter "We Do Not Live the Right Life" from his novel-even-now-still-in-the-works, *The Tunnel,* with its astonishing descriptions of Dakota's astonishing weather, and of the great prairie there outside our windows. One could ask for no better demonstration of the truth that when a *place* is central to a good writer's imagination, it is because that place has become a metaphor for larger concerns.

Reviewing my symposium remarks, I see that I was fumbling toward a notion of "postmodernism" set forth more fully in a later Friday-piece called "The Literature of Replenishment."

Ernest Hemingway remarked that every writer owes it to the place of his birth either to immortalize it or to destroy it. He himself did neither for Oak Park, Illinois (I believe he made the remark apropos of Thomas Wolfe). It is an idle remark anyhow, as is every generalization beginning with the words "Every writer . . ."

A good writer may be inspired in part by the *locus genii* of the place where he was born or raised: The "heart of the country" is near the heart of William Gass's fiction, though he depends on place less literally than Flannery O'Connor or William Faulkner did. His is a Dakota of the mind, an Ohio or Indiana of the heart. But at least as often, the writer's place of origin may be of little or no significance to the work: We note in passing that Ishmael Reed escaped from Buffalo, New York, or that Donald Barthelme was born in Philadelphia and raised in Houston; but Reed's "place" is wherever his hoodoo leads him—Harlem, New Orleans, Berkeley—and some of the best of Barthelme's fiction takes place no-where, not even in that Manhattan-of-the-nerve-ends where he lives.

The very notion of place, or "setting," realistically evoked as a main ingredient of fiction, is no doubt as suspect at this hour of the art as are the conventions of realistic characterization or linear plot as practiced by our literary great-grandparents. Our modernist grandparents and parents long since outgrew such parochialism and left us free to choose from three basic attitudes toward the realistic rendition of place in short stories and novels, as toward the other traditional components of prose fiction. I find two of these attitudes regrettable, the third admirable.

First, out of innocence or conservative inclination we may write as though Joyce and Kafka and Beckett and Borges and company had not written—as though the phenomenon of modernism and all that gave rise to it in the history of Western art hadn't happened, or was a regrettable aberration—and try to carry on where Henry James or Emile Zola or John Galsworthy left off. More Anglo-American writers than not (and about four-fifths of my students) write like this. The attitude strikes me as irresponsible to history, though I acknowledge that it does not preclude good work. A really fine artist can rise above his/her own aesthetics.

Second, we may fall into the opposite error of confusing change in the arts with progress in the empirical sciences, and imagine that because the great modernists turned away from conventional realism, linearity, and continuity, we may never legitimately again paint ravishing nudes, or compose moving melodies, or tell marvelous stories in which are included recognizable places and people. Many of those who practice what is called "meta-fiction" or "sur-fiction" espouse this attitude, and those who misread my 1967 essay "The Literature of Exhaustion" would include me among them. But I deplore this position, too: It is not only sterile and dec-adent; it's unintelligent, and it robs the bank of human experience, in which we all have a greater or smaller deposit.

Third, we may regard ourselves as being not irrevocably cut off from the nineteenth century and its predecessors by the accomplishment of our artistic parents and grandparents in the twentieth, but rather as free to come to new terms with both realism and antirealism, linearity and non-linearity, continuity and discontinuity. If the term "postmodern" describes anything worthwhile, it describes this freedom, successfully exercised. It used to be that an unmarried woman was immoral if she said Yes; for a while it seemed she was a prude if she said No; nowadays, she is free not only to say yes or no as she intelligently decides, but to do the asking. Similarly, the "postmodern" writer may find that the realistic, even tender evocation of place (for example) is quite to his purpose, a purpose which may partake of the purposes of both his modernist fathers and his pre-modern remoter ancestors without being quite the same as either's. The Joyce of *Finnegans Wake,* after all, is every bit as Irish as Sean O'Casey, without being, like O'Casey, every bit Irish. And Borges explicitly reminds us that one needn't write about gauchos on the Pampas or the *fervor* of Buenos Aires to be an Argentine writer.

In his recent book *Invisible Cities,* Italo Calvino—one of the most appealing of the "postmodernists"—imagines a Marco Polo who describes for a weary Kublai Khan a great many fantastical, no doubt imaginary cities; at one point the Khan observes that perhaps all these invisible cities are variations of Venice: that Marco Polo has never left home.

That is the sort of *Landgeist* which may still haunt and inspire us in the closing decades of twentieth-century fiction.

Getting Oriented

THE STORIES THUS FAR

―――――――――

PARTLY in order to say hello to William Gass again and to meet his St. Louis colleagues Stanley Elkin and Howard Nemerov, in the September after that spring conjunction in Grand Forks, I went to Washington University in Missouri to address the student body in connection with that university's undergraduate orientation program. As the date approached, I fixed my imagination duly upon the subject of Orientation—and then learned that what I was really expected to do was read from and chat about my novels and stories.

I wound up more or less reviewing My Fiction Thus Far: a kind of self-orientation prompted by the *LETTERS* project, which for better or worse—and against my personal shop rules—happened to involve a character from each of my previous six books.

The talk was delivered in Washington U's Graham Chapel, which is also by way of being Bill Gass's classroom. So popular a teacher is he, I was told, it is the only hall on campus commodious enough to seat all the students who sign up for his courses.

The *LETTERS* novel was published in 1979; the project of self-orientation is ongoing. What follows is an amended text of my "orientation lecture," bringing that project up to date. It appeared in the *New York Times Book Review* in 1984.

We meet this morning under a mutual misapprehension. You had been led to expect that I would read from and talk about my fiction; I had been led to believe that I'd be addressing the new freshman class as part of their orientation program, and that is what I originally prepared to do. I shall see whether I can do both at once.

As to my orienting university freshpeople to their new academic environment, it is the blind leading the blind. I know very little about Washington University beyond the fact that there are on its faculty at least two excellent writers of fiction and two excellent poets—William

Gass, Stanley Elkin, Howard Nemerov, and Mona Van Duyn—all of whom are reported to be fine teachers as well. Enroll in their courses before you graduate. As they are also quite famous, hit them for letters of recommendation for your job-placement files, and you'll be a shoo-in to graduate school if that is whither you incline. But do this only after you have done brilliant, even astonishing work in their courses; otherwise take your *C* and don't be pushy.

That's all I can think of in the way of specific practical advice for Washington University undergraduates. Speaking more generally, I remind you that *orientation* literally means determining which way is east, whether for architectural purposes (if you're building a medieval Christian church, you aim it in that direction, as Graham Chapel is properly aimed) or for funerary purposes (a well-oriented corpse lies with its feet to the rising sun). Apparently it wasn't until the end of the nineteenth century that *orientation* came to mean getting one's bearings, literally or figuratively, and not until well into the twentieth that it was used specifically to name the project of suggesting to new American college students that they're not high-school kids any longer, but responsible young adults commencing a major phase of their intellectual apprenticeship; taking a tour as it were of the lunchrooms and classrooms, lavatories and laboratories of the Western cultural conglomerate of which Washington University, for example, is one wholly owned subsidiary among many others, and we hope you'll enjoy your stay here.

In short, the word *orientation* came to mean finding out where in the occidental world we are as more and more of us came to suspect we didn't know. I feel on familiar ground. Indeed, when I set about to find something from my fiction suitable for this occasion, I realized that the general project of orientation—at least the condition of *dis*orientation which the project presumes—is my characteristic subject matter, my fictionary stock in trade. Intellectual and spiritual disorientation is the family disease of all my main characters—a disease usually complicated by ontological disorientation, since knowing where you're at is often contingent upon knowing who you are.

It is a malady, of course, epidemic in the literature of the last hundred years: one of its *orientations,* you might say, as they use the term in crystallography. What's more, the specific malaise of *academic* disorientation I find recurring from book to book of mine like a flu virus one had thought oneself done with. William Carlos Williams remarks in his autobiography that after years and years as both a practicing physician and a practicing poet, it occurred to him one day in a brow-slapping swoop of insight that the word *venereal* is related to the goddess Venus: It was a connection too obvious for him to have noticed. In the same way, I hadn't quite realized how *academic,* in this special sense, my life's work as a writer of stories has been. All of my books, I see now, are in the genre the Germans call *Erziehungsromane:* "upbringing-novels," education novels— a genre I had not found especially interesting after *David Copperfield* except as a vehicle for satire or an object of parody. And the satirical and parodical possibilities have been pretty well exhausted too, I'm sure.

More dismaying, when I reviewed my six offspring under this aspect, I realized that what I've been writing about all these years is not only orientation and education (rather, disorientation and education), but imperfect or unsuccessful or misfired education at that: not *Erziehungsromane* but *Herabziehungsromane:* "down-bringing novels." That I failed to recognize this before last week is exemplary: I am obliged to reorient myself to my own bibliography, as one must occasionally revise one's view of oneself retrospectively in the light of some new self-knowledge, usually bad news. And this reorientation is the more timely because my work in progress involves for better or worse the systematic reprise, reorchestration, reorientation of themes and characters from that bibliography: a sure sign that a novelist has passed forty.

The themes of that work in progress, I suppose, are regression, reenactment, and reorientation; like an ox-cart driver in monsoon season or the skipper of a grounded ship, one must sometimes go forward by going back. As an amateur sailor and navigator myself, I like the metaphor of dead reckoning: deciding where to go by determining where you are by reviewing where you've been. Aeneas does that, in Carthage and in Hades; many of the wandering heroes of mythology reach an impasse at some crucial point in their journey, from which they can proceed only by a laborious retracing of their steps. This is the process, if not the subject, of my novel-in-*regress*, and it is the substance of this orientation talk.

Todd Andrews, the hero of my first novel (*The Floating Opera*), goes to college originally—that is, he enrolls in a particular curriculum in a particular university—in order to fulfill his father's expectations more than his own. His own expectation is to drop dead before he finishes this sentence, from a certain kind of heart disease he learned he had while serving in the army in World War I. It takes him most of his undergraduate career (and most of a chapter) to discover what on earth he's doing there in the university; his orientation period, you might say, lasts almost to the baccalaureate. Even postgraduately, he is given to unpredictable shifts of life-style: In successive decades he plays the role of a libertine, an ascetic, a practicing cynic; he ends up at 54 (his present age in the novel) a sexually feeble small-town nihilist lawyer with an ongoing low-grade prostate infection and subacute bacterial endocarditis tending to myocardial infarction, writing long letters to his father, who committed suicide a quarter-century since. The fruit of his education, formal and informal, is one valid syllogism:

1. There is no absolute and ultimate justification for any action.
2. Continuing to live is a variety of action.
3. Therefore etc.

Whence he moves, less validly, to the resolve not only to kill himself that very evening, but to take a goodly number of his townspeople, friends, lovers, and such with him: He means to blow up the showboat of the novel's title by opening the acetylene gas tanks under the stage that fuel the house and stage lights at landings without electricity. The attempt fails; the show goes on; Todd Andrews's deductive faculty is restored, perhaps by the gas, and he understands (but neglects to inform Albert Camus) that, given his premises, he's likely to go on living because there's finally no more reason to commit suicide than not to.

If this sounds to you like the thinking more of a 24-year-old than of a 54-year-old, that is because the author was 24 at the time. Todd Andrews is a moderately successful lawyer—he lucks out on the two major legal cases in the plot—but he couldn't have done better than a gentleman's C+ in Logic 1, and he must have flunked The Chemistry of Gases cold. I hope your education will be more successful.

Novel #2, *The End of the Road,* is set on and around the campus of a seedy little state teachers college at the opening of the fall term. (In the film version, the campus sequences were shot at Swarthmore, of all inappropriate places: one of the loveliest campuses in the east. This was the first in a series of ruinous mistakes made by the film makers, who, as film makers sometimes do, combined considerable cinematographical expertise with considerable dramaturgical ignorance.) The central character is a grad-school dropout and ontological vacuum named Jacob Horner, who is subject to spells of paralysis because he suffers from the malady *cosmopsis,* the cosmic view. He is teaching English grammar on orders from his doctor, as a kind of therapy; but the prescription fails, as did his education. He becomes involved with a colleague's wife, a kind of na-ture-girl on the wrong trail: Nature may abhor a vacuum, but she shows her abhorrence by rushing to fill it. The novel ends with an illegal and botched abortion fatal to the young woman (this was the 1950s) and a final abdication of personality on Horner's part. The film critic John Simon accurately remarked that the principal difference between the novel and the film is that whereas the novel concludes with a harrowing abortion, the film is an abortion from start to finish. But I see now that it is Horner's aborted education that originally wound the mainspring of the plot: his total disorientation in the concourse of Baltimore's Penn Station, where he first becomes immobilized because he can't think of any reason to go anywhere—and, apparently, can't go anywhere without a reason.

Those two novels make a little duet: a nihilist comedy and, if not a nihilist tragedy, at least a nihilist catastrophe. I am a twin—an opposite-sex twin—and I see in retrospect that I've been oriented as a writer to the same iteration-with-variation that my sister and I exemplify: a sort of congenital redundancy. There followed a pair of very long novels, *The Sot-Weed Factor* and *Giles Goat-Boy,* each of whose heroes begins with a radically innocent orientation of which he is disabused in successive chapters. Ebenezer Cooke, the hero of *The Sot-Weed Factor,* matriculates at Cambridge University near the end of the seventeenth century; he has been ruinously disoriented by a tutor who professes *cosmophilism,* the sexual love of everything in the world: men, women, animals, plants, al-gebra, hydraulics, political intrigue. Cooke, like Jacob Horner, tends to-ward paralysis; he copes with the tendency by a radical assertion of his innocence and his fondness for versifying: He declares himself program-matically to be a virgin and a poet, as one might choose a double major, and sets out for the New World with a commission as Poet Laureate of the Province of Maryland. But the commission is spurious, his talent is questionable, the New World isn't what he'd been led to suspect and commissioned to eulogize; his innocence grows ever more technical and imperfect. In the end he has to marry a whore and contract a social dis-ease in order to regain the estate he didn't recognize as his until he'd lost it. His poetry gets a little better, but it's written figuratively in red ink—his own blood—and it's admired for the wrong reasons. By the time he is legitimately appointed Poet Laureate, he couldn't care less. Ebenezer Cooke would recommend that you choose some other major than Inno-cence, which he comes to see he has been guilty of.

Giles Goat-Boy, raised by the goats on one of the experimental stock-farms of an enormous, even world-embracing university, takes as *his* orientation program the myth of the wandering hero: He majors, as it were, in mythic heroism. It is not a gut course, though Giles has to descend into the very bowels of knowledge, and of the Campus, in order to earn his degree. And after nearly 800 pages, the main thing he seems to have learned is that what he's learned can't be taught: In his attempts to eff the ineffable, his truths get garbled in transmission, misconstrued, betrayed by verbalization, institutionalization. He almost ceases to care— as, I'm sure, many serious teachers do. But the *almost* is important.

After those two long books came a pair of short ones, my favorites. Both are about orientation, disorientation, reorientation. Both involve wandering heroes from classical mythology, usually lost. (One reason why classical mythic heroes need to know which way is east is that they traditionally travel west. But they *always* lose their way.) The first book of the pair is a series of fictions for print, tape, and live voice called *Lost in the Funhouse*. The title speaks for itself, orientationwise. The other is a series of three novellas, called *Chimera*. I'll glance at those novellas briefly through the lens that this occasion has given me, and then we'll have done.

"Dunyazadiad," the opening panel of the *Chimera* triptych, is a reorchestration of one of my favorite stories in the world: the frame-story of *The Thousand and One Nights*. You know the tale: how King Shahryar is driven so mad by sexual jealousy that he sleeps with a virgin every night and has her killed in the morning, lest she deceive him; and how that wonderful young woman Scheherazade, the Vizier's daughter, beguiles him with narrative strategies until he comes to his senses. For a time, I regarded the *Nights* as an insightful early work of feminist fiction: Scheherazade is called specifically "the Savior of her Sex"; the king's private misogyny is shown to be dangerous not only to his women but to his own mental health and, since he's the king, to the public health as well. Later in my own education as a writer, I came to regard the story as a kind of metaphor for the condition of narrative artists in general, and of artists who work on university campuses in particular, for a number of reasons:

1. Scheherazade has to lose her innocence before she can begin to practice her art. Ebenezer Cooke did, too; so do most of us.

2. Her audience—the king—is also her absolute critic. It is "publish or perish," with a vengeance.

3. And no matter how many times she has pleased the king before,

her talent is always on the line. That is as it should be, up to a point, with all of us.

4. But this terrifying relation is also a fertilizing one; Scheherazade bears the king three children over those 1001 nights, as well as telling all those stories. Much could be said about those parallel productions. . . .

5. Which, however, cease—at least her production of stories ceases—as soon as the king grants her the "tenure" of formal marriage. So it goes.

My version of the story, told by Scheherazade's kid sister, Dunyazade, echoes some of these preoccupations. Dunyazade reviews their history for her young bridegroom, the king's brother, Shah Zaman of Samarkand:

> "Three and a third years ago, when King Shahryar was raping a virgin every night and killing her in the morning, and the people were praying that Allah would dump the whole dynasty, and so many parents had fled the country with their daughters that in all the Islands of India and China there was hardly a young girl fit to fuck, my sister was an undergraduate arts-and-sciences major at Banu Sasan University. Besides being Homecoming Queen, valedictorian-elect, and a four-letter varsity athlete, she had a private library of a thousand volumes and the highest average in the history of the campus. Every graduate department in the East was after her with fellowships—but she was so appalled at the state of the nation that she dropped out of school in her last semester to do full-time research on a way to stop Shahryar from killing all our sisters and wrecking the country.
>
> "Political science, which she looked at first, got her nowhere. Shahryar's power was absolute, and by sparing the daughters of his army officers and chief ministers (like our own father) and picking his victims mainly from the families of liberal intellectuals and other minorities, he kept the military and the cabinet loyal enough to rule out a coup d'état. Revolution seemed out of the question, because his woman-hating, spectacular as it was, was reinforced more or less by all our traditions and institutions, and as long as the girls he was murdering were generally upper-caste, there was no popular base for guerrilla war. Finally, since he could count on your help from Samarkand, invasion from outside or plain assassination were bad bets too: Sherry figured your retaliation would be worse than Shahryar's virgin-a-night policy.
>
> "So we gave up poly sci (I fetched her books and sharpened her quills and made tea and alphabetized her index cards) and tried psychology—another blind alley. Once she'd noted that *your* reaction to

being cuckolded by your wife was homicidal rage followed by despair and abandonment of your kingdom, and that Shahryar's was
the reverse; and established that *that* was owing to the difference in
your ages and the order of revelations; and decided that whatever
pathology was involved was a function of the culture and your position as absolute monarchs rather than particular hang-ups in your
psyches, et cetera—what was there to say?

"She grew daily more desperate; the body-count of deflowered
and decapitated Moslem girls was past nine hundred, and Daddy
was just about out of candidates. Sherry didn't especially care about
herself, you understand—wouldn't have even if she hadn't guessed
that the King was sparing her out of respect for his vizier and her
own accomplishments. But beyond the general awfulness of the situation, she was particularly concerned for my sake. From the day I
was born, when Sherry was about nine, she treasured me as if I were
hers; I might as well not have had parents; she and I ate from the
same plate, slept in the same bed; no one could separate us; I'll bet
we weren't apart for an hour in the first dozen years of my life. But I
never had her good looks or her way with the world—and I was the
youngest in the family besides. My breasts were growing; already I'd
begun to menstruate: any day Daddy might have to sacrifice me to
save Sherry.

"So when nothing else worked, as a last resort she turned to her
first love, unlikely as it seemed, mythology and folklore, and studied
all the riddle/puzzle/secret motifs she could dig up. 'We need a
miracle, Doony,' she said (I was braiding her hair and massaging her
neck as she went through her notes for the thousandth time), 'and
the only genies *I've* ever met were in stories, not in Moormen's-rings
and Jews'-lamps. It's in words that the magic is—Abracadabra,
Open Sesame, and the rest—but the magic words in one story aren't
magical in the next. The real magic is to understand which words
work, and when, and for what; the trick is to learn the trick.' "

In other words—as Dunyazade and Scheherazade and the Author
come to learn in the pages that follow—the *key* to the treasure may *be* the
treasure.

The tuition for that sort of lesson can be very high. Retracing one's
steps—"becoming as a kindergartener again," as the goat-boy puts it—
may be necessary to a fruitful reorientation, but one runs the risk of losing oneself in the past instead of returning to the present equipped to
move forward into the future. Perseus (in the second *Chimera* novella,
called "Perseid") understands this, though he's not sure for a while what
to do with his understanding. He too has retraced his heroical route, re-

capitulated his mythic exploits, and not for vanity's sake, but for reorientation. As he says one night to the nymph Calyxa, as she and he are making love:

> "Well, now, perhaps it was a bit vain of me to want to retrace my
> good young days; but it wasn't *just* vanity; no more were my nightly
> narratives: Somewhere along that way I'd lost something, took a
> wrong turn, forgot some knack, I don't know; it seemed to me that if
> I kept going over it carefully enough I might see the pattern, find the
> key."
> "A little up and to your left," Calyxa whispered.

And a bit farther on:

> "Thus this endless repetition of my story: As both protagonist and
> author, so to speak, I thought to overtake with understanding my
> present paragraph as it were by examining my paged past, and, thus
> pointed, proceed serene to the future's sentence."

Perseus's research is successful: He finds the Key and moves on to his proper destiny, which is to become a constellation in the sky, endlessly reenacting his story in his risings and settings. Perseus "makes it" because his vocation is legitimate: He doesn't major in Mythic Heroism; he happens to *be* a mythic hero, whose only problem is what to do for an encore. And if his ultimate stardom is ambivalent (he can't embrace the constellation he loves, which hangs right next to him forever), it is the ambivalence of immortality, as Keats tells us in his "Ode on a Grecian Urn."

More cautionary is the lesson of Bellerophon, the hero of the final *Chimera* novella. Like Giles the goat-boy, Bellerophon aspires to be a mythic hero; it is his only study. When Perseus reaches middle age, he researches his own history and the careers of other mythic heroes in order to understand what brought him to where he is, so that he can go on. Young Bellerophon's orientation, on the other hand, is that by following perfectly the ritual pattern of mythic heroism—by getting all A's and four letters of recommendation, as it were—he will become a bona fide mythic hero like his cousin Perseus. What he learns, and it is an expensive lesson, is that by perfectly imitating the pattern of mythic heroism, one becomes a perfect imitation of a mythic hero, which is not quite the same thing as being Perseus the Golden Destroyer. Hence the novella's title, "Bellerophoniad." Something similar may befall the writer too fixated upon his/her distinguished predecessors; it is a disoriented navigator indeed who mistakes the stars he steers by for his destination.

He is not, however, my Bellerophon, entirely phony: He is too earnest for that, too authentically dedicated to his profession, whatever the limits of his gift. What's more, he really does kill the Chimera—that fictive monster or monstrous fiction—to the extent that it ever really existed in the first place. Bellerophon's immortality is of a more radically qualified sort: What he becomes is not the story of his own exploits, as Perseus does up there among the other stars, but the *text* of the story "Bellerophoniad." Pegasus, the winged horse of inspiration on which Bellerophon has flown, gets to heaven (in fact, he's one of the constellations in the Perseus group); his rider is thrown at the threshold of the gate, falls for a long time (long enough to tell his long tale), and is transformed just in the nick of time into the pages, the sentences, the letters of the book *Chimera*. To turn into the sound of one's own voice is an occupational hazard of professional storytellers; even more so, I imagine, of professional lecturers.

That brings us to the present, appropriately, just at the end of my allotted hour. All these retracements, recapitulations, rehearsals, and reenactments really would be simply regressive if they didn't issue in reorientation, from which new work can proceed. But that, as Scheherazade says, is another story, for another night.

I wish you good luck in your own orientation. East is over that way.

POSTSCRIPT 1984, FOR THE CLASS OF 1988

The novel *LETTERS,* alluded to above and published some while after that orientation lecture, centers upon an enormous (and hypothetical) third-rate American university, Marshyhope State, constructed for my purposes on the freshly filled saltmarsh of my native Dorchester County, in Maryland. The year is 1969, the heyday of U.S. academic imperialism and gigantism. Marshyhope's architectural symbol and intended beacon to the world, The Tower of Truth, on the eve of its dedication already shows signs of subsiding into the fenlands whence it sprang, like the Hancock Tower into Back Bay Boston.

As R. D. Laing rationalizes schizophrenia, at least in certain cases, as a sane response to a deranged but inescapable set of circumstances, so the cautionary example of Marshyhope State suggests that—in certain cases, at least—the fault of disorientation may lie not in ourselves, Horatio, but in our alma maters and paters. To disoriented undergraduates (and to readers bogged down in *LETTERS*) I say: By all means allow for that possibility—but do not jump to that conclusion, as it is most likely mistaken.

My little novel *Sabbatical: A Romance* (1982) carries the Laingian scenario farther. Todd Andrews in *The Floating Opera* (and again in *LETTERS*) wonders sentence by sentence whether his heart will carry him from subject to predicate; in *Sabbatical,* set on Chesapeake Bay in 1980, the background question is whether the world will end before the novel does.

More specifically, the question is whether one can responsibly bring children into the disoriented powder-keg wherein we dwell. The prospective parents in *Sabbatical* are literal navigators, of a seaworthy cruising sailboat (she is a proper young academic, on sabbatical leave; he is a decent, middle-aged ex-CIA officer, between careers). *They* are oriented; the course they steer is accurate, if not always straightforward. What's more, after years of marriage and trials large and small they remain happily in love with each other. In an oriented world, their landfall—and progeny—would be assured. In the troubled and dangerous waters through which they, like the rest of us, necessarily sail, however, no degree of skill in navigation or of seaworthiness in the vessel guarantees that the destination will still be there at our Estimated Time of Arrival.

This being the more or less apocalyptical case—the Sot-Weed Factor supplanted as it were by the Doomsday Factor—why set a course at all, whether toward graduation or procreation or distinguished career or further fiction? This is the approximate subject of my next effort at self-orientation: my novel presently in the works.

But that, as Scheherazade says, is etc.

My Two Problems: 1

THROUGH the rest of the academic year 1975/76, my once-a-month fiction readings were a program of excerpts from and around the *LETTERS* novel, still under construction. Reading ''live'' from that book presented a small problem, set forth below; but at one of the first tryouts of the program, that small problem was overshadowed by another more considerable.

In October 1975, Michigan State University staged an elaborate homage to Jorge Luis Borges. The elderly writer was flown up to East Lansing from Buenos Aires, together with his secretary-guide-companion-nurse, and established in a year's residency, from which he would make frequent excursions about the country. Borges translators and Borges critics were assembled to read papers and tributes.

By reason of my ''Literature of Exhaustion'' essay, I was invited to the feast, but given permission to read from my fiction instead of preparing yet another essay in praise of Borges. I accepted, pleased to pay my respects again to the great man, whom I hadn't crossed paths with for seven years, and confidently assuming that my reading from *LETTERS* would be but one more of the preliminaries to Sr. Borges's own public presentation, the culmination of the festivities.

However, in an exquisite lapse of good judgment, the orchestrators of the homage climaxed the several-day celebration by scheduling Borges's main appearance in the afternoon of the final day, to be followed by a testimonial banquet, to be followed in turn and presumably wrapped up by . . . my reading. I was appalled at that impossible programming, and said so. No help for it, my hosts explained: The old chap is 77; he tires easily and therefore prefers to do his number in the afternoon.

He did, impressively indeed, stringing together anecdotes and comments upon his work in an informal but practiced spiel to a large, reverent audience which he could not see. Well, I said to myself: Hard as this act will be to follow, at least Borges himself will tire early as promised and not attend my anticlimactic coda to the main event. Alas, dinner gave the man new energy; he insisted not only upon coming to my reading, but upon sitting front row center, flanked by his companion and his American translator, where I could see his reaction to every line. For that hour I could almost have wished myself blind; but the show had to go on.

Good evening.

Our situation tonight is of course impossible.

In 1966, in an effort to come to terms with the fiction of Jorge Luis Borges, which I admired more than my own, I wrote an essay called "The Literature of Exhaustion." Among other remarks which have risen from that essay to haunt or embarrass me since—whether because they were marvelously misunderstood or because they were understood correctly— was this one: "Our century is more than two-thirds done; it is dismaying to see so many of our writers still following Dostoevsky or Flaubert, when the real problem seems to me to be how to follow not even Joyce and Kafka, but those who've *followed* Joyce and Kafka and are now in the evenings of their own careers." How does one follow Nabokov, Beckett, Borges?

I did not imagine in 1966 that I would have to confront the problem in this literal a fashion. It delights me that the writer I was praising nine years ago "in the evening of his career" has spoken to us today in the vigorous afternoon and left the evening to us poor epigones. I am in the position of the heroine of my novella about Scheherazade's younger sister, Dunyazade, who sat at the foot of the king's bed for 1001 nights, watching Scheherazade and him make love and listening to all those stories. The Genie in my story exclaims at one point:

> "All those nights at the foot of the bed, Dunyazade! . . . You've had the whole literary tradition transmitted to you—and the whole erotic tradition, too! There's no story you haven't heard; there's no way of making love that you haven't seen again and again. I think of you, little sister, a virgin in both respects: All that innocence! All that sophistication! And now it's your turn: Shahryar has told [his younger brother] Shah Zaman about his wonderful mistress, how he loves her as much for herself as for her stories—*which he also passes on;* the two brothers marry the two sisters; it's your wedding night, Dunyazade. . . . But wait! Look here! Shahryar deflowered and killed a virgin a night for a thousand and one nights before he met Scheherazade; Shah Zaman has been doing the same thing, but it's only now, a thousand nights and a night later, that *he* learns about Scheherazade—that means he's had two thousand and two young women at the least since he killed his wife, and not one has pleased him enough to move him to spend a second night with her, much less

spare her life! What are you going to do to entertain *him,* little sister?
Make love in exciting new ways? There are none! Tell him stories,
like Scheherazade? He's heard them all! Dunyazade, Dunyazade!
Who can tell *your* story?"

Well, one must try. Like the mountebank in Anatole France's story
"The Juggler of Our Lady," I can pay tribute only by doing my tricks,
and must pray that you—and Señor Borges—will accept them in that
spirit.

My second problem is less serious by comparison. I want to read to
you from work in progress, since you can read my works in print for
yourself. But alas, after spending several years writing fiction for the ear,
out of my interest in the oral narrative tradition, I have—as André Gide
used to say—walked to the opposite corner of my imagination: The work
in hand really is for print, not for reading aloud. Therefore I shall talk
about it a bit and read *around* it some: hors d'oeuvres served up too late,
after the *chef d'oeuvre* of this afternoon.

My Two Problems: 2

THAT little introductory gambit soon turned into a formula. When, as happened several times that season, I was asked to address some particular topic, I would explain that as I hadn't five minutesworth to say just then on anything except my novel in progress, and as that novel was not really meant for reading aloud from, my inviters had better find another guest lecturer. Sometimes they did; more often, for one reason or another, they said Come say your five minutesworth and then read whatever you please. By October 1976, when I revisited Penn State in a lecture series called ''The Impact of Contemporary Literature on Contemporary Society,'' the formula was full-fledged.

I have two problems this evening, each less serious than the other. The first is that I was invited back to Penn State to address the subject "The Impact of Literature Upon Contemporary Society," your general visiting-lecture-series topic this season. You have set aside your usual and normal evening pursuits to hear what this particular novelist has to say upon that particular subject. But (*a*) after twenty-five years of professing literature and presiding over apprentice writers—twelve of those years here at University Park, PA—I've yet to master the art of formally lecturing on anything, or for that matter of talking and writing on a blackboard simultaneously. Furthermore, (*b*) I suspect that literature *has* no impact, or even any measurable effect, on contemporary society. I am reminded of a colleague from my Penn State days who went to India on a Fulbright grant to study the influence of communism on outlying villages in northern India. Having investigated the matter on location for a full year, he urgently applied for and was awarded a renewal of his research grant in order to continue his field investigations. At the end of two years, he returned to this university and published a report which declared, in essence, that there *was* no significant influence of communism on outlying villages in northern India.

With respect to literature's impact upon contemporary society, W. H. Auden said it right: "Poetry makes nothing happen." Neither does fiction, as a rule, even *engagée* fiction. The sort of fiction that *does* affect the world of affairs is likely not to be first-rate art, even when, like Alexander Solzhenitsyn's *Gulag Archipelago,* it is first-rate moral propaganda. Many of us would put *Uncle Tom's Cabin* in this category: it is not *War and Peace,* but Abraham Lincoln is said to have remarked, upon meeting Harriet Beecher Stowe during the American Civil War: "So you're the little lady who caused all this." The best fiction of Vladimir Nabokov is in my opinion incomparably better stuff than Solzhenitsyn's; yet Nabokov's declared objective—so far from changing the world or "impacting" contemporary society, as they say nowadays—is "mere aesthetic bliss."

So. I have asked and been granted permission to turn the topic around, since contemporary society indisputably has an impact upon contemporary literature. Here is what I have to say:

First of all, as any bulletin from Amnesty International or the literary organization P.E.N. will attest, when Contemporary Society is not actively suppressing, coercing, censoring, or otherwise bullying and silencing the authors of our contemporary literature, as happens in more nations of the world than not, it is likely to assist them in their self-destruction or self-corruption—a circumstance not entirely society's fault, to be sure. The fate of numerous American best-selling novelists moved Leslie Fiedler to observe, "Nothing fails like success." Second, when doing neither of the above to its writers, it may yet corrupt, distract, miseducate, or otherwise deprive them of their audiences, and a writer without readers is a tree falling without hearers: It is a moot question whether he has made any noise at all. But I have no idea what if anything is to be done about that.

Finally, of course, contemporary society is what all writers write *about,* and its history affects the way we write about it. The experience of being human beings, alive in this world now, is what even solipsists, historical novelists, science-fiction writers, concrete poets, and art-for-art's-sakers write about—if only as the suicide makes his little comment upon life by declining to live it.

Having said this, which no doubt went without saying, I have said my total say upon the matter. If the Barth line on The Impact of Literature Upon Contemporary Society is the extent of your interest in me, I here excuse you from the remainder of the hour.

Well. Being unable to dissertate, I have further asked and received permission to *illustrate* The Impact of Et Cetera upon at least one writer—this one—and so I now turn with some relief to my second problem, which is as follows:

For several years in the 1960s I was interested in oral narrative, both with the live authorial voice and with electronic tape: fiction for the ear, the spring from which written literature sprang. And being a musician-gone-wrong, I like to choose for occasions like this a piece of my fiction that *performs* well, whatever its other merits and shortcomings, and then perform it enough times to get fairly good at it. For a year or so I did the tape-and-live-voice pieces out of the series called *Lost in the Funhouse;* more recently I've been reading from the novellas in a book of mine called *Chimera:* novellas about the mythical Greek heroes Perseus and Bellerophon and about Scheherazade's kid sister.

Unfortunately, my fiction in progress has nothing whatever to do with oral narrative. It is meant absolutely for the printed page. But I want to try a little bit of it anyhow, because I've been working on it for several years now in that peculiar vacuum that a novelist has to sustain in order to get his work done.

Here are some things I don't mind telling you about the project: It is a book-length fiction, more a novel than not. In fact, muse help me, it's in the most venerable and vulnerable of English novel-forms, the *epistolary novel*—made so popular by Samuel Richardson in the second third of the eighteenth century that it was already worked to death by the third third of the eighteenth century. The jury may still be out on the famous and unimportant question of the death of the novel, but that the novel-in-letters has long since run its course, even Samuel Richardson was declaring by 1759, in a pair of remarkable letters which may well be the first mention of the Novel's demise.

The title of my novel-in-letters is *LETTERS*. It consists of letters between several correspondents, and it is preoccupied with the role of epistles—real letters, forged letters, doctored letters, mislaid and misdirected letters—in the history of history. It is also concerned with, and of course constituted of, alphabetical letters, the atoms of which the universe of print is made. (There is a charming Cabalistical tradition that the primordial Torah was a jumble of letters, just as the primordial universe was a chaos of atoms, and that the Hebrew letters arranged themselves into words and sentences as the events they describe came to pass.) Finally, to some extent the book is addressed to the phenomenon of literature itself, the third main sense of our English word *letters*.

Letters is a seven-letter word. *LETTERS* is my seventh book of fiction. The letters in *LETTERS* are from seven correspondents, some of them recruited from my earlier books, and they're dated over the seven months from March through September of 1969 (for some exquisite reason that I have forgotten), though they also involve the 1976 U.S. Bicentennial, the War of 1812, the American Revolution, revolutions and recyclings in general, and other things. There are to be 88 letters in all, and since I have as of this hour drafted 54 of them, I am about four-sevenths of the way through, serenely confident that the first four-sevenths of any project are the hardest.

By 1968 I knew at least one other detail about the enterprise: that at a point *six*-sevenths of the way through there should occur two stories within the main story: one about Perseus and Medusa, to be written by Ambrose Mensch, a character from *Lost in the Funhouse* who is also one of our correspondents; and a story about Bellerophon and the original Chimera to be written by one Jerome Bonaparte Bray, another of our correspondents and the putative editor of *Giles Goat-Boy*. I decided to write those little off-central texts first, and they grew into the *Chimera* book aforementioned, which is thus to some extent contaminated from the future by the project that was meant to give it birth.

Ah, the artist's life.

My reading tonight will be an illustration of that contamination, followed by a sample of the contaminant-in-progress.

In the opening of the novella "Perseid," the centerpiece of *Chimera*, the hero Perseus, now a constellation in the sky, recalls the day he tried to repeat his youthful exploits and crashed into the Libyan desert. As I read it, you are to nudge your neighbor and say "Get it? Letters."

> Good evening.
> Stories last longer than men, stones than stories, stars than stones. But even our stars' nights are numbered, and with them will pass this patterned tale to a long-deceased earth.
> Nightly, when I wake to think myself beworlded and find myself in heaven, I review the night I woke to think and find myself vice-versa. I'd been long lost, deserted, down and out in Libya; two decades past I'd overflown that country with the bloody Gorgon's

head, and every drop that hit the dunes had turned to snake—so I
learned later. At twenty years and twenty kilometers high, how could
I have known? Now there I was, sea-leveled, forty, parched and
plucked, every grain in my molted sandals raising blisters, and beleaguered by the serpents of my past. It must have been that of all
the gods in heaven, the two I'd never got along with put it to me:
sandy Ammon, my mother-in-law's pet deity, who'd first sent Andromeda over the edge, and Sabazius the beer-god, who'd raised the
roof in Argos till I raised him a temple. Just then I'd've swapped
Mycenae for a cold draught and a spot of shade to sip it in; I even
prayed to the rascals. Nothing doing. Couldn't think where I'd been
or where was headed, lost track of me entirely, commenced hallu-
cinating, wow. Somewhere back in my flying youth I'd read how to
advertise help wanted when you're brought down: I stamped a
whopping *PERSEUS* in the sand, forgot what I was about, writing
sets your mind a-tramp; next thing I knew I'd printed *PERSEUS
LOVES ANDROMED* half a kilometer across the dunes. Wound up
in a depression with the three last letters; everything before them
slipped my mind; not till I added *USA* was I high enough again to
get the message, how I'd confused what I'd set out to clarify. I fried
awhile longer on the dune-top, trying to care; I was a dying man: so
what if my Mayday had grown through self-advertisement to an
amphisbane graffito? But O I was a born reviser, and would die one:
as I looked back on what I'd written, a fresh East breeze sprang from
the right margin, behind, where I'd been aiming, and drifted the *A*
I'd come to rest on. I took its cue, erased the whole name, got lost in
the vipered space between object and verb, went on erasing, erasing
all, talking to myself, crazy man: no more *LOVES,* no more *LOVE,*
clean the slate altogether—me too, take it off, all of it. But I'd forgot
by that time who I was, relost in the second space, my first draft's
first; I snaked as far as the subject's final *S* and, frothing, swooned,
made myself after that seventh letter a mad dash—

Very well. And in the novella called "Bellerophoniad," Bellerophon's
account of his childhood tutor, Polyeidus, echoes this same preoccupation with letters:

"Our tutor he became, Polyeidus, Polyeidus, after being prophet
laureate to the court of Corinth. Though featured in several other
myths, on the strength of which Dad had hired him, he declared to
us he had no memory of his pre-Corinthian past, or any youth. Some
said he'd been Proteus's apprentice, others that he was some
stranded version of The Old Man of the Sea himself. At such stories
Polyeidus shrugged, saying only that all shape-shifters are revisions
of tricky Proteus. But he dismissed the conventional Protean trans-

formations—into animals, plants, and such—as mere vaudeville entertainment, and would never oblige us with a gryphon or a unicorn, say, howevermuch we pled, or stoop to such homely predictions as next day's weather. For this reason, among others, he was demoted to tutor; and he urged upon us, even as boys, a severer view of magic. By no means, he used to insist, did magicians necessarily understand their art, though experience had led him to a couple of general observations on it. For example, that each time he learned something new about his powers, those powers diminished, anyhow altered. Also, that what he "turned into" on those occasions when he transformed was not altogether within his governance. Under certain circumstances he would frown, give a kind of grunt, and turn into something, which might or might not resemble what if anything he'd had in mind. Sometimes his magic failed him when he called upon it; other times it seized him when he had no use for it; and the same was true of his prophesying. 'It will be alleged that Napoleon died on St. Helena in 1821,' he would announce, with no more notion than we of the man and place and date he meant, or the significance of the news; 'in fact he escaped to the Eastern Shore of Maryland, to establish his base for the Second Revolution.' Most disappointingly to Deliades and me, his transformations were generally into what he came to call 'historical personages from the future': this same Napoleon, for example, or Captain John Smith of the American plantation of Virginia: useless to our education. But no sooner did he see this pattern than he lost the capacity, and changed thenceforward only into documents, mainly epistolary: Napoleon's imaginary letter from King Theodore to Sir Robert Walpole, composed after the Emperor's surrender; Plato's Seventh Letter; the letter from Denmark to England which Hamlet transferred to Rosencrantz and Guildenstern; the Isidorian Decretals; the *Protocols of the Elders of Zion;* Madame de Staël's *Lettres sur Jean-Jacques Rousseau;* the 'Henry Letters' purchased for $50,000 by President Madison's administration from the impostor Compte de Crillon in 1811 to promote the War of 1812; the letter from Vice Admiral Sir Alexander Cochrane, commander of the British fleet at Halifax, to that same president, warning that unless reparations were made for the Americans' destruction of Newark and St. Davids in Canada, the British would retaliate by burning Washington—a letter said to be either antedated or intentionally delayed, as it reached its address when the capital was in ashes; the false letter describing mass movements of Indian and Canadian forces against Detroit, planted by the Canadian General Brock so that the U.S. General Hull would discover it, panic, and surrender the city; a similar letter dated September 11, 1813, which purported to be from Colonel Fossett of Vermont to General MacComb, advising him of massive reinforcements on the way to aid him against the Canadian General Prévost in the Battle of

Plattsburg: it was entrusted to an Irishwoman of Cumberland Head whom the U.S. Secret Service, its actual author, knew to be loyal to the British; Prévost, when she dutifully turned it over to him, took it to be authentic and retreated into Canada, though no such reinforcements existed. Et cetera. Doctored letters. My brother and I were not very interested."

Later in that same novella, Bellerophon, wandering in the marshes, "far from the paths of men," Homer tells us, "devouring his own soul," actually receives a sort of letter from the author, washed up in an empty bottle, in which letter the author reviews the myth of Bellerophon and then remarks:

> ... the two central images—Pegasus and the Chimera—appealed to me profoundly. I envisioned a comic novella based on the myth; a companion-piece to "Perseid," perhaps. To compose it I set aside a much larger and more complicated project, a novel called *LETTERS*: It seemed anyway to have become a vast morass of plans, notes, false starts, in which I grew more mired with every attempt to extricate myself.

Are writers supposed to put stuff like that into their fiction? Don't ask me. In any case, that was 1968: Things are slogging along nicely now, thank you—though I'm not sure what I'll do when I reach that spot six-sevenths of the way through *LETTERS* where these two stories were designed to go.

The artist's life; the artist's life.

My Two Problems: 3

COULD I still have been doing the Two Problems bit in 1977? Evidently so, though as with all literary formulas, repetition had rendered it by then more than a touch perfunctory. At the University of Louisville, Kentucky, in February 1977, for example, the general topic of the university's annual Conference on Twentiety-Century Literature was "Speed, Time, and Change" . . .

I have two problems this evening.

The first, of which I gave our hosts fair warning, is that I haven't much to say directly upon the subject of our conference: Speed, Time, and Change in Twentieth-Century Literature. The reason for this is that although I read impertinent critics now and then who suggest that John Barth has fallen silent, a victim of the Literature of Exhaustion, I have in fact been hard at work for a number of years at top *speed,* on a literary project that has turned out to demand more *time* than I'd expected, and which, Proteus-like, has *changed* its nature under my hands while I, like Menelaus on the beach at Pharos, wrestle to hold onto it—and, in the wrestling, grow wiser but no younger.

Among the hazards of composing long works is the Heraclitean one: The Proust who finished *The Past Recaptured* was not the Proust who began *Swann's Way.* My novel-so-long-in-progress bids to take seven years to complete: long enough for every cell in the author's body to replace itself. Long enough for a young person to matriculate as a college freshman and complete a Ph.D. And just long enough, Horace tells us, for the composition of a proper epic.

So much for my first problem. Our hosts have kindly given me leave to *illustrate* the subject that I cannot *dissertate* upon, by excerpting from this protean project and growing older before your very eyes. As for the second problem . . .

My Two Uncles

HERE'S a switch on the old routine that I rather like, delivered in Walt Whitman's house in Camden, New Jersey, on Walt Whitman Day—May 5—1976, at the annual homage to the good gray poet sponsored by the Camden branch campus of Rutgers University.

My first problem this afternoon is that your guest speakers on Walt Whitman Day, normally and properly, should be either eminent American poets or scholars of classical American literature, both of whom will have had to come to some sort of professional terms with their great gray literary ancestor. Thus for example Professor Donald Davie, in a recent review of John Berryman's posthumously collected papers, says, "It cannot be denied that at some point in mid-career Berryman momentously shifted his stance toward his art and the experience his art fed upon. . . . And the shift seems to have to do, not surprisingly, with that inescapable figure in every American poet's heritage, Walt Whitman."

Professor Davie's own forthcoming book is a new critical study of Ezra Pound; as he wrote that sentence about John Berryman, he was perhaps remembering Pound's explicit reconciliation with his ancestor: the early poem called "A Pact":

A PACT

I make a pact with you, Walt Whitman—
I have detested you long enough.
I come to you as a grown child
Who has had a pig-headed father;
I am old enough now to make friends.

It was you that broke the new wood,
Now is a time for carving.
We have one sap and one root—
Let there be commerce between us.

But me, I'm neither a poet nor a scholar of American literature. I have had no particular quarrel with Walt Whitman; therefore I feel no particular urge for atonement with him. The spiritual fathers I've had to make my own pacts with are mainly European. Indeed, Leslie Fiedler, in an early essay on my "historical" novel *The Sot-Weed Factor,* in the course of commending me for staying as it were in the Maryland marshes, made this remark: "Only such a European-oriented writer as Walt Whitman at his worst believes that to portray America one must encompass its imaginary vastness, its blurred totality." I agreed with Fiedler then; I still agree with him.

In a moment I'll pay my respects to Walt Whitman in the only way I competently can: by reading to you a few leaves of my own grass, from a project that perhaps suffers from some Whitmanesque ambition. Before I do, though, I want to tell you a complicated story of my discovery of two artistic uncles, one figurative and one literal: a discovery prompted by that remark of Leslie Fiedler's.

It is a curious remark, after all: to say of our archetypal American poet, "Only such a *European*-oriented writer as Walt Whitman at his worst . . ." etc. That epithet reminded me of me. My memory of *Leaves of Grass* was an undergraduate memory; I reread it and recognized some kinship after all. Whitman's project of going forward by going *back,* beyond the immediate European conventions of verse and their American imitations, to something older, looser, freer, more epical and rough— there were surely some resemblances there to *my* project of returning to the inventors of the English novel for my long story of Ebenezer Cooke, the misfortunate poet laureate of Maryland, in order as it were to make an end run around Flaubert and the modernist novel. So I discovered in Walt Whitman not a lost father, for better or worse, but a kind of mislaid literary uncle, who seemed to me to ratify, after the fact—benignly, avuncularly—my own project.

All right; that's simple enough. Now comes the complicated part.

In 1873, in his fifty-fifth year, Walt Whitman suffered a partial paralytic stroke and retired from Washington here to Camden. Among his friends for the next number of years, here and across the river in Philadelphia, was a jolly circle of businessmen, physicians, clergymen, and more or less professional artists and goodfellows organized by and around the studio of one Colonel John R. Johnston, himself an artist of sorts. Johnston lived at 434 Penn Street in Camden, one block from this lecture hall; his Philadelphia studio became such a popular hangout for the wits of the area that they formed a mock society—after the model of the eighteenth-century Hartford Wits or the even older Tuesday Club of Annapolis, and all the earlier such mock orders in England and Europe, back at least to Plato's Symposium crowd. Colonel Johnston dubbed himself The Chief; there were a Lieutenant General, a Marshal, an Attorney General, a Commissary, a Surgeon General, a Chaplain, a Chief of Old Pensioners, and a Poet Laureate. Not surprisingly, the Poet Laureate of the Studio was Walt Whitman.

They socialized; they drank; the artists drew serious or satiric drawings; the wits composed mock autobiographies, mock insults, mock book-reviews. All of it was pretty ponderous stuff, not nearly so witty as Joel Barlow's Hartford crowd or the minutes of the Annapolis Tuesday Club. Whitman's own contributions were rather straight: In 1880, at the peak of the group's flourishing, he was sixty, fatigued, in indifferent health, and preoccupied with what was to be the big 1881 edition of *Leaves of Grass.* That same year, Colonel Johnston and his "Chaplain" (T. D. Caulston) availed themselves of a new invention called the hectograph to duplicate the sketches and the autograph inscriptions of the group, and published them as a handsomely bound volume called "*The Studio Souvenir* of John R. Johnston, Artist, First & Only Edition, Published in Philadelphia, February, 1880." They ran off enough copies for each of the Studio's habitués: those chief officers aforementioned plus a group listed as "Attendants on the Chief & Staff, as follows: Noblemen, Princes, rich men's sons and millions expecting to be rich . . ." That last sounds like Whitman's democratic touch, doesn't it? Each copy—the printing numbered about three dozen in all—bore the owner's name stamped in gold.

Here are a couple of Whitman's entries, in his hand:

Feb. 9 '80
　　Loafing around for a couple of hours this fine sunny crispy day—cross'd the Delaware—walk'd up Chestnut St—every thing lovely—look'd in at my friend Col. Johnston's studio—the sun shining bright, & I feeling all right

　　　　　　　　　　　　　　　Walt Whitman

Camden N J
   At 434 Penn Street
      Sunday Evening
         Feb 15th '80—
   Another fresh, dear, social evening here, with Col. & Mrs.
Johnston, & Ida, & John (an evening fine as I have had, over & over
again for six years). Next summer early (May 31), I shall be 61 years
old.
   —I have just return'd from a four months' trip to the Rocky
Mt's, and over the Great Plains, & through Colorado, Missouri,
Kansas, Illinois, Indiana, Ohio, &c.
   Am well for me—
                                          Walt Whitman

And a final one, undated, toward the end of the book:

   Nothing does me more good than to have a little shake up with
the boys of the Studio.
                                          Walt Whitman

   Now the plot thickens. One of those "boys" Whitman refers to happened to be a forty-year-old Baltimorean named James H. Wilson (I am
reading from his copy; he is listed among the Attendants), who describes
himself as being "in the steamboat business." By 1908, twenty-eight years
after *The Studio Souvenir* was published and sixteen years after Whitman's death, Wilson's copy was evidently floating around another sort of
studio, a more serious one: the old Maryland Institute of Art on Mount
Royal Avenue in Baltimore. That year, somehow, it came into the pos-
session of a young sculpture student at the Institute named Herman
Barth. After the manner of Colonel John Johnston and his friends, young
Herman inscribed and dated the book with elaborate nineteenth-century
flourishes and had many of his studio friends do the same. On some of the
flyleaves, superimposed upon their signatures, they made Rorschach-
style ink blots (Hermann Rorschach himself was twenty-four at the time,
working in Switzerland, and hadn't yet developed his famous ink-blot
test).
   I never met this uncle of mine—my father's older brother and the
only artist I know of among my ancestors. Herman Barth graduated from
the Maryland Institute of Art, worked a few years in Baltimore as a stonecutter while practicing the art of sculpture, went to France in 1918 with
the American Expeditionary Force, looked foward to visiting the Louvre

(so says one of his last postcards home), but died before he got there, in the great influenza pandemic of 1918/19, a dozen years before I was born. But I have thought about him a lot, this young sculptor sprung from the large family of a German immigrant tombstone-cutter, my grandfather, whose arrival in America coincided with the '81 edition of *Leaves of Grass.* I've wondered whether Uncle Herman would have "made it" as an artist, had he lived: whether he'd have outgrown the academic conventions of his time and gotten in on the ground floor of modernism, for example, or become just another master mason. And whether, in either case, he might have taught me useful things.

Just about the time of Leslie Fiedler's review of *The Sot-Weed Factor,* when I was beginning to find my own way in my own medium, my father gave me some of my late uncle's effects: a few pieces of Beaux-Arts plaster statuary—classical copies and imitations, student work—and a couple of his books, including James Wilson's copy of John Johnston's *Studio Souvenir,* in which I found the Whitman holographs, my uncle's flourishing autographs and doodles, and those proto-Rorschach ink blots.

Well. Jorge Luis Borges says in his essay on Kafka that every writer creates his own precursors. This is the opposite of Professor Harold Bloom's argument that great writers are as it were created *by* their precursors—by their struggles against and pacts with their spiritual fathers. Borges also says, in an essay on Walt Whitman, that Whitman, who *had* no immediate precursors, invented himself: the colossal democrat, the Good Gray Poet who no doubt shared a few characteristics with the Camden invalid who bore his name, as Borges admits to sharing a few with the Argentine writer named Jorge Luis Borges.

As for me, I didn't invent, nor was I invented by these two uncles, the figurative and the literal, whom I rediscovered together by this curious chain of coincidences; by whom I feel obscurely but benignly—that is to say, *avuncularly*—ratified; to whom I give this nephewlike wave of the hand.

Now, for my *second* problem . . .

My Two Muses

FALL, 1978: the *LETTERS* novel all but done at last, and this final variation on the twin-problem theme, at a conference on Myth and Modernism sponsored by the Classics Department at the University of Wisconsin at Milwaukee.

In a university as programmatically contemporary as this one, with its distinguished and formidable Institute for Twentieth Century Studies, I find it a comfort to be the guest of the Classics Department. As an undergraduate at Johns Hopkins in the 1940s, while I was cutting my writerly teeth on Joyce and Kafka and discovering that literature existed, it was my good fortune to work part-time as a book-filer in the library stacks of Greek and Latin classical literature and of W. F. Albright's Oriental Seminary. I read so much of what I was supposed to be reshelving that to this day I don't know whom to blame the more for my own literary productions: the High Modernists or the tale-tellers of antiquity.

My particular interest in classical mythology, as distinct from classical literature, is a tale quickly recounted. When my novel *The Sot-Weed Factor* appeared in 1960, several critics remarked that it showed the influence of Otto Rank and the comparative mythologists. I had not in fact read Rank and company; I quickly did, and found the critics to be correct. Indeed, as I wandered through Jung and Lord Raglan and Joseph Campbell and the rest—the way I'd once wandered through the Classics stacks—I became fairly obsessed by the detailed abstract pattern, the actuarial profile, of wandering heroes in the myths of the world's cultures. That cyclical model tyrannized my imagination. I was quite aware that one arrives at such a level of generality as the *Ur-Mythe,* or Monomyth, only by ignoring enough particularity; I knew that to a cultural anthropologist, say, the *differences* between the adventures of Perseus and those of Watu Gunung might be more significant than their similarities. No matter. I was also aware of the several profound things that this general model was alleged to signify, or at least to correspond to: the circuit of the seasons, the rites of passage, the crisis of individuation, the psychoanalytical deep-dive, the mystic transcension of categories into undifferentiated Being. But I confess that it was the model itself I loved, quite apart from its multiple significations, and whether or not it turned out to be, after all, just another fallible nineteenth-century-style synthesis.

That is the confession, I suppose, of an unreconstructed formalist. It is also the confession of a failed musician whose youthful ambition was to be neither a composer nor a performer, but an orchestrator—what in those big-band days was called an *arranger.* And that's my real bond with the authors of antiquity, for whom originality was chiefly a matter of rearrangement. I wrote a long comic orchestration of the abstract model (*Giles Goat-Boy*) and a number of short stories and novellas based on particular manifestations of it: the story of Menelaus and the Old Man of the Sea; the story of Narcissus and Echo; the story of Perseus and Medusa; the story of Bellerophon and the Chimera. These are beautiful, wonderful stories—I mean the originals. Indeed, my problem—since my muse is ineluctably the comic muse—was not to trivialize, in my reorchestrations, those splendid melody-lines that moved and touched me so profoundly: the great myths themselves.

I'm not sure I succeeded. In any case, that particular obsession is behind me now, replaced by others. But the capital-P Pattern continues to reverberate through the long work that I have been holding by the tail—and it me by the throat—since 1972, when the last of those "mythological" stories was published.

Tonight I want to read to you two excerpts: one from the mythological comedies, as advertised, and one from the novel in progress. That novel, I almost blush to report, is a reorchestration of one of the oldest and riskiest of novel-forms: the epistolary novel, long since pronounced *kaput* by the coroners of literary criticism. But it happens that in addition to being a disappointed orchestrator, I am a bona fide honorary Doctor of Letters, who likes to take that distinction in its medical sense (Johns

Hopkins is, after all, both my alma mater and my present employer), and who therefore makes it part of his business to administer artificial respiration to the apparently dead, whether the patient is the classical myths or certain exhausted conventions of the novel. So . . .

The Future of Literature and the Literature of the Future

AT A SYMPOSIUM on the subject above, held at the University of North Carolina at Chapel Hill in 1976, I seem actually to have spoken to the topic, perhaps for mere relief.

To speculate about the literature of the future, what it might be like, is to beg at least two much larger questions. Let's do it, breathtaking as those twin presumptions are: namely, that the future will contain, in some no doubt attenuated form, that we have got used to calling Western Civilization; and that in that civilization the survivors will continue to produce and consume something like what we have got used to thinking of as literature.

Cleanth Brooks and Robert Penn Warren's textbook definition of literature will do: "the artistic rendering of human experience into words." I shall qualify it with the adjective *written* words, to distinguish what I imagine to be our subject from, on the one hand, stage plays, operas, films, television dramas, and laser holography or whatever gets invented next, and on the other hand from the oral tradition out of which written literature springs and toward which, in a modest way, it has been inclining since the 1960s, when live readings became more popular than they'd been since the nineteenth century and some of us began to explore the possibilities of electronic tape as a medium for fiction and poetry.

I am no prophet. Furthermore, I'm not very *interested* in prophesying the future of the arts: a category of speculation wherein—unlike energy development or international relations—the consequences of erroneous prediction approach zero. On the Baltimore Beltway, between Exit 19 and Exit 20, there is another exit sign very plainly marked *FUTURE;* but if you spend your time looking for the ramp, you just go around and around Baltimore instead of getting where you want to go. My profession is the opposite of soothsaying: A writer of fiction spends his time making up stories attractive enough to induce people to spend their time reading what he writes precisely despite the presumption that it's all made up in his head. That is a mystery I only half understand, though my living depends upon it.

There is a historical connection between prophesy and poetry. Between prophesy and prose fiction, that connection gets debased (some would say elevated) into "science fiction": fiction *about* the future, which of course is no more the same thing as the fiction *of* the future than science fiction is the same as scientific fiction. I shall not concern myself here with science fiction.

For what one storyteller's opinion is worth, I'll hazard a *yes,* at least a *probably,* to both of our great presumptions aforementioned. As to the first: I am not particularly optimistic about the rest of this century and the next one, to look no farther, but I'm not quite apocalyptic about them, either. The only view of history that squares with my experience, education, and intuitions is the tragic view; I see no reason not to extend it to the future as well. Elizabeth Bishop has called ours "the most dreadful human century," and perhaps she's right: To think about what we've done to our planet and to one another in the last seventy-five years is almost unbearable. But the nineteenth century was a horror show, too: the butchery of the Napoleonic wars, the butchery of imperial colonialization. And consider the centuries before that: catastrophic, every one of them. I try to believe Jacob Bronowski's affirmation (in his television series *The Ascent of Man*) that humankind is in fact ascending despite Dachau and Auschwitz and the "Gulag archipelago"; I guess I finally *do* believe it, if only because I'm a healthy, moderately successful white American with a color TV set and enough leisure to watch *The Ascent of Man.* But oh, my: Capitalism really does seem to be ruinously exploitative and inherently self-destructive; large-scale socialism is dreary, bureaucratic, inefficient, stifling; anarchy is impossible; everything else is repressive and authoritarian at best, totalitarian at worst, and especially noxious for artists and intellectuals. I fear that we're in for catastrophic nuclear accidents before the century's done; maybe even at least limited thermonuclear wars, heaven forfend. Surely cataclysms of overpopulation, inadequate food production and distribution, and insufficient energy lie down the road for our children if not ourselves to suffer. We may be ascending, but the cost is immeasurable and the ascent so gradual that we'll need all the Bronowskis we can find to assure the survivors that they're going up at all. That's what I mean by the tragic view.

Compared to the first, the second presumption seems insignificant, though for some of us it would be a necessary condition of civilization that it have a written literature. Literature will no doubt be indispensable as long as language is indispensable, and written literature is important, if not necessary, exactly for its peculiar limitations, which people like Marshall McLuhan made so much of in the 1960s. These limitations (I'm going to call them virtues, but *characteristics* is a more accurate term than either) can be summed up in four adjectives: written literature is *semiotic, anesthetic, linear,* and *solitary.* I shall now speak to these adjectives one at a time, in reverse order.

First, *solitary.* Literature is the only art I can think of that is normally both produced and consumed, or received, by individuals as individuals. Its audience is one person at a time even when everybody on the beach is reading *Jaws* or *Ragtime* (they're not at all at the same word at the same moment; even if by extraordinary coincidence they were, their experience wouldn't be communal as the experience of a concert or even a symposium is). Reading is as private as thinking or dreaming, exactly; one imagines that it will be valued (and permitted) as long as private thinking and dreaming are valued and permitted.

As to literature's *linearity*—the literal lines of print on the page and the normal one-word-at-a-timeness of language—some of us believe, Dr. McLuhan to the contrary notwithstanding, that to be linear, even continuous, is not necessarily to be wicked. While many important aspects of experience are no doubt "gestaltic," discontinuous, or otherwise nonlinear, many other aspects are in fact linear and more or less continuous. Other media may deal more effectively than writing with the nonlinear and the discontinuous, but it may be that writing is uniquely suited to deal with the linear and the continuous aspects of human experience. To be less than absolute is not to be obsolete; to be unable to do everything is not to be unable to do anything. And in fact we writers can even suggest, in our linear and continuous way, the experience of nonlinearity and discontinuity. Such suggestion was part of the program of literary modernism. But it is only a suggestion, just as a statement about the sea, or a metaphor for the sea, or for that matter the mere word *sea,* is a different thing from the sea itself.

Solitary, linear, anesthetic. When I say that literature is *anesthetic,* I don't mean that it numbs sensation or puts us to sleep, though either of the two novels I mentioned a while back might have that effect upon readers who enjoyed the other. What I mean is that written literature, remarkably, is the only one of the arts that appeals directly to none of the physical senses, though it may appeal indirectly to all of them. One needs the faculty of sight to read the print, or the faculty of touch if you're reading in Braille, and there is a very real but incidental pleasure (ever rarer) in reading well designed and well manufactured books. But except for the few poets and fewer fiction-writers who deploy typography, layout, and other graphic effects as an essential part of their sense, the visual and tactile aspects of reading aren't central to the experience of the literary text. Obviously that's not the case with oral literature: One would have enjoyed hearing Dylan Thomas read the alphabet (some good declaimers have done it, as a stunt); the man in charge of the Library of Congress program of recordings for the blind tells me that his clients don't ask "What else do you have written by James Joyce?" but "What else do you have narrated by Alexander Scourby?" Nobody ever asked a bookseller what else he had by Alfred A. Knopf in Janson or Caslon typefaces.

Written literature, most especially prose fiction, is ineluctably anesthetic because it is essentially *semiotic*. It transpires in the mind. It can't deal directly with qualities, sensations, emotions, actions, things; it can't even deal directly, as theater can, with *imitations* of actions and emotions. It can deal only with their signs, their names: *pain, blue, courage, Venezuela, walking around, once upon a time*. Writers who are also philosophers, like William H. Gass, have explored the metaphysical implications of this state of affairs. As a professional writer who is only an interested amateur of metaphysics, indeed of reality, I find the chief implication to be that written literature can deal most appropriately—at least more effectively than any other art—with just those aspects of our experience that are at some remove from direct sensation: not only the whole silent life of the mind—cognition, reflection, speculation, recollection, calculation, and the rest—but even the registration of sensation, so to speak: what perception is *like*.

That's the famous fact about metaphor, of course, a main property of language and mainly a property of literature (nonverbal metaphors, like the ones film makers sometimes attempt, seem to me to be metaphors for metaphors): to call the sea "wine-dark" and the dawn "rosy-fingered" is to say something about the sea and the dawn (and about wine, roses, and fingers) that can't really be photographed, just as photographs and paintings show us things that can't finally be said. As long as the private, verbal registration of experience has a future—and, just as important, the registration of *verbal experience,* the experience of language, which can take us beyond the possibilities of reality—literature has a future.

"Sun so hot I froze to death; Susanna don't you cry." " 'Twas brillig, and the slithy toves / Did gyre and gimble on the wabe. / All mimsy were the borogoves, / And the mome raths outgrabe." Try making a movie out of those.

I have now said more than I had thought I had to say, in the general way, about the future of literature. I have a few other opinions about the short-range future of my particular branch of literature—long and short prose fictions—but they'll keep till some future conversation.

Algebra and Fire

A CHAT WITH THE DOCTORS

HISTORICALLY, the Johns Hopkins University has been the distinguished tail upon a very large dog: the Johns Hopkins Medical Institutions, across town. In 1972, Stephen Muller became the first president of the JHU in nearly 100 years also to preside over the JHMI; he initiated a program of rapprochements between the two, which came eventually to include a series of talks at the medical institutions by professors at the university's Homewood Campus and its Peabody Conservatory of Music. The series, which still continues, was popular from the start, not least because it affords a wine-and-cheese break at afternoon's end for hosts of weary medical students and staff on duty in the enormous, rambling East Baltimore medical complex.

I did my bit in November 1977.

I have been assured that the speakers in this series need not address themselves to matters medical, and I've decided to half-believe that assurance. Only half, because among our premedical undergraduates over at the university, the distinction between the artistic interest of a literary text and its symptomological interest is by no means always clear.

So I learned when I joined the Hopkins faculty in 1973 and gave an undergraduate lecture course in modernist and postmodernist short fiction. Our analysis of Franz Kafka's beautiful story "A Hunger Artist," for example, turned into a knowledgeable discussion—knowledgeable on the students' part—of *anorexia nervosa,* which clearly appealed to the science majors as much as did the theme of the problematical position of saints and artists in a post-traditional culture: what I take to have been the author's principal concern. And among their liveliest interests in Thomas Mann's novella *Death in Venice* was the question whether, given the incubation period of the cholera virus, Mann's hero could *really* have contracted the disease from eating those overripe strawberries in the pi-azza, as Visconti's film version of the story seems to imply.

I confess that both as a teacher and as a writer of fiction I was as in-terested in these clinical footnotes to literature as the premedical people were. More than once—in fact, twice—I have called upon friends and rel-atives at the Hopkins Medical Institutions to help me find metaphorically appropriate diseases to inflict upon my characters. Todd Andrews, for example, the hero of my first published novel, *The Floating Opera,* suffers from subacute bacterial endocarditis with incipient myocardial infarc-tion, along with a low-grade prostatic infection. Get it? And a fellow in my novel in progress is terminally afflicted with osteosarcoma as a com-plication of Paget's Disease. If those are the wrong pathologies for what I intend them to represent in the novels, the fault may be that my infor-mants over here were reading fiction or attending cultural lectures when they ought to have been studying medicine.

Well. As I am not obliged to draw connections between the arts of healing and of storytelling, I mean to talk briefly about two other subjects and then illustrate them even more briefly with a passage from my fic-tion. The first subject will be the *multifariousness* of literary texts: the way they frequently spring from a multiplicity of motives and constraints on their author's part, not all of them of a "literary" or "serious" or even a conscious sort. The second subject is the way a literary text meant to be seriously comic or impassioned or at least emotionally energetic may de-rive a fair part of its energy from strictly formal or technical considera-tions. And my illustration will be the opening pages of a comic novella from the book *Chimera:* a novella about the later adventures of the mythical Greek hero Perseus—Perseus the Golden Destroyer—and his girlfriend Medusa, whom he had earlier mistaken to be his adversary.

I should explain that the title of this talk—"Algebra and Fire"—is borrowed from the Argentine writer Jorge Luis Borges, one of whose stories is about the encyclopedia of an imaginary world, exhaustively de-scribed in twenty meticulous volumes. Everything about this nonexistent world is set forth there, Borges imagines, in perfectly cogent terms: everything from its medicine to its mythology, from its algebra to its fire. Let Algebra stand for technique, or the technical and formal aspects of a work of literature; let Fire stand for the writer's passions, the things he or she is trying to get eloquently said. The simple burden of my sermon is that good literature, for example, involves and requires both the algebra and the fire; in short, passionate virtuosity. If we talk mainly about the algebra, that is because algebra lends itself to discussion. The fire has to speak for itself.

Multifariousness. It is generally agreed that there is some analogy, maybe even some connection, between what we all do when we dream and what poets and fiction-writers do when they're awake. Freud's famous description of the Dreamwork, for example, in *The Interpretation of Dreams,* could apply very well to a television-serial scriptwriter taking orders from his producer: Throw together something old (i.e., memories of early childhood), something new (events of the past twenty-four hours), something borrowed (the disguised fulfillment of a repressed wish), and something blue (the repressed wish is typically of an erotic character); work into the plot that traffic noise from outside your bedroom and the fact that you need to urinate but don't want to wake up; don't forget a walk-on part for the sponsor's mistress; make the whole thing reasonably plausible to a semicomatose viewer—and have it ready for the cameras in two hours, before the alarm goes off.

The fact is that capital-L Literature, no less than dreams and hackwork, comes out of a multiplicity of motives and constraints—with the differences that most of them are self-imposed, many are relatively conscious, and at least a few may have to do with the author's medium and his sense of himself as a practitioner of it, instead of with things like gratifying ambition, earning more money, meeting deadlines, shooting down the competition, or getting past the censors—all which motives may also play their part. Donald Barthelme winds up one of his stories ("Rebecca") with the remark: "It was written for several reasons. Nine of them are secrets." What I propose to do now is catalogue for you at least seven things that I was trying to do all at the same time in that novella about Perseus and Medusa and then read its opening pages so that you can hear them through my eyes, so to speak.

First: For a number of years I've been at work upon a fat novel called *LETTERS,* the title of which has three senses: literature itself (as in *belles lettres*), post-office-type letters (it is an epistolary novel), and the alphabetical letters of which both epistles and novels are constituted, as combinations of atoms constitute the physical universe. At a point six-sevenths of the way through *LETTERS*—that is to say, in the neighborhood of section *R*—my early plans called for two substantial stories-within-the-main-story: one about Perseus, another about his misfortunate cousin Bellerophon. In fact, I wrote those "inside" stories first, and they grew into the book *Chimera,* which is therefore infected with some of the preoccupations of the *LETTERS* novel—notably with the three senses of its title, as you will presently observe. At my writing-desk up on North Charles Street I am just now approaching the consequent great pothole in section *R* of *LETTERS,* which I must find some way to patch. Do not envy me that labor.

Second, I had never before written a *novella*—a literary genre that I define as too long to sell as a short story and too short to sell as a book— and I wanted to attempt that interesting space, just for the hell of it. The novella was a popular form once upon a time; but having perpetrated a novella in contemporary America, about the only thing you can do with it is perpetrate a couple more and sell the package to your publisher as a book. This I did.

But (the third item in this catalogue of motives and constraints) volumes of novellas are even more anathematical in the literary marketplace than volumes of short stories. Hence, in part, my decision to compose not merely three novellas, but a *series* of three novellas: three novellas related both formally and thematically to make what I believe is called a nonsummative system and what my editor believed could be called a novel and marketed as one. I sympathized: To sell a novel must unquestionably be easier than to sell a nonsummative system.

Points Four, Five, Six, and Seven comprise these formal and thematic relations among the three novellas.

One of them is *phi,* the classical "Golden Ratio" expressed in the number-series called Fibonacci Numbers and ubiquitous throughout nature and culture. The façade of the Parthenon, the relation of the three to the five in a three-by-five card, the average height of the navel from the floor in perpendicular Caucasian women as a proportion of their total height, the disposition of seeds around a pine cone and of chambers in a chambered nautilus—all these are manifestations of the Golden Ratio, as is the ratio of increasing length among the *Chimera* novellas. The third of them ("Bellerophoniad," a story about Bellerophon and Pegasus) is as proportionately larger than the second ("Perseid") as the second is larger than the first ("Dunyazadiad," a story about Scheherazade's kid sister)— that proportion being such that "Dunyazadiad" and "Perseid," combined, equal "Bellerophoniad," pagewise. Expressed formulaically, A:B::B:C such that A+B=C.

Of such is the kingdom of letters now and then made.

Next, the specific Fibonaccian instance of the logarithmic spiral—as embodied in the chambered nautilus, for example, and as contrasted with a closed circle—appealed to me and Perseus metaphorically, because (we're up to Point Six now) a ground-theme of both *Chimera* and the *LETTERS* novel is reenactment versus mere repetition. The spiral reenacts the circle, but opens out—if you're going in the right direction. The nautilus's latest chamber echoes its predecessors, but does not merely repeat them, and it is where the animal lives; he carries his history on his back, but as a matter of natural-historical fact, that history is his Personal Flotation Device, not a dead weight carrying him under. Middle-aged Perseus in my novella sets out to revisit the scenes of his earlier mythical adventures, but ends up reenacting and finally transcending them. Some novelists have similar ambitions.

Finally, this transcension-by-reenactment may in human instances correspond to the second half or second cycle of one's life, after Carl Jung's and Erik Erikson's celebrated crisis of individuation (it happens at ages 35, 34, or 33⅓, depending upon which Jungian you subscribe to). Such is Perseus's case. I myself was on the cusp of 40 when I wrote the "Perseid" story, and so safely past that particular pothole in the North Charles Street of life.

To this soup of preoccupations (and stew of metaphors) must be added my long-standing one with the ritual pattern of mythic wandering-heroism, itself a closed cycle, and my newer curiosity about non-literary phenomena which have a sort of narrative or quasi-dramaturgical aspect: human coitus, for example, when all goes well, or a wave breaking upon a beach, or my electric coffee-percolator (which builds up through chuckling foreplay to a virtual orgasm of percolation and then settles down to its afterglow), or the nightly passage of constellations in the sky, including those we call Perseus, Andromeda (with her spiral galaxy M33), and—in Perseus's left hand—the eclipsing binary star Algol, which is Medusa's winking eye.

The myth of Perseus being classical, I borrowed from classical literature one further formal constraint: beginning Perseus's story *in medias res*—in the middle of things, rather than at Square One. In fact, the ancients usually began nearer the end—the ninth year of the Trojan War or of Odysseus's homeward voyage—and then fed in their exposition of the story thus far, and then proceeded to climax and denouement. In keeping with my own number system, I decided to start Perseus's story six-sevenths of the way through its plot, and by this decision I set myself a pretty task of what might be called double exposition: My hero is six-sevenths of the way, not through his original adventures, but through his reenactment of them, and the reader has therefore to be briefed not only upon what has happened this time around, but upon the episodes of the original myth, which no contemporary reader can be presumed to remember from his/her schooldays.

This classical constraint, modernistically compounded, I addressed with a classical device, borrowed in the classical manner from Virgil's borrowings from Homer. Some of you will remember the set-piece, early in Virgil's *Aeneid,* of the Carthaginian frescoes, whose panels depict the Trojan War and in which, reviewing them in Dido's Carthage, Aeneas is moved to find not only his story thus far but even himself, who has yet to complete that story. It is a neat device for retrospective exposition; Virgil took it from Homer's description of the low-relief scenes on Achilles's shield, which serve a similar purpose in the *Iliad.* To accomplish my duple exposition in "Perseid," I borrowed Virgil's Carthaginian frescoes and applied them to the walls of an out-spiraling temple whose first revolution comprises seven panels (each Fibonaccily longer than its predecessor) depicting my hero's first cycle of adventures, and whose second revolution—not yet completed—depicts his ongoing reenactment of them. Applying the formula rigorously (and it's no fun if you don't) gives us a temple in which, if Perseus had Superman's X-ray vision, he could see behind any given episode of his original adventures the panel depicting its reorchestration in his current story—up to the point where he must leave that temple of hero-worship, address his future, and bring his story to its climax and its close.

Here are the first seven pages of my "Perseid":

Speaking of *LETTERS*

THE INTERVIEW is not my métier: I have never once regretted saying No to interview-requests, and have more than once regretted saying Yes. But when the novel *LETTERS* was finally done in 1979 and my publisher made a bet on its commercial success—a bet as unprofitable in the event as it was handsome at the time—I did my bit with the interviewers to help the book along. The best of the lot was a friend from Buffalo days, Angela Gerst, then working in Boston. Our conversation, in a considerably expanded version, first appeared in the Boston *Globe's* Sunday magazine section and has since been reprinted here and there. It is more chatty but less efficient than this initial tapescript, from which it grew.

GERST: You don't enjoy interviews.

BARTH: As a rule, no.

G: Why do you suppose so many writers feel that way?

B: No doubt because our business is the considered word, not the spontaneous. We care as much for the *how* as for the *what* gets said, in print. Talking with audiences can be enjoyable; talking tête-à-tête can be enjoyable. But talking tête-à-tête for the record . . .

G: Yet you've agreed to this tête-à-tête for the record. . . .

B: The rules, as Jesus says about the Sabbath, are made for us, not we for them. I have a big new novel done, which I'm excited about and may now speak of without risking the muse's disfavor. Finally, you're both a former student of mine and an old friend. Shoot.

G: Even so, you'll want to review the transcript?

B: To put it gently.

G: My questions as well as your responses?

B: Inevitably. Otherwise it all comes out late-Eisenhower. Another reason for interviewing rarely: It's work.

G: And you have a good many former students.

B: Several thousand, after nearly three decades of full-time teaching. But not so many who are also friends. Of those, I've married one; I stay in reasonably close touch with half a dozen others at a time; and I read the published writings of a few dozen more, products of my seminars over the years at Penn State, Buffalo, Boston, and especially Johns Hopkins.

G: You read only their published work?

B: Absolutely. No hopeful typescripts once they've graduated. Otherwise I'd drown. My current students keep me adequately supplied in the hopeful-typescript way. Since they're chosen for their ability—I mean the graduate students—their work is generally quite interesting, thank God. But it *is* advanced-apprentice typescript, and there are so many fine things one hasn't read yet in print, and so many other agreeable things to do besides write, read, and teach. . . .

G: Such as?

B: Sailing on the Chesapeake. Snorkeling in the Caribbean. Tennis, skiing, eating, drinking, sleeping, et cetera. Maintaining the property and a flotilla of small watercraft. Writing letters to my parents and in-laws and grown-up children. Listening to jazz—I used to play it, but don't anymore—and Baroque music. Thinking, daydreaming, loafing. Avoiding harm to myself, my fellow humans, and the planet. Avoiding interviews except with former students who are also old friends.

G: Shall we talk about the new novel?

B: Yup.

G: Let's begin with its title.

B: *LETTERS.* Seven caps, please. Subtitled *An old time epistolary novel by seven fictitious drolls & dreamers, each of which imagines himself actual.* Eighty-seven lower-case letters plus an ampersand.

G: ". . . each of *which* . . ."?

B: Unavoidable. *Whom* doesn't have enough letters.

G: To total eighty-eight?

B: And to put the *g* of *imagines* in the right position in a certain pattern, an alphabetical acrostic. Don't ask. Perfectly clear in the novel.

G: Seven authors?

B: Seven correspondents, including the capital-A Author. Six of the seven happen to be men; The seventh—and most important—is a wonderful middle-aged British-Swiss gentlewoman and scholar: one Germaine Gordon Pitt, Lady Amherst, now widowed and reduced to teaching History of the Novel 101 in a third-rate American college—

G: Anywhere in particular?

B: Marshyhope State University, Redmans Neck, Maryland, 21612. An imaginary city of learning built in and upon the Dorchester County marshes, on Maryland's Eastern Shore.

G: I think I get the idea. Your first woman protagonist, not counting Scheherazade?

B: Yup. And she's a jim dandy, in her author's opinion.

G: What's she like?

B: Ms. Pitt traces her descent from Lord Jeffrey Amherst, of French-and-Indian War fame; also from an unrecorded dalliance between the aging Madame de Staël and her young friend Lord Byron. Highly unlikely, given Byron's sexual pickiness, but all things are possible to the novelist. It isn't true, by the way, that Lord Jeffrey Amherst distributed smallpox-infected blankets to the Indians to speed them to the Happy Hunting Grounds.

G: I'm relieved to hear that.

B: He only authorized the distribution of such blankets, in a letter to one of his officers at Fort Pitt who had proposed the stratagem. Our first adventure into bacteriological warfare. As for my Lady A: In better days she has been the Great Good Friend of a number of this century's celebrated novelists. She has even been impregnated by a few of them, though all the pregnancies have failed to reach term for one reason or another. In 1969, the present time of the novel, she's fifty and has a new young American lover, who does not always manifest his love with the dignity and courtesy she deserves. He's a failed last-ditch provincial modernist and avant-gardist; a sort of marsh-country mandarin. But he is possessed of an unreasoning obsession to impregnate my heroine one last time and bear a child with her, despite her age and their unimpressive track records. You get the idea.

G: I do.

B: All twenty-four of her letters are to the Author, who for the most part does not reply. Who's got time to answer all the mail? *I* do, but not the capital-A Author of *LETTERS*. That's a pity, because Germaine Gordon Pitt is a remarkable woman, whom I'm proud to have conceived and brought to light. You'd like her.

G: I hope so. Who are the other six correspondents? I mean the other five, after Lady Amherst and the Author?

B: In order, after Lady A, whose letters open each of the novel's seven sections: Todd Andrews (the lawyer-hero of my first novel, *The Floating Opera*): He's sixty-nine now and reconsidering suicide, but for all new reasons. Jacob Horner of *The End of the Road,* whose Remobilization Farm is presently located in Fort Erie, Ontario, and has become a haven for U.S. Vietnam War escapees as well as for the immobilized. Andrew Burlingame Cook the Sixth, lineal descendant of Maryland's Colonial virgin poet laureate in *The Sot-Weed Factor;* he is searching for his son, a Quebec terrorist, and for his ancestors, particularly from the time of the British Chesapeake invasion in the 1812 War. Washington burned! Baltimore threatened! Let's see . . .

G: Two more.

B: Jerome Bonaparte Bray, putative editor of *Giles Goat-Boy,* who works with a peculiar computer in Lily Dale, New York, the Spiritualist Capital of America, and who himself may be a great big bug mimicking a postmodern writer. . . .

G: Mm *hm.*

B: And Ambrose Mensch, from *Lost in the Funhouse,* currently Lady A's lover aforementioned. Then there's the Author, a self-effacing chap whose letters to the other six are generally polite requests for information. The several plots soon become one plot, of course: a good one, in my judgment.

G: That is to say, in "the Author's" judgment?

B: In a sense, Angela. In a sense.

G: Characters from all your previous books . . .

B: I know: One shouldn't. But it is a rule in our house that you needn't have read or even have heard of the other books in order to enjoy this one. Important rule.

G: *LETTERS* in both senses, then? Alphabetical letters and written messages?

B: In the third sense, too: literature, which I've heard a film-freak call "that mildly interesting historical phenomenon, of no present importance."

G: You don't agree.

B: My interest in movies is not great, particularly since the filming of *The End of the Road.* But I often think about the strengths and limitations of print versus film, TV, and theater—and, for that matter, opera, ballet, cartoon strips, tape, and live voice. All the various ways of "telling" stories, which is my passion and vocation.

G: Should we talk about that? The differences between media?

B: Sure. It mostly goes without saying, but it doesn't always go without doing. Certain things are easier to do in one medium than in another.

G: Couple of examples?

B: Metaphor: very clumsy in the visual media; very easy, almost inherent, in words, if you have the gift (Aristotle says it's the only aspect of writing that can't be taught). The whole universe inside our heads and under our skins: at your disposal in verbal narrative; only indirectly approachable in drama and film and the rest. Print, on the other hand, appeals directly to none of the physical senses. I've written about this elsewhere, so I won't natter on. But no doubt this is why even a second-rate film often moves us to physical tears and laughter, while even a great novel almost never does. Especially to tears. How many times have you wept real salt tears upon the printed page?

G: My copy of *Ulysses* is pretty dry. But my *Anna Karenina* is all but unglued from having been wept into. Maybe you're just hard-hearted.

B: That may be. And yet great fiction can change our lives; turn us around corners. No movie ever did that to me. I might walk and talk a bit differently for a few minutes after leaving an effective film, but that's about it. Novels have heft; films are filmy.

G: What's the heft of *LETTERS*? I mean what's it about?

B: All the foregoing, for one thing: I mean the three senses of *letters,* and the word-versus-image business, and Can the old girl bear one more offspring at this advanced hour of the world, and if so will it be a monster or what. Madame de Staël's own fifth and last child was unfortunately imbecilic. She and her young husband called it *Petit Nous,* pretended it was American, and invented fictitious U.S. parents for it: "Mr. and Mrs. Giles, of Boston." . . .

G: Oy. What else?

B: The doctoring of the documents of history, from the Isidorean Decretals to the Tonkin Gulf Resolution. False letters, doctored letters, concealed or misdirected letters. Letters consigning the bearer to death (they're called "Bellerophontic letters" in the trade). Letters crossed in the mails.

G: What else?

B: 1969. 1812. The genocide of aboriginal Americans. The French and American revolutions. Revolutions, recyclings, and reenactments generally. The compulsion to repeat: its hazards and possibilities. Um: "second cycles" in our lives and histories. The Tragic View of Everything, including of the tragic view.

G: Anything else?

B: Everything else. The passions of the human heart. Second chances. Lost loves, last loves. Language; the novel itself. God bless novels, Angela! Room to swing a cat in!

G: You took a while writing this one. *Sot-Weed* and *Giles,* I believe, took four years apiece. . . .

B: Long enough to start from scratch and take a bachelor's degree in anything.

G: *LETTERS* evidently took longer. *Chimera* came out in '72 . . .

B: It took my whole fucking forties, is what *LETTERS* took. Let's say seven years, since the story runs to sevens, and it's my seventh book. Long enough to conceive a child and see it into grade school! Or, Horace tells us in the *Ars Poetica,* long enough to write an epic.

G: Is *LETTERS* an epic?

B: I think of it as a medium-size principality. It's fairly fat, but I've done fatter.

G: Yet you've said you don't like long novels.

B: Other things equal, certainly not. *Ars longa,* et cetera. But one's loyalty, as William Gass has said, is finally neither to oneself nor to one's readers. It's to the object: the project in the womb, excuse the metaphor. Some objects want to be terse little stories: I've published one ten words long. Some want to be novellas: that delicious, unmarketable literary space. Some want to be lean, Flaubertian novels. And some demand to be enormous creatures like *Gargantua and Pantagruel,* or Burton's *Anatomy of Melancholy,* or the other Burton's *1001 Nights,* or Richardson's *Clarissa.* The fact is, my *LETTERS* novel is efficient. But lean it isn't, except as you might imagine a tidy giant. *Tant pis.* I think it's terrific. Anyhow, it's out of the house, and every cell in my body has replaced itself since I began it, and now I'm threatening fifty. Shall we change the subject?

G: Earlier on, you mentioned house rules.

B: Shop rules, actually. Like not recycling characters from your earlier works.

G: What are some others in your shop?

B: Oh . . . no titles or epigraphs taken from other literature. Why remind readers of things that they might be reading instead? No dedications. No autobiography, except in the Nabokovian way.

G: What is that?

B: His remark, in an interview, that while he deplores autobiographical fiction, he will on occasion bestow upon one of his invented characters a detail from his own life, "as one might award a medal." I like that.

G: It must be tiresome to be interrogated even about those occasional "medals."

B: Prurient curiosity. Irrelevant to the text even in the case of "confessional" fiction, from which muse spare us. An insult to the inventive capacity of us nonconfessional writers, and to the capacity of transmutation in the others, if they happen to be artists as well as confessors. Confessees? Once upon a time a chap in Virginia, I believe it was, pressed me publicly on the recurrence of adulterous triangles in my earlier novels. Had I myself been a vertex in such a triangle? "Only once," I told him: "with your mother." I'm glad you're free of that sort of curiosity.

G: Why no dedications?

B: Clutters up the book, as a rule. But as Jesus said, et cetera. In fact, *LETTERS* is dedicated to Shelly: former student, present wife. And a first-class editor. So I discovered only last year, when after seven years of work-without-feedback I asked her to go through the next-to-last draft of *LETTERS* before final typing. Doesn't miss a trick, or hardly any, even in a 1700-page script. I'm sure there are still problems in there, but a lot fewer than there would have been if Shell hadn't leaned on it. It's like discovering that the person you love is also rich. So I broke that particular shop rule, and may again in future, as I have broken others.

G: Want to speak of the future?

B: Only the Tragic View will do, and it not perfectly.

G: I mean your "shop." What's next after *LETTERS*?

B: Postscripts for a while, no doubt.

G: What are you writing right now?

B: Replies to your gentle questions. An appeal of our property-tax reassessment. An itinerary for a sailing cruise through the Virgin Islands next March. Remarks on postmodern American Fiction for a lecture-tour through Germany and Austria next June with Bill Gass and Jack Hawkes and our wives. Maybe a birthday letter to our first grandchild, due in Gemini.

G: Seriously.

B: Serious matters, every one.

G: Fictively, then. What's the next "object"?

B: No more long novels, I think; after *LETTERS* I'm ready for a sabbatical from such sustained imposition upon civilized attention. I have a couple of literary ambitions not yet fulfilled, but those are shop secrets. The fact is, I've never known in advance what's next in the works, or been frightened at the prospect of blank paper. Experience is calming, in that line. What artists do, even quite conscious artists, really *is* mysterious at bottom, even to them. And so we speak of the Muse. I've learned to trust her. The blank gets filled.

G: So, when the postscripts are cleared away and it's serious blank-paper time . . .

B: I await her next visitation with impassioned, but serene, curiosity.

Historical Fiction,
Fictitious History,
and Chesapeake Bay Blue Crabs,
or,
About Aboutness

WHILE making notes toward the novel that was to follow *LETTERS*, I wrote a few more Friday-pieces. This one was first delivered to the 1979 winter dinner-meeting of the Dorchester County Historical Society in Cambridge, Maryland. A spectacular blizzard, rare for my hometown, raged outside that evening and delayed the caterers' delivery of the entrée, but not the ministrations of the bar, with the amiable result that all hands were fairly sozzled before the dinner was served, not to mention the after-dinner talk. An amended version was subsequently published in the Washington *Post* Sunday Magazine for July 15, 1979, with the appropriate illustrative plates. The nature of the subject makes it unnecessary to reproduce those plates here: At that high-spirited historical-society dinner, in a much larger hall than I had anticipated, the much-larger audience than I had anticipated couldn't see the plates either.

My talk this evening will not quite be about what its title says it's about: historical fiction, fictitious history, and Chesapeake Bay blue crabs.

The fact is, I am about to publish a novel called *LETTERS* that happens to involve the Chesapeake Bay area and to some extent its history, particularly the late 1960s and the period of the 1812 War; and twenty years ago I published a novel called *The Sot-Weed Factor*, set mainly in Colonial Maryland. Both are more or less "historical" fiction, and for both I did a respectable amount of homework on the historical periods involved. But it was a novelist's homework, not a historian's, and novelists are the opposite of icebergs: Eight-ninths of what I once knew about this region's history, and have since forgotten, is in plain view on the surface of those two novels, where it serves its fictive purposes without making the author any sort of authority. Since *The Sot-Weed Factor* isn't finally "about" Colonial Maryland at all, any more than *LETTERS* is really "about" the burning of Washington in 1814 or the burning of Cambridge in 1967, I'm already uncertain which of their historical details are real and which I dreamed up.

For example, I recall a fine anecdote about the first murder ever committed by white folks in Colonial Maryland. It happened not long after the original settlers disembarked from the *Ark* and the *Dove* in 1634: Fellow killed his wife, or vice-versa. No problem apprehending the murderer, who obligingly confessed at once. The trouble was, there were no courts to try him in, no statutes to try him under, and no jails to sentence him to. They had just got off the boat. So the Governor's Council, by a rap of the gavel, turned itself into a board of inquest, took depositions, and found a true bill; then turned itself into a court, heard the case, and found the defendant guilty of murder; then turned itself into a legislative body and ruled that murder is against the law; then turned itself back into a court and sentenced the guilty party to hang; then commuted the sentence lest there be, in all this improvising, some miscarriage of justice. That solved *their* problem; *my* problem is an occupational hazard of storytellers: I can't remember now how much of this story is history and how much is fiction.

Fictitious history is something that my *LETTERS* novel *is* more or less about: false documents, falsified documents, forged and doctored letters, mislaid and misdirected letters and the like, in the history of History. But I would rather you read the novel than listen to me talk about it.

The next thing that these remarks will emphatically not be about is Mr. James A. Michener's recent best-selling novel *about* the Chesapeake Bay/Choptank River area: my native turf, or bog. Mr. Michener and I are respectful acquaintances, but I won't comment about his novel about the Chesapeake for the excellent reason that I haven't read it; and I haven't read it, as I've explained to the author, mainly because I've been too busy thinking about the subject myself.

But my fiction, I've declared, is *not* finally about tidewater Maryland and its history. There are obvious differences in the way history and fiction are about what they're about; there are differences just as important, but maybe less obvious, in the way different kinds of fiction are about what they're about. These different kinds of "aboutness" will be my topic here: I want to speak to you about aboutness.

Now, storytellers and Chesapeake Bay blue crabs have something in common: They usually approach what they're after sideways. With your indulgence I shall say what I have to say about *aboutness* by way of five different Chesapeake Bay blue crabs—or rather, five pictures or other representations of crabs. Never mind if you can't see them from where you're sitting: I'll describe them to our purpose. Anyhow, the first of the five crab-representations I don't have with me, and the last one doesn't exist. We shall use our imaginations, as both novelists and historians have to do, in their different ways.

The first rendition of a blue crab that I want you to imagine is one of those large preserved ones mounted on a plaque on the wall of any seafood restaurant in the tidewater area. I wasn't able to lay hands on such a specimen: The best I could come up with is this horseshoe-crab shell that my wife and I picked up off a beach on the Choptank River a couple of years ago when we dinghied in from our sailboat for lunch. Please pretend that it's a blue crab instead, mounted on the wall of the Crab Claw Restaurant over in St. Michaels, say, and then let's notice certain things about it.

First and obviously, it isn't "fiction": It's made from the mortal remains of an actual, "historical" animal, preserved by a taxidermist in the case of our restaurant crab; held together with sea-tape in the case of this one. The degree of realism in the representation is therefore considerable, though it's relative and, so to speak, "historical": We have only the skeleton; the living, breathing beast is gone, and with it the feel, taste, and smell of the real thing. Its sensory aspects have been reduced to just one, really: the visual aspect. It looks a lot like a crab, even though the colors are a sort of mortician's approximation of life; there can be no question about its general external accuracy. If we consider what the *purposes* of such a representation are—which is another way of asking what this crab is *about*—I think we'll agree that it has at least five: (1) to help decorate the restaurant; (2) in doing so, to evoke the tidewater atmosphere by means of a bit of natural-historical realism, and thereby (3) to whet our appetites for what we've come there for; in other words, and on the bottom line, (4) to sell seafood dinners at an acceptable profit to the owners of the crab and of the restaurant, while incidentally (5) standing as a historical record of an actual crab caught somewhere in the surrounding waters. We shall return to these purposes presently.

Our second and third blue crabs were both rendered by staff artists of the *National Geographic Magazine* as illustrations for accompanying texts. Number Two is this detail from a color foldout entitled "Marsh Fauna." It has a lot of other fauna in it besides the blue crab; he or she is tucked down here in the lower right-hand corner, about to grab an anchovy for lunch. Number Three, an ad for the magazine itself, is this pen-and-ink drawing entitled "Blue crab: main cog in an 'immense protein factory.' " (The metaphor is H. L. Mencken's.) In both of these representations, as in the first one, there is considerable realism in the way of anatomical or biological accuracy. The colors aren't quite right, of course, even in the foldout, and the drawing is in black and white, as no actual blue crab ever was. Both of them translate the three dimensions of historical blue crabs into two dimensions. And both, unlike the first one, represent no individual, "historical" crab, but rather a generalized, typical, you might say "fictitious" crab. The foldout painting adds an improbable amount of other simultaneous ecological action—all sorts of marsh fauna engaged in eating one another up; more such action than anybody ever saw at once, even in Indian times—and it presumes further to show us in cross-section what's going on under the water and inside the mudflats. But we don't object to this exaggeration of the "historical" facts, because we understand the instructional-scientific purpose of the foldout: namely, to illustrate the actual ecology of a Chesapeake marsh by distorting the time-frame, by cutting away certain factual barriers to normal human vision, and by moving the whole scene from the inconvenient reality of three physical dimensions (plus scale, motion, smell, feel, taste, and sound) to the convenience of two visual dimensions, scaled down, frozen in action, and approximated in color. We don't mistake it for reality, though it is inspired by reality. We don't mistake it for science, though it grows out of science. We don't mistake it for fine art, either, though the artist (Mr. Ned Seidler) is properly called a staff artist and is good at his trade. We would not likely frame and hang the original on our walls as art, much less expect to see it in the National Gallery or the Louvre or the Metropolitan—though I confess that my particular copy was carried around with Shelly and me for some seven years, from Buffalo to Boston to Baltimore, to remind me, while I was writing the *LETTERS* novel, of all the life and death besides historical human life and death that goes on all the time in the place I was writing about.

The pen drawing, Crab Number Three, is even more striking, and our reaction to it is interesting to think about. It is a meticulously realistic drawing; we're likely to admire it even more than the color foldout, not only because the detail is finer, but because, paradoxically, it is at the same time more realistic and farther removed from reality than those other crab images. Not only are feel, taste, sound, smell, scale, depth, motion, and environment removed (not to mention literal life), but also any attempt to approximate the actual color of the subject. The very black-and-whiteness of the drawing, and the absence of any background, make us sharply aware that this is an ink drawing, not the real thing; and that awareness enhances rather than diminishes our pleasure in it. In fact, this drawing (by Mr. Paul Breeden) might be said to be not only about the Chesapeake Bay Blue Crab, but about pen and ink as well, and shading and foreshortening and such. In other words, it's partly *about* the art of drawing; and we admire it, if we do, precisely because the artist is able to evoke the reality of blue crabs with material so far removed from that reality as a pen and black ink and white paper. Number Three here we might actually hang with pleasure on the wall of our office, or our kitchen, if we had the original well matted and framed, even though its bottom-line purpose, like that of the mounted crab earlier, is to sell us something: in this case, not restaurant meals for profit, but subscriptions to the organ of a nonprofit scientific and educational society. And even though we realize, consciously or intuitively, that Crab Number Three is "about" line and shape and shading as well as "about" the blue crab and, by extension, about the life and culture of the Chesapeake Bay estuarine system, we don't expect to see this drawing in a museum of fine art, for the simple but important reason (which I'll come back to) that it's more *about* the crab than *about* the medium of drawing, and while it's professionally excellent draftsmanship, something tells us that there's a difference between competent, accurate draftsmanship and fine art.

Our fourth crab image is the one crawling up my necktie: a gold-plated tie-tack in the semblance of a crab, purchased and worn as a souvenir. It is not *Callinectes sapidus,* the Chesapeake blue crab. Its carapace more resembles something in the dungeness or purple marsh crab family—but of course it isn't purple, and there's no detail to speak of beyond the correct number and location of the legs. It is a stylized version of a crab, designed for inexpensive manufacture and retail sale at a high profit margin to people like myself who may like to be reminded, when they put their neckties on, or remind others whom they then see, that the world contains objects somewhat like this called *crabs,* fun to catch and good to eat, and maybe, by extension, that the world contains the Chesapeake Bay, and the Eastern Shore thereof: interesting and even beautiful places to work and play and live in, with more or less colorful human inhabitants as well as blue crabs, and a more or less interesting cultural, political, and geological history; and, by further extension yet, that the wearer of the tie-tack, while he knows the difference not only between it and a real crab, but also between it and a realistic representation of a crab, nevertheless enjoys being reminded, even crudely, of the real thing and its associations, and reminding others likewise. He might even be reminding you that he's *part* of the real thing, or once was, or wishes he were: a member of the tidewater culture, or a familiar of it.

In this case, the purpose of the designer is to make some money by trading on these innocent wishes and pleasures of ours. My tie-tack is not *about* crabs in any remarkable, thoughtful, interesting, or even careful way. Nor is it *about* the art of costume jewelry in any remarkable, thoughtful, interesting, or careful way—as a gold brooch by Benvenuto Cellini cast by the lost-wax method from an actual fly or scarab beetle might be, for example. What my tie-tack is *about,* from the designer's point of view, is low-budget commercialized nostalgia; from the wearer's point of view, it's about the gratification or advertisement of that nostalgia. The wearer's motives, we might notice in passing, are relatively innocent; the manufacturer's are relatively mercenary. To this point, too, we shall return.

There is a curious phenomenon involved here that can make artists tear their hair, though it's perfectly understandable and, up to a point, forgivable. Any of you who happen to have traveled through the Netherlands will have found that Dutch gift shops are as full of toy wooden shoes and cheap china windmills as Chesapeake Bay gift shops are full of junk-art mallard duck prints and fake goose decoys and so much stuff with cattails and oyster-boats on it, often so clumsily or cheaply rendered, that one feels like setting out at once for Honolulu or Montreal or even Ohio, where folks have scarcely heard of such things; or else for the Eastern Shore marshes, where there's nothing between oneself and the real McCoy. But the curious thing is that the main purchasers of this sentimental-picturesque junk, after the tourists, are the natives. The Dutch happen to love very much their dikes and canals and windmills and wooden shoes and tulips; so much so that even when the outside of a Dutch farmhouse is surrounded by the genuine article, the inside is likely to be decorated with plastic tulips stuck in simulated *Klompen* made out of imitation Delftware imported from Hong Kong. The same goes for Eastern Shore of Marylanders, I've noticed, and I daresay it goes for any other people who happen to enjoy their culture and/or its history.

What may drive an artist bananas is certainly not this innocent pleasure in their culture by its natives, even where that culture has been trivialized, vulgarized, and commercially exploited by outsiders or by insiders (often the worst offenders). When the artist tears his hair, or at least rolls his eyes, is when people mistake the junk for the quality stuff: when they lose sight of the difference between a true and honest crabcake, for example, and some third-rate restaurant's version of the same thing, whether that restaurant is a low-overhead fast-food joint or a pretentious, high-overhead rip-off. Third rate is third rate, no matter how impressive the packaging and promotion. Not many Eastern Shore folk can be taken in by a third-rate crabcake masquerading as gourmet food—and gourmet food is what a *first*-rate crabcake is. I wish I could be as confident of native judgment in the other matter, to which we now return.

The fifth and last rendition of a blue crab in this series, like the first, I don't have with me, but for a different reason: I don't believe it exists yet. It's the one which, if it did exist, might very well hang in the Louvre, or the National Gallery, or the Amsterdam Rijksmuseum, even though the people who came to see it might never have seen a blue crab, live or steamed, or know where Chesapeake Bay is, unless they looked it up or came around the world to visit because they loved the drawing so. I wish there were a Rembrandt drawing of a crab, blue or otherwise, to illustrate my point; but they don't have *Callinectes sapidus* in the North Sea, and Rembrandt didn't go in much for still lifes anyhow, though he was very big on windmills and canal boats. The best I could find is this reproduction of a Rembrandt pen-and-wash drawing of a different animal: two birds of paradise, done in whites and gray-yellows about 1637, three years after Lord Baltimore's people stepped ashore in Maryland and committed the first recorded murder in the Old Line State. The original of this drawing does in fact hang in the Louvre. I invite you to notice two things about it, and then we'll get to our own bottom line.

The first thing is that there's much less *information* about birds of paradise in Rembrandt's drawing than there is about the Common Egret or the Long-Billed Marsh Wren in the "Marsh Fauna" foldout. The Rembrandt would not be of much use to a birdwatcher for field identification, whereas the foldout even shows us what the birds eat and where they find it. The second thing to notice is the caption commentary by the critic who put together the volume from which I took this plate, a professor of fine arts at Harvard's Fogg Museum. "The way these exotic birds fill the page," Professor Seymour Slive remarks, "is as admirable as Rembrandt's depiction of the different weights and textures of the feathers on their heads, necks, bodies, and great tails."

This is an extension of what we noted about the blue-crab drawing in pen and ink: A lot of the reality of birds of paradise is in Rembrandt's drawing, no doubt; maybe even more than of crab-reality in the *National Geographic* staff artist's. But it isn't there by meticulous copying of detail (not to mention color, size, depth, feel, sound, smell, motion, and lice under the wings). The Rembrandt is certainly *about* birds of paradise, but, as Professor Slive's commentary makes clear, it is at least as much *about* the composition of forms on the page, the arrangements of darks and lights, the *suggestion* of weights and textures by quick and masterful strokes of the pen and the brush. In other words, it's about as much *about* the art of drawing as it is about what it's a drawing *of,* and since it's about both of these things in a masterful way, it hangs in the Louvre instead of in a highway emporium for the ocean resort trade.

We could go farther and imagine a version by some twentieth-century Rembrandt in which that former kind of aboutness, the bird of paradise itself, might fly the coop altogether. If the second kind of aboutness were still powerful and fine enough, the work mightn't be in the Louvre, but it might well be in the Museum of Modern Art or the National Gallery's new East Wing, with the other abstractionists: art that is entirely, or almost entirely, about itself and its materials; in which the "subject," if any, is just a point of departure, like the melody line among good jazz musicians.

The aim of these remarks is plain: the analogy between these several categories of crab-art and some different ways in which a piece of writing can be about a place, such as the Chesapeake Bay region, and/or about a historical moment, such as the invasion of Washington, D.C., by British forces during the War of 1812, or the Cambridge race riots of the 1960s.

The mounted prize crabs on the walls of the seafood restaurant, let's say, are like the documents of history: those antebellum wills in the Dorchester County courthouse, for example, in which black human beings and bedroom furniture are given away in the same sentence. From such documentary shucks and sheds, the historiographer tries to infer what happened in a human place and time: He reconstructs the political, social-economic, and cultural past; how things hung together and were done, their causes and effects. If he's knowledgeable and scrupulous, he keeps speculation and conscious bias to a minimum and tries to beware the unconscious biases and cultural assumptions that he can doubtless never entirely avoid. The result will be the verbal equivalent of that *National Geographic* foldout: a good deal of information efficiently, attractively, and authoritatively presented, which we might even read for

pleasure as well as for reference. It usually isn't Literature, in the capital-L sense of the term, but it's honest and useful work, done mainly for
the love of knowledge, like pure science.

The historical novelist, too, might make use of those documentary
crabshells and dramatize not only what happened, but what it might have
felt like to be a live human being experiencing that history in that place.
There's a much greater likelihood here that the author will project
his/her contemporary sensibility back onto our ancestors—that's one
large reason why most historical fiction is a pretty fishy rendition of a
crab—but we're talking about *fiction* now, and since our bottom line in
reading fiction is to illuminate our own experience of life, a case can be
made for that kind of distortion. Anyhow, if the novelist happens to be a
fine literary artist like Charles Dickens (I'm thinking now of his novel
"about" the French Revolution), what he turns out won't be a proper historical novel at all, but a work of literature. *A Tale of Two Cities* is not
about the French Revolution in the way that Carlyle's *History of the
French Revolution* is, not to mention the actual documents of the Reign of
Terror: It is about love, loyalty, and self-sacrifice among human beings
pungently observed, not among puppets sent down from Central Casting.
The same goes for Tolstoy's *War and Peace* or Stendhal's *Charterhouse of
Parma:* They're *about* the Napoleonic wars, for sure—but so is Puccini's
opera *Tosca*—and for most of us that fact is the least interesting thing
about those works of art, even though their authors happen to have done
their homework.

It should be added, before we leave the crabshells and the foldouts,
that the forged and doctored and suppressed documents of history—from
the ninth-century Donation of Constantine, which "justified" the Holy
Roman Empire, to the twentieth-century faked reports that "justified"
the Tonkin Gulf Resolution—share the same bottom line with faked restaurant atmosphere: to sell us a bill of goods. Even the honest historian,
to be sure, wants to sell us his point of view, though not particularly for
gain, and not by distorting the evidence systematically to fit a thesis. And
good historical novelists such as Marguerite Yourcenar or Mary Renault
are like good restaurateurs: They're not in business simply for their
health, but they enjoy what they're doing and do it well, at a small or
large profit, and they don't stuff their crab imperial full of breadcrumbs
and cheap mayonnaise. Their books might be compared to that pen-and-
ink drawing in the *National Geographic* advertisement. So might that
lovely nonfiction work of William Warner's, *Beautiful Swimmers:* full of

honest information about *Callinectes sapidus* and its environment, skill-fully presented, rich in detail, ably written, and attractively illustrated. Great literature it may not be, in the Louvre/National Gallery sense, but like Gilbert Klingel's fine book on the Bay of twenty-eight years ago,* or Hulbert Footner's of thirty-five years ago,† it surely ranks with the best writing about the Chesapeake area.

Now: About the literary equivalent of my tie-tack, the less said the better: Its perpetrators are overpublicized already. These are your flat-out, big-time, big-money book-of-the-monthers, who move in on a culture or a subject and "work it up" like a real-estate developer, with high-rise megabucks under a low profile. It's tempting to say "under a low-*brow* profile," but your tie-tack writers are often smart cookies in-deed, even civilized and likeable, though the size of their egos can be breathtaking. Their belief that what they manufacture is *literature* is as remarkable as if Mr. Levitt were to mistake his Levittowns for Athens and Rome; rather, it *would be* remarkable, if not that so many innocent readers (but almost no critics or other writers) make the same mistake. I daresay Mr. Levitt never confused himself with Pericles of Athens; but to hear Mr. Leon Uris talk about his novel *Exodus,* for example, is to won-der whether he's not confusing his version with Moses's. It ought to be astonishing that the same people who can't be fooled when it comes to overcooked rockfish or adulterated crabmeat—that these same sturdy and expert native citizens can read a trite commercial novel and believe that they've taken in a genuine work of art about their place and its his-tory, even about themselves, when in fact they've *been* taken in by a su-perficial—though not necessarily cynical—piece of giftshop merchandise.

I say it *ought* to be astonishing. Of course, it isn't, for the innocent reason I mentioned before. If we enjoy our territory, we're apt to enjoy being reminded of it. We ought to be indignant at a stock rendition of it into novels or films or TV miniserieses—but alas, most of us know more about our local seafood, and about whatever our regular daily business is, than we know about the human language in which the human heart, the human spirit, the human passions of our fellow women and men can be expressed. So instead of making something honest out of a tie-tack novel—like a doorstop—we're apt to think, "Now, by golly, he's got *that* part right: Your skipjack has one mast and your bugeye has two," and

---

* *The Bay* (New York: Dodd, Mead, 1951).
† *Rivers of the Eastern Shore* (New York: Rinehart, 1944).

feel sort of proud to see it said in best-selling print. God forgive and assist us.

I mentioned the human passions and human language: We have arrived at the Louvre and those Rembrandt birds. But instead of describing the literary equivalent of our imaginary Rembrandt blue crab, I shall close with what seem to me to be three reasonable rules of thumb for culling beautiful literary swimmers from the other kind. I hope three rules of thumb won't make us all thumbs; this culling is important to our literary ecology.

Rule #1: *Fiction about history almost never becomes part of the history of fiction.* To put it another way: Novels that are mainly and directly *about* a particular culture and its heritage seldom become part of that culture's cultural heritage. There are exceptions—we think of Faulkner's fiction about the American South, or Isaac Bashevis Singer's fiction about Polish-Jewish life before the Holocaust—but I believe that such apparent exceptions prove the rule: namely, that the more a novel's *main* interest is in the time and place it's *about,* the less likely it is to be a significant work of literature in its own right—though it might certainly be good light entertainment of the costume-drama sort. Aristotle, the first writer in history to describe the difference between historians and poets, says in the *Poetics* that the historian tells us how things were, while the poet tells us how they might have been, or ought ideally to have been. The trouble with much official history, by this famous and useful distinction, is that it is poetry: It tells us how its sponsor wishes things had been. "History is the propaganda of the winners," etc. And the trouble with much historical fiction is that it's so concerned with getting the "facts" straight—as given in the documents of history—that the artistic truth gets lost. The data might be correct, but the hearts and minds and souls of the characters come from Hollywood, not from human history. On the other hand, high-school students reading Shakespeare's *Julius Caesar* like to point out the anachronism of the clock's striking in Act II: There were no clocks in Caesar's Rome. But of course Shakespeare's play isn't *about* Caesar's Rome: It's about Caesar and Brutus, and the poet has them right. Even if he didn't, in detail, it wouldn't matter, since the *real* subjects are pride and conflicting loyalties, not Caesar and Brutus, and the play is one of the treasures of English literature, not of Roman history.

Rule #2 is Rule #1 turned inside out: *The literature that finally matters in any culture is almost never principally* about *that culture.* The eighteenth-century historian Edward Gibbon remarks that in the Koran there is no mention of camels. The contemporary Argentine writer Jorge Luis Borges once quoted this remark of Gibbon's when he himself was being criticized for not being Argentinian enough, because he never wrote about tangos and about gauchos riding over the pampas. Borges went on to say that if the Koran had been written by Arab nationalists, there would no doubt be caravans of camels on every page; but the actual authors of the Koran were so unselfconsciously Arabian that they took camels for granted, and didn't feel pressed to turn the holy book of Islam into a regional zoo. The same might go for blue crabs and Canada geese in the Great Chesapeake Bay Novel, if one ever gets written, and the reason for this Aristotle also tells us plainly: It is that the true subject of literature is not the events of history or the features of a particular place, but "the experience of human life, its happiness and its misery." That is what Faulkner's and Singer's stories are truly about: not Southern life or Jewish life, but human life, which they get at by making use of their intimate knowledge of Southerners and of Jews, respectively, and then by writing fiction that rises above its Southernness or its Jewishness.

This is what another Nobel Prizewinner, Thomas Mann, meant when he wrote in 1903: "What an artist talks *about* is never the main point; it is the raw material, in and for itself indifferent, out of which, with bland and serene mastery, he creates his work of art." The contemporary French writer Alain Robbe-Grillet goes even farther: ". . . the genuine writer," he declares, "has nothing to say. . . . He has only a way of speaking." And Homer, the daddy of us all, is equally radical on the subject of poetry and history: He makes the famous remark in the *Odyssey* that "wars are fought so that poets will have something to sing about"—with the clear implication that the songs are finally more important than the wars which are their ostensible subject. Most fiction *about* a place and time never rises above that place and time. When real artists such as Faulkner or Singer or Mark Twain or Nathaniel Hawthorne or Homer happen to find inspiration in a particular region or period, it is likely to be because they find in that region or period a symbol of their real concerns, which will be the passions of the human breast and the possibilities of human language.

That fetches us to Rule #3, illustrated both by Crab Number Three (that *National Geographic* graphic) and by the Rembrandt drawing: *Whatever else it is about, great literature is almost always also about itself.*

On rare occasions it may even be mainly about itself, though it is almost never exclusively about itself, even when it seems to be. And the same may go for such remarks as these, even when they claim to be about "aboutness."

The Literature of Replenishment

POSTMODERNIST FICTION

ANOTHER Friday-piece from 1979, meant as a companion and corrective to my 1967 essay ''The Literature of Exhaustion'' and published in *The Atlantic* in January, 1980. In 1982 the Lord John Press of Northridge, California, brought out the twin essays in a slim, handsome volume for which I wrote the following headnote:

Not every storyteller is afflicted with the itch to understand and explain, to himself and others, why he tells the stories he tells the way he tells them, rather than some other sort of stories some other way. It is well that this is so. The gifts of doing and explaining are notoriously not the same: An eloquent artist may sound like a mumbler, a crank, a soulless pedant—may *be* those unadmirable things—when he sets about accounting for what he has perhaps brilliantly done. And first-rate critics may write fifth-rate fiction.

But there are those who are thus afflicted; who for better or worse want every dozen years or so not only to get a working perspective on what they and their contemporaries are up to, but to publish their ruminations. I am of that number. The two essays which constitute this book were written in that spirit and published less to share my convictions than to share my speculations, so that others more expert in the matters dealt with could improve my working perspective. In this respect they have succeeded quite.

''The Literature of Exhaustion'' was written in 1967 in Buffalo, New York, during the troubles at the state university there and in our land. (See my headnote to it earlier in this *Friday Book*.) ''The Literature of Replenishment'' was written twelve years later in a calmer place and time—Johns Hopkins, Jimmy Carter—and has a more tenured, middle-aged air about it. My purpose was to define to my satisfaction the term *postmodernism*, which in 1979 was everywhere in the air. Almost no one agrees with my definition, but I remain satisfied with it.

Both essays appeared originally in *The Atlantic*; each has been several times reprinted and translated. Readers in countries like Romania and mainland China find such pieces fascinating less for their arguments, which may strike them as unintelligible or hopelessly luxurious, than for the particular artists and artworks mentioned in passing, unavailable to them but possibly

touchstones among us—just as their interest in American films may be less in
the stars and stories than in details of dress, furniture, the passing scene. It is
sad, for a storyteller, to see his opinions read where his stories cannot be.

   But it is pleasing to have these essays, separated since birth, here for the
first time reunited. May their two-part harmony make clear their song: that
what matters is not the exhaustion or the replenishment, both of which may
be illusory, but the literature, which is not.

The word is not yet in our standard dictionaries and encyclopedias,
but since the end of World War II, and especially in the United States in
the latter 1960s and the 1970s, "postmodernism" has enjoyed a very considerable currency, particularly with regard to our contemporary fiction.
There are university courses in the American postmodernist novel; at
least one quarterly journal is devoted exclusively to the discussion of
postmodernist literature; at the University of Tübingen last June (1979),
the annual meeting of the Deutsche Gesellschaft für Amerikastudien
took as its theme "America in the 1970s," with particular emphasis on
American postmodernist writing. Three alleged practitioners of that
mode—William Gass, John Hawkes, and myself—were even there as live
exhibits. The December annual convention of the Modern Language Association, just held in San Francisco, likewise scheduled a symposium on
"the self in postmodernist fiction," a subtopic that takes the larger topic
for granted.

   From all this, one might innocently suppose that such a creature as
postmodernism, with defined characteristics, is truly at large in our land.
So I myself imagined when, in preparation for the Tübingen conference,
and in response to being frequently labeled a postmodernist writer, I set
about to learn what postmodernism is. I had a sense of *déjà vu:* About my
very first published fiction, a 1950 undergraduate effort published in my
university's quarterly magazine, a graduate-student critic wrote: "Mr.
Barth alters that modernist dictum, 'the plain reader be damned': He removes the adjective." Could that, I wondered now, be postmodernism?

   What I quickly discovered is that while some of the writers labeled as
postmodernists, myself included, may happen to take the label with some
seriousness, a principal activity of postmodernist critics (also called
"metacritics" and "paracritics"), writing in postmodernist journals or
speaking at postmodernist symposia, consists in disagreeing about what
postmodernism is or ought to be, and thus about who should be admitted
to the club—or clubbed into admission, depending upon the critic's view
of the phenomenon and of particular writers.

Who are the postmodernists? By my count, the American fictionists most commonly included in the canon, besides the three of us at Tübingen, are Donald Barthelme, Robert Coover, Stanley Elkin, Thomas Pynchon, and Kurt Vonnegut, Jr. Several of the critics I read widen the net to include Saul Bellow and Norman Mailer, different as those two writers would appear to be. Others look beyond the United States to Samuel Beckett, Jorge Luis Borges, and the late Vladimir Nabokov as engendering spirits of the "movement"; others yet insist upon including the late Raymond Queneau, the French "new novelists" Nathalie Sarraute, Michel Butor, Alain Robbe-Grillet, Robert Pinget, Claude Simon, and Claude Mauriac, the even newer French writers of the *Tel Quel* group, the Englishman John Fowles, and the expatriate Argentine Julio Cortázar. Some assert that such filmmakers as Michelangelo Antonioni, Federico Fellini, Jean-Luc Godard, and Alain Resnais are postmodernists. I myself will not join any literary club that doesn't include the expatriate Colombian Gabriel García Márquez and the semi-expatriate Italian Italo Calvino, of both of whom more presently. Anticipations of the "postmodernist literary aesthetic" have duly been traced through the great modernists of the first half of the twentieth century—T. S. Eliot, William Faulkner, André Gide, James Joyce, Franz Kafka, Thomas Mann, Robert Musil, Ezra Pound, Marcel Proust, Gertrude Stein, Miguel de Unamuno, Virginia Woolf—through *their* nineteenth-century predecessors—Alfred Jarry, Gustave Flaubert, Charles Baudelaire, Stéphane Mallamé, and E. T. A. Hoffmann—back to Laurence Sterne's *Tristram Shandy* (1767) and Miguel de Cervantes's *Don Quixote* (1615).

On the other hand, among certain commentators the sifting gets exceedingly fine. Professor Jerome Klinkowitz of Northern Iowa, for example, hails Barthelme and Vonnegut as the exemplary "postcontemporaries" of the American 1970s and consigns Pynchon and myself to some 1960ish outer darkness. I regard the novels of John Hawkes as examples of fine late modernism rather than of postmodernism (and I admire them no less for that). Others might regard most of Bellow, and Mailer's *The Naked and the Dead,* as comparatively *pre*modernist, along with the works of such more consistently traditionalist American writers as John Cheever, Wallace Stegner, William Styron, or John Updike, for example (the last of whom, however, Ihab Hassan calls a modernist), or those of most of the leading British writers of this century (as contrasted with the Irish), or those of many of our contemporary American women writers of fiction, whose main literary concern, for better or worse, remains the eloquent issuance of what the critic Richard Locke has called "secular news reports." Even among the productions of a given writer, distinctions can be and often are invoked. Joyce Carol Oates writes all over the aesthetical map. John Gardner's first two published novels I would call distinctly modernist works; his short stories dabble in postmodernism; his polemical nonfiction is aggressively reactionary. Italo Calvino, on the other hand, began as an Italian new-realist (in *The Path to the Nest of Spiders,* 1947) and matured into an exemplary postmodernist (with e.g., *Cosmicomics,* 1965, and *The Castle of Crossed Destinies,* 1969) who on occasion rises, sinks, or merely shifts to modernism (e.g., *Invisible Cities,* 1972). My own novels and stories seem to me to have both modernist and postmodernist attributes, even occasional premodernist attributes.

One certainly does have a sense of having been through this before. Indeed, some of us who have been publishing fiction since the 1950s have had the interesting experience of being praised or damned in that decade as existentialists and in the early 1960s as black humorists. Had our professional careers antedated the Second World War, we would no doubt have been praised or damned as modernists, in the distinguished company listed above. Now we are praised or damned as postmodernists.

Well, but what *is* postmodernism? When one leaves off the mere recitation of proper names, and makes due allowance for the differences among any given author's works, do the writers most often called postmodernist share any aesthetic principles or practices as significant as the differences between them? The term itself, like "post-impressionism," is awkward and faintly epigonic, suggestive less of a vigorous or even interesting new direction in the old art of storytelling than of something anticlimactic, feebly following a very hard act to follow. One is reminded of the early James Joyce's fascination with the word *gnomon* in its negative geometrical sense: the figure that remains when a parallelogram has been removed from a similar but larger parallelogram with which it shares a common corner.

My Johns Hopkins colleague Professor Hugh Kenner, though he does not use the term postmodernist, clearly feels that way in his study of American modernist writers (*A Homemade World,* 1975): After a chapter on William Faulkner entitled "The Last Novelist," he dismisses Nabokov, Pynchon, and Barth with a sort of sigh. The later John Gardner goes even farther in his tract *On Moral Fiction* (1978), an exercise in literary kneecapping that lumps modernists and postmodernists together without

distinction and consigns us all to Hell with the indiscriminate fervor char-
acteristic of late converts to the right. Irving Howe (*The Decline of the
New,* 1970) and George P. Elliott (*The Modernist Deviation,* 1971) would
applaud—Professor Howe perhaps less enthusiastically than Professor
Elliott. Professor Gerald Graff of Northwestern University, writing in
Tri-Quarterly in 1975, takes a position somewhat similar to Kenner's, as
the titles of two of his admirable essays make clear: "The Myth of the
Postmodernist Breakthrough" (*Tri-Quarterly 26*) and "Babbitt at the
Abyss" (*Tri-Quarterly 33*). Professor Robert Alter of Berkeley, in the
same magazine, subtitles *his* essay on postmodernist fiction "reflections
on the aftermath of modernism." Both critics proceed to a qualified sympathy for what they take to be the postmodernist program (as does Professor Ihab Hassan of the University of Wisconsin-Milwaukee in his 1971
study *The Dismemberment of Orpheus: towards a postmodern literature*),
and both rightly proceed *from* the premise that that program is in some
respects an extension of the program of modernism, in other respects a reaction against it. The term *postmodernism* clearly suggests both; any discussion of it must therefore either presume that modernism in its turn, at
this hour of the world, needs no definition—surely everybody knows
what modernism is!—or else must attempt after all to define or redefine
that predominant aesthetic of Western literature (and music, painting,
sculpture, architecture, and the rest) in the first half of this century.

Professor Alter takes the former course: His aforementioned essay
opens with the words "Over the past two decades, as the high tide of modernism ebbed and its masters died off . . ." and proceeds without further
definition to the author's reflections upon the ensuing low tide. Professor
Graff, on the other hand, borrowing from Professor Howe, makes a useful quick review of the conventions of literary modernism before discussing the mode of fiction which, in his words, "departs not only from
realistic conventions but from modernist ones as well."

It is good that he does, for it is not only *post*modernism that lacks definition in our standard reference books. My *Oxford English Dictionary*
attests *modernism* to 1737 (Jonathan Swift, in a letter to Alexander Pope)
and *Modernist* to 1588, but neither term in the sense we mean. My
American Heritage Dictionary (1973) gives as its fourth and last definition
of *modernism* "the theory and practice of modern art," a definition which
does not take us very far into our American Heritage. My *Columbia Encyclopedia* (1975) discusses modernism only in the theological sense—the
reinterpretation of Christian doctrine in the light of modern psychologi-

cal and scientific discoveries—and follows this with an exemplary entry
on *el modernismo,* a nineteenth-century Spanish literary movement which
influenced the "Generation of '98" and inspired the *ultraísmo* of which
Jorge Luis Borges was a youthful exponent. Neither my *Reader's Encyclopedia* (1950) nor my *Reader's Guide to Literary Terms* (1960) enters
modernism by any definition whatever, much less *postmodernism.*

Now, as a working writer who cut his literary teeth on Eliot, Joyce,
Kafka, and the other great modernists, and who is currently branded as a
postmodernist, and who in fact has certain notions, no doubt naïve, about
what that term might conceivably mean if it is to describe anything very
good very well, I am grateful to the likes of Professor Graff for not regarding his categories as self-defining. It is quite one thing to compare a
line of Verdi or Tennyson or Tolstoy with a line of Stravinsky or Eliot or
Joyce and to recognize that you have put the nineteenth century behind
you:

> Happy families are all alike; every unhappy family is unhappy in its
> own way. (Leo Tolstoy, *Anna Karenina,* tr. Constance Garnett)

> riverrun, past Eve's and Adam's, from swerve of shore to bend of
> bay, brings us by a commodius vicus of recirculation back to Howth
> Castle and Environs. (James Joyce, *Finnegans Wake*)

It is quite another thing to characterize the differences between those two
famous opening sentences, to itemize the aesthetic principles—premodernist and modernist—from which each issues, and then to proceed to a
great *post*modernist opening sentence and show where its aesthetics resemble and differ from those of its parents, so to speak, and those of its
grandparents, respectively:

> Many years later, as he faced the firing squad, Colonel Aureliano
> Buendia was to remember that distant afternoon when his father
> took him to discover ice. (Gabriel García Márquez, *One Hundred
> Years of Solitude,* tr. Gregory Rabassa)

Professor Graff does not do this, exactly, though no doubt he could if
pressed. But I shall borrow his useful checklist of the characteristics of
modernist fiction, add a few items to it, summarize as typical his and
Professor Alter's differing characterizations of *post*modernist fiction, disagree with them respectfully in some particulars, and then fall silent, except as a storyteller.

The ground motive of modernism, Graff asserts, was criticism of the nineteenth-century bourgeois social order and its world view. Its artistic strategy was the self-conscious overturning of the conventions of bourgeois realism by such tactics and devices as the substitution of a "mythical" for a "realistic" method and the "manipulation of conscious parallels between contemporaneity and antiquity" (Graff is here quoting T. S. Eliot on James Joyce's *Ulysses*); also the radical disruption of the linear flow of narrative, the frustration of conventional expectations concerning unity and coherence of plot and character and the cause-and-effect "development" thereof, the deployment of ironic and ambiguous juxtapositions to call into question the moral and philosophical "meaning" of literary action, the adoption of a tone of epistemological self-mockery aimed at the naïve pretensions of bourgeois rationality, the opposition of inward consciousness to rational, public, objective discourse, and an inclination to subjective distortion to point up the evanescence of the objective social world of the nineteenth-century bourgeoisie.

This checklist strikes me as reasonable, if somewhat depressing from our historical perspective. I would add to it the modernists' insistence, borrowed from their romantic forebears, on the special, usually alienated role of the artist in his society, or outside it: James Joyce's priestly, self-exiled artist-hero; Thomas Mann's artist as charlatan, or mountebank; Franz Kafka's artist as anorexic, or bug. I would add too, what is no doubt implicit in Graff's catalogue, the modernists' foregrounding of language and technique as opposed to straightforward traditional "content": We remember Thomas Mann's remark (in *Tonio Kröger,* 1903), ". . . what an artist talks *about* is never the main point"; a remark which echoes Gustave Flaubert's to Louise Colet in 1852—". . . what I could like to do . . . is write a book about nothing . . ."—and which anticipates Alain Robbe-Grillet's *obiter dictum* of 1957: ". . . the genuine writer has nothing to say . . . He has only a way of speaking." Roland Barthes sums up this fall from innocence and ordinary content on the part of modernist literature in *Writing Degree Zero* (1953):

> . . . the whole of literature, from Flaubert to the present day, became the problematics of language.

This is French hyperbole: It is enough to say that one cardinal preoccupation of the modernists was the problematics, not simply of language, but of the medium of literature.

Now, for Professor Alter, Professor Hassan, and others, *post*modernist fiction merely emphasizes the "performing" self-consciousness and self-reflexiveness of modernism, in a spirit of cultural subversiveness and anarchy. With varying results, they maintain, postmodernist writers write a fiction that is more and more about itself and its processes, less and less about objective reality and life in the world. For Graff, too, postmodern fiction simply carries to its logical and questionable extremes the antirationalist, antirealist, antibourgeois program of modernism, but with neither a solid adversary (the bourgeois having now everywhere co-opted the trappings of modernism and turned its defiant principles into mass-media kitsch) nor solid moorings in the quotidian realism it defines itself against. From this serious charge Graff exempts certain postmodernist satire, in particular the fiction of Donald Barthelme, Saul Bellow, and Stanley Elkin, as managing to be vitalized by the same kitschy society that is its target.

I must say that all this sounds persuasive to me—until I examine more closely what I'm so inclined to nod my head yes to.

It goes without saying that critical categories are as more or less fishy as they are less or more useful. I happen to believe that just as an excellent teacher is likely to teach well no matter what pedagogical theory he suffers from, so a gifted writer is likely to rise above what he takes to be his aesthetic principles, not to mention what *others* take to be his aesthetic principles. Indeed, I believe that a truly splendid specimen in whatever aesthetic mode will pull critical ideology along behind it, like an ocean liner trailing seagulls. Actual artists, actual texts, are seldom more than more or less modernist, postmodernist, formalist, symbolist, realist, surrealist, politically committed, aesthetically "pure," "experimental," regionalist, internationalist, what have you. The particular work ought always to take primacy over contexts and categories. On the other hand, art lives in human time and history, and general changes in its modes and materials and concerns, even when not obviously related to changes in technology, are doubtless as significant as the changes in a culture's general attitudes, which its arts may both inspire and reflect. Some are more or less trendy and superficial, some may be indicative of more or less deep malaises, some perhaps healthy correctives of or reactions against such malaises. In any case, we can't readily discuss what artists aspire to do and what they end up doing except in terms of aesthetic categories, and so we should look further at this approximately shared impulse called postmodernism.

In my view, if it has no other and larger possibilities than those noted by, for example, Professors Alter, Graff, and Hassan, then postmodernist writing is indeed a kind of pallid, last-ditch decadence, of no more than minor symptomatic interest. There is no lack of actual texts illustrative of this view of the "postmodernist breakthrough"; but that is only to remind us that what Paul Valéry remarked of an earlier generation applies to ours as well: "Many ape the postures of modernity, without understanding their necessity." In my view, the proper program for postmodernism is neither a mere extension of the modernist program as described above, nor a mere intensification of certain aspects of modernism, nor on the contrary a wholesale subversion or repudiation of either modernism or what I'm calling premodernism: "traditional" bourgeois realism.

To go back a moment to our catalogue of the field-identification marks of modernist writing: Two other conspicuous ones are not yet there acknowledged, except by implication. On the one hand, James Joyce and the other great modernists set very high standards of artistry, no doubt implicit in their preoccupation with the special remove of the artist from his or her society. On the other hand, we have their famous relative difficulty of access, inherent in their antilinearity, their aversion to conventional characterization and cause-and-effect dramaturgy, their celebration of private, subjective experience over public experience, their general inclination to "metaphoric" as against "metonymic" means. (But this difficulty is *not* inherent, it is important to note, in their high standards of craftsmanship.)

From this relative difficulty of access, what Hassan calls their aristocratic cultural spirit, comes of course the relative unpopularity of modernist fiction, outside of intellectual circles and university curricula, by contrast with the fiction of, say, Dickens, Twain, Hugo, Dostoevsky, Tolstoy. From it comes also and notoriously the engenderment of a necessary priestly industry of explicators, annotators, allusion-chasers, to mediate between the text and the reader. If we need a guide, or a guidebook, to steer us through Homer or Aeschylus, it is because the world of the text is so distant from our own, as it presumably was not from Aeschylus's and Homer's original audiences. But with *Finnegans Wake* or Ezra Pound's *Cantos* we need a guide because of the inherent and immediate difficulty of the text. We are told that Bertolt Brecht, out of socialist conviction, kept on his writing desk a toy donkey bearing the sign *Even I must understand it;* the high modernists might aptly have put on their desks a professor-of-literature doll bearing, unless its specialty happened to be the literature of high modernism, the sign *Not even I can understand it.*

I do not say this in deprecation of these great writers and their some-times brilliant explicators. If modernist works are often forbidding and require a fair amount of help and training to appreciate, it does not fol-low that they are not superbly rewarding, as climbing Mount Matterhorn must be, or sailing a small boat around the world. To return to our sub-ject: Let us agree with the commonplace that the rigidities and other limi-tations of nineteenth-century bourgeois realism, in the light of turn-of-the-century theories and discoveries in physics, psychology, anthropol-ogy, technology, etc., prompted or fueled the great adversary reaction called modernist art—which came to terms with our new ways of think-ing about the world at the frequent expense of democratic access, of im-mediate or at least ready delight, and often of political responsibility (the politics of Eliot, Joyce, Pound, Nabokov, and Borges, for example, are notoriously inclined either to nonexistence or to the far right). But in North America, in western and northern Europe, in the United Kingdom, in Japan, and in some of Central and South America, at least, these nine-teenth-century rigidities are virtually no more. The modernist aesthetic is in my opinion unquestionably the characteristic aesthetic of the first half of our century—and in my opinion it *belongs* to the first half of our cen-tury. The present reaction against it is perfectly understandable and to be sympathized with, both because the modernist coinages are by now more or less debased common currency and because we really don't *need* more *Finnegans Wake*s and *Pisan Cantos,* each with its staff of tenured profes-sors to explain it to us.

But I deplore the artistic and critical cast of mind that repudiates the whole modernist enterprise as an aberration and sets to work as if it hadn't happened; that rushes back into the arms of nineteenth-century middle-class realism as if the first half of the twentieth century hadn't happened. It *did* happen: Freud and Einstein and two world wars and the Russian and sexual revolutions and automobiles and airplanes and tele-phones and radios and movies and urbanization, and now nuclear weap-onry and television and microchip technology and the new feminism and the rest, and except as readers there's no going back to Tolstoy and Dickens. As the Russian writer Evgeny Zamyatin was already saying in the 1920s (in his essay *On Literature, Revolution, and Entropy*): "Euclid's world is very simple, and Einstein's world is very difficult; nevertheless, it is now impossible to return to Euclid's."

On the other hand, it is no longer necessary, if it ever was, to repudiate *them,* either: the great premodernists. If the modernists, carrying the torch of romanticism, taught us that linearity, rationality, consciousness, cause and effect, naïve illusionism, transparent language, innocent anecdote, and middle-class moral conventions are not the whole story, then from the perspective of these closing decades of our century we may appreciate that the contraries of those things are not the whole story either. Disjunction, simultaneity, irrationalism, anti-illusionism, self-reflexiveness, medium-as-message, political olympianism, and a moral pluralism approaching moral entropy—these are not the whole story either.

A worthy program for postmodernist fiction, I believe, is the synthesis or transcension of these antitheses, which may be summed up as premodernist and modernist modes of writing. My ideal postmodernist author neither merely repudiates nor merely imitates either his twentieth-century modernist parents or his nineteenth-century premodernist grandparents. He has the first half of our century under his belt, but not on his back. Without lapsing into moral or artistic simplism, shoddy craftsmanship, Madison Avenue venality, or either false or real naïveté, he nevertheless aspires to a fiction more democratic in its appeal than such late-modernist marvels (by my definition) as Beckett's *Texts for Nothing* or Nabokov's *Pale Fire*. He may not hope to reach and move the devotees of James Michener and Irving Wallace—not to mention the great mass of television-addicted non-readers. But he *should* hope to reach and delight, at least part of the time, beyond the circle of what Mann used to call the Early Christians: professional devotees of high art.

I feel this in particular for practitioners of the novel, a genre whose historical roots are famously and honorably in middle-class popular culture. The ideal postmodernist novel will somehow rise above the quarrel between realism and irrealism, formalism and "contentism," pure and committed literature, coterie fiction and junk fiction. Alas for professors of literature, it may not need as much *teaching* as Joyce's or Nabokov's or Pynchon's books, or some of my own. On the other hand, it will not wear its heart on its sleeve, either; at least not its whole heart. (In a recent published exchange between William Gass and John Gardner, Gardner declares that he wants everybody to love his books; Gass replies that he would no more want his books to be loved by everybody than he'd want his daughter to be loved by everybody, and suggests that Gardner is confusing love with promiscuity.) My own analogy would be with good jazz or classical music: One finds much on successive listenings or close examination of the score that one didn't catch the first time through; but the first time through should be so ravishing—and not just to specialists—that one delights in the replay.

Lest this postmodern synthesis sound both sentimental and impossible of attainment, I offer two quite different examples of works which I believe approach it, as perhaps such giants as Dickens and Cervantes may be said to anticipate it. The first and more tentative example (it is not meant to be a blockbuster) is Italo Calvino's *Cosmicomics* (1965): beautifully written, enormously appealing space-age fables—"perfect dreams," John Updike has called them—whose materials are as modern as the new cosmology and as ancient as folktales, but whose themes are love and loss, change and permanence, illusion and reality, including a good deal of specifically Italian reality. Like all fine fantasists, Calvino grounds his flights in local, palpable detail: Along with the nebulae and the black holes and the lyricism, there is a nourishing supply of pasta, bambini, and good-looking women sharply glimpsed and gone forever. A true postmodernist, Calvino keeps one foot always in the narrative past—characteristically the Italian narrative past of Boccaccio, Marco Polo, or Italian fairy tales—and one foot in, one might say, the Parisian structuralist present; one foot in fantasy, one in objective reality, etc. It is appropriate that he has, I understand, been chastized from the left by the Italian communist critics and from the right by the Italian Catholic critics; it is symptomatic that he has been praised by fellow authors as divergent as John Updike, Gore Vidal, and myself. I urge everyone to read Calvino at once, beginning with *Cosmicomics* and going right on, not only because he exemplifies my postmodernist program, but because his fiction is both delicious and high in protein.

An even better example is Gabriel García Márquez's *One Hundred Years of Solitude* (1967): as impressive a novel as has been written so far in the second half of our century and one of the splendid specimens of that splendid genre from any century. Here the synthesis of straightforwardness and artifice, realism and magic and myth, political passion and nonpolitical artistry, characterization and caricature, humor and terror, are so remarkably sustained that one recognizes with exhilaration very early on, as with *Don Quixote* and *Great Expectations* and *Huckleberry Finn,* that one is in the presence of a masterpiece not only artistically admirable, but humanly wise, lovable, literally marvelous. One had almost forgotten that new fiction could be so *wonderful* as well as so merely important. And the question whether my program for postmodernism is achievable goes happily out the window, like one of García Márquez's characters on flying carpets. Praise be to the Spanish language and imagination! As Cervantes stands as an exemplar of premodernism and a great precursor of much to come, and Jorge Luis Borges as an exemplar of *dernier cri* modernism and at the same time as a bridge between the end of the nineteenth century and the end of the twentieth, so Gabriel García Márquez is in that enviable succession: an exemplary postmodernist and a master of the storyteller's art.

A dozen years ago I published in these pages a much-misread essay called "The Literature of Exhaustion," occasioned by my admiration for the stories of Señor Borges and by my concern, in that somewhat apocalyptic place and time, for the ongoing health of narrative fiction. (The time was the latter 1960s; the place Buffalo, N.Y., on a university campus embattled by tear-gassing riot police and tear-gassed Vietnam War protesters, while from across the Peace Bridge in Canada came Professor Marshall McLuhan's siren song that we "print-oriented bastards" were obsolete.) The simple burden of my essay was that the forms and modes of art live in human history and are therefore subject to used-upness, at least in the minds of significant numbers of artists in particular times and places: in other words, that artistic conventions are liable to be retired, subverted, transcended, transformed, or even deployed against themselves to generate new and lively work. I would have thought that point unexceptionable. But a great many people—among them, I fear, Señor Borges himself—mistook me to mean that literature, at least fiction, is *kaput;* that it has all been done already; that there is nothing left for contemporary writers but to parody and travesty our great predecessors in our exhausted medium—exactly what some critics deplore as postmodernism.

That is not what I meant at all. Leaving aside the celebrated fact that, with *Don Quixote,* the novel may be said to *begin* in self-transcendent parody and has often returned to that mode for its refreshment, let me say at once and plainly that I agree with Borges that literature can never be exhausted, if only because no single literary text can ever be exhausted— its "meaning" residing as it does in its transactions with individual readers over time, space, and language. I like to remind misreaders of my earlier essay that written literature is in fact about 4,500 years old (give or take a few centuries depending on one's definition of literature), but that we have no way of knowing whether 4,500 years constitutes senility, maturity, youth, or mere infancy. The number of splendid sayable things— metaphors for the dawn or the sea, for example—is doubtless finite; it is also doubtless very large, perhaps virtually infinite. In some moods we writers may feel that Homer had it easier than we, getting there early with his rosy-fingered dawn and his wine-dark sea. We should console ourselves that one of the earliest extant literary texts (an Egyptian papyrus of ca. 2000 B.C., cited by Walter Jackson Bate in his 1970 study *The Burden of the Past and the English Poet*) is a complaint by the scribe Khakheper-resenb that he has arrived on the scene too late:

> Would I had phrases that are not known, utterances that are strange,
> in new language that has not been used, free from repetition, not an
> utterance that has grown stale, which men of old have spoken.

What my essay "The Literature of Exhaustion" was really about, so it seems to me now, was the effective "exhaustion" not of language or of literature, but of the aesthetic of high modernism: that admirable, not-to-be-repudiated, but essentially completed "program" of what Hugh Kenner has dubbed "the Pound era." In 1966/67 we scarcely had the term *postmodernism* in its current literary-critical usage—at least I hadn't heard it yet—but a number of us, in quite different ways and with varying combinations of intuitive response and conscious deliberation, were already well into the working out, not of the next-best thing after modernism, but of the *best next* thing: what is gropingly now called postmodernist fiction; what I hope might also be thought of one day as a literature of replenishment.

The Self in Fiction,
or,
"That Ain't No Matter.
That Is Nothing."

THE PRECEDING Friday-piece mentions a Modern Language Association symposium in San Francisco on the subject "The Self in Postmodernist Fiction." By the time the symposium was held—December 27, 1979—the topic had been broadened to "The Self in Fiction," a subject too general for meaningful discourse. The symposium was, therefore, like many another, no symposium at all: However individually interesting the presentations, they had little to do with one another. Their most apparent common ground was their authors' wish to spend a few days in San Francisco.

That was a wish I shared, and so like my fellow symposiasts—the rest of them high-tech scholars indeed—I rode my hobby-horse of the moment. Norman Holland, of SUNY/Buffalo, spoke of psychoanalysis and fairy tales. My Johns Hopkins colleague Stanley Fish spoke of the act of reading. J. Hillis Miller, of Yale, spoke of Hegel and Nietzsche. Benjamin DeMott, of Amherst, disapproved of both narcissism and incest. I spoke as best I could of the self in fiction.

Our topic is The Self in Fiction. In order to speak to it from the only competence I can bring to the subject—as a self myself who in fact writes fiction in the second half of the twentieth century—I shall set three limitations upon my remarks.

First, I'll consider only one category of the self in fiction: namely, the authorial self: the self of the writer him- or herself, participating in his or her own inventions.

Second, I'll consider only one aspect of the authorial self in fiction: namely, authorial self-consciousness, often manifested as narrative self-reflexiveness and usually condemned as the last-ditch decadence of modern self-consciousness in general.

Third, I'll consider this authorial self-consciousness in only one category of fiction: namely, what's called postmodern or postmodernist fiction (the terms are used so interchangeably that I've come to think of it
myself as P.M. fiction; it is after all a phenomenon of the evening of our
century, and I happen to do most of my reading after supper).

More specifically yet, my concern will be the proper role of authorial
self-consciousness in what I consider to be *exemplary* postmodernist fiction, whether extant or yet to be written; and the burden of my argument
is so simple that I can take as my text the opening of Mark Twain's epistolary novel *The Adventures of Huckleberry Finn:*

> You don't know about me [Huck writes], without you have read
> a book by the name of "The Adventures of Tom Sawyer," *but that
> ain't no matter.* That book was made by Mr. Mark Twain, and he
> told the truth, mainly. There was things which he stretched, but
> mainly he told the truth. *That is nothing.*

Italics by yours truly, not by the "Yours Truly, Huck Finn," who
signs off the single long letter to the reader which is Twain's novel.

About the first of my qualifiers—the *author's* self in his/her fiction—
I make two simple observations. The first is that as a narrative convention
it has a very long provenance. The contemporary appearance of the author, or of authorial surrogates, in the fiction of Kurt Vonnegut, Philip
Roth, John Updike, and Bernard Malamud, for example—to mention
only a few American novelists published last year—reminds us of our
near contemporaries' similar inclination to make cameo appearances,
sometimes even to take major roles, in their own productions: Borges's
Borges, Nabokov's Van Veen, and the rest. And they of course are echo-
ing the great modernists' preoccupation with author-heroes, authorial
surrogates, and the *Künstlerroman* in general: Joyce's Dedalus, Mann's
Kröger and Aschenbach, Proust's Marcel, Kafka's Samsa (at whose simple vowel-and-consonant correspondence to his own surname Kafka felt
such an odd, sly, uncharacteristic, *undergraduate* excitement). But the
modernists were of course only escalating that foregrounding of authorial
self-consciousness which runs from Flaubert through Henry James: that
"fall from innocence" on the part of literature which Roland Barthes
seems to date from about 3 P.M. on a Tuesday in 1853 or thereabouts and
which he exaggerates as follows a hundred years later in *Writing Degree
Zero:*

. . . the whole of literature, from Flaubert to the present day, became the problematics of language.

It would have been enough to say that *one* characteristic preoccupation, among others, of the modernists and protomodernists was the problematics, not only of language, but of the medium and processes of literature: a manifestation of their heightened authorial self-consciousness. But these protomodernists, to be sure, are anticipated by the late eighteenth- and nineteenth-century romantics, not to mention such "performing selves" as Mister Mark Twain and Mister Charles Dickens. The romantics' confessional fiction and not-always-subtle *romans à clef*, from Kafka/Samsa in 1912 back to Goethe/Werther in 1774—are a genus easily recognized through its mutations, even without Goethe/Werther's declaring, in the very first letter of *his* epistolary novel, ". . . one might wish himself metamorphosed into a cockchafer. . . ."

But weren't the romantics themselves merely reorchestrating the early eighteenth-century conventions of the author-as-maître-d' (Fielding's chatting with the reader through the whole first chapter of *Tom Jones*), and the author-surrogate as protagonist (Smollett's rehearsing his biography and settling old scores in the guise of *Roderick Random*—not to mention the proto-postmodern self-reflexiveness of Laurence Sterne's *Tristram Shandy* (1767) and that spookily contemporary sense, which all the inventors of the English novel seemed to share, of the documentary nature of their enterprise: novels in the form of journals, of letters, of diaries, of confessions—of almost anything except novels, as if to say, "It is not life we imitate, but writing: life's enscripted epiphenomena." But where did these eighteenth-century conventions come from, if not from such seminal seventeeth-century prefigurations as *Don Quixote*—especially the vertiginous opening of Part II, where the characters criticize the translation of Part I from Arabic into Spanish? And does not Cervantes's fictitious historian Cid Hamete Benengeli remind us of another artificial Arab from the sixteenth century, Alcofribas Nasier, the anagrammatical author of *Gargantua and Pantagruel* (1532)? And doesn't Goethe/Werther, that aspiring cockchafer, writing his letters and reading his Homer in the woods of Wahlheim, remind us of Dante/Dante in a darker wood, somewhere outside Florence, chatting with Virgil and even with Homer, confirming his advance reservation at the table of immortals, and checking in with his agent Beatrice, who has connections with the best-selling Author of all, in hopes of eventual metamorphosis into a different species of winged creature? But who is it that Dante/Dante chats with and Goethe/Werther reads, and Borges/Borges so frequently invokes, if not the inventor of this whole tradition of author-characters and self-reflexive narrative? I mean, of course, blind Homer/Demodocus, led onstage in the *Odyssey* in order to perform the *Iliad* and, by making disguised Odysseus weep, to spring the next episode of the plot of his work-in-progress.

One is tempted to push on, push on, back to the antecedent of the *I* in one of the earliest extant literary documents: an Egyptian papyrus of circa 2000 B.C., cited by W. J. Bate in his 1970 study *The Burden of the Past and the English Poet*—but that would be to leave narrative for lyric conventions. (In fact the "I" is the scribe Khakheperresenb, and the fragment, which I quote at every opportunity, is a complaint that he has arrived upon the scene too late; that literature is already exhausted:

> Would I had phrases that are not known, utterances that are strange, in new language that has not been used, free from repetition, not an utterance which men of old have spoken.

Every authorial intuition tells me that Khakheperresenb's complaint was itself a literary convention, with an already long provenance of its own by circa 2000 B.C.)

The other remark I want to make about these authorial selves and surrogates as characters in their own fictions is that, often as not, they're just as fictitious as their fellow characters. Everybody grants that the relation between Dante in the poem and Dante the poet is at most participatory, almost Platonic: The Dante character is merely somewhat closer to Dante the writing poet than the Beatrice character is, or the Virgil character, or the God character. "Madame Bovary, c'est moi"—et aussi Charles Bovary, Monsieur Homais, et tout le monde of the author's imagination. What's more (to move from Plato to Schopenhauer), fiction-making is a two-way street: If the world is our idea, we are the world's idea, too. It is not speaking mystically to say that our dreams dream us; that our fictions construct us, at least as sub-contractors. I hear Madame Bovary replying, "Monsieur Flaubert, c'est moi." Even Borges admits that he doesn't know which Borges invented which—and, as Huck Finn says, that ain't no matter.

Self-consciousness itself has an even grander provenance than the

authorial-self-as-character: a provenance nowhere better traced than in a
recent *Georgia Review* essay by James Sloan Allen called "Self-Consciousness and the Modernist Temper." Having commenced with a line
from a certain so-called postmodernist author—"Oh God comma I abhor
self hyphen consciousness"*—and having then made the easy connection
through the modernists and the romantics, Allen declares:

> Self-consciousness has seemingly had as many cultural births
> as, say, Romanticism or modernity. The Enlightenment may be seen
> as the fount of that intellectual self-awareness that dissolves naive
> certainties, as evidenced by Hume's agonizing scrutiny of knowing,
> Rousseau's and Kant's demand for moral self-determination, and
> the rise of an aesthetic sensitivity which, in W. J. Bate's words, intro-
> duced "a self-consciousness unparalleled in degree at any time be-
> fore." Yet the seventeenth century has impressive claims to priority
> in self-consciousness with the birth of modern philosophy in Des-
> cartes' self-reflecting *cogito;* the unabashed critical psychology of La
> Rochefoucauld and La Bruyère; and the conflict between "moderns"
> and "ancients" in the Battle of the Books. But then no student of the
> sixteenth century could fail to assert that modern self-consciousness
> had its origins in the subjectivity of that age: aesthetic Mannerism
> and Montaigne's self-searching; the Protestant Reformation and the
> revival of Pyrrhonian skepticism; the perfection of the mirror and
> the emergence of autobiography and the self-portrait; Cervantes' in-
> vention of what Robert Alter calls "the self-conscious novel" and
> Shakespeare's self-absorbed heroes; the cult of sincerity and the rise
> of the role-playing self. Nor could students of the Italian Renais-
> sance resist placing the source of self-consciousness in the Quattro-
> cento's high valuations of man, new assertive ego, and cultivation of
> secular intellectual and artistic pursuits.
>
> Yet even before the modern individualism of the Renaissance,
> the reforms of Gregory VII had given life to a type of man who was,
> in the words of the great historian Marc Bloch, "more self-con-
> scious" than any Christian before him and whose "self-conscious-
> ness indeed extended beyond the solitary human being to society,"
> where it stimulated the art and thought of the High Middle Ages.
> But Christianity itself may also be credited with introducing into
> Western culture a self-reflectiveness unknown to ancient times
> through its psychological definition of sin—as formulated in The
> Sermon on the Mount and Paul's Epistles and reflected in the spir-
> itual autobiographies and confessional day books of believers. But
> no sooner has the novelty of Christian self-awareness been recog-
> nized than classical antiquity asserts new priorities with the meta-

---

* The line is from my story "Title," in *Lost in the Funhouse.*

physical self-consciousness of Plotinus; the critical, secular spirit of Latin literature; and beyond these the rise of philosophical skepticism and heterodoxy among Hellenistic philosophers and of an educated cosmopolitan personality in the Hellenistic cities. Even earlier still, there are manifestations of self-consciousness in Aristotle's ideal of self-contemplating intellect, Plato's intuitive rationalism, Socrates' irony, and—unavoidably—the motto at Delphi: Know Thyself. In fact, no search for the historical origins of self-consciousness could stop before that awakening of human self-knowledge in the Garden of Eden when Adam and Eve lost not only moral purity and hallowed sanctuary but psychological innocence: they clutched at fig-leaves, having become painfully conscious of themselves.

About this wonderful history of lost innocence, I offer two remarks.

First, it is in my opinion an innocence well lost. One should be no great admirer of innocence, in either narratives, individuals, or cultures. Where it's genuine, after a certain age it's unbecoming, off-putting, even freakish and dangerous. Where it's false, it's false. To admire it much is patronizing and sentimental; to aspire to it is self-defeating. Let us admire—in cultures, narratives, and people—not innocence, but experience and grace.

Second, and on the other hand, self-consciousness, even self-reflexiveness, are so much in the cultural air we breathe now that they can have a kind of innocence of their own. I am reminded of this paradox by every Woody Allen movie, every television news show opening shot of the cameras filming the cameras filming John Chancellor or Walter Cronkite watching the monitors showing the cameras, etc.: naïve, unselfconscious self-consciousness. And so perhaps of self-consciousness, too, we may say with Huck Finn: That is nothing.

But if self-consciousness goes back to Adam and Eve, and authorial self-consciousness back at least to Flaubert if not to the scribe Khakheperresenb, surely *postmodernist* authorial self-consciousness has a shorter pedigree, at least if we detach it from the modernism of which it is variously regarded as an extension, an attenuation, an aftermath, an anticlimax, or an adversary reaction. I have been told that Arnold Toynbee uses the term "post-modern" somewhere in his vast *Study of History:* I haven't the heart to check. Let's content ourselves that in 1967 or thereabouts, certain literary critics seem to have borrowed the term from their colleagues in the graphic and plastic arts, as their forebears borrowed the term modernism.

Now, my notion of postmodernist fiction is rather different from the other notions of it that I've encountered: enough so that I was moved not long ago to a little essay on the subject.* Its purpose was to investigate for myself whether this clumsy term postmodernism describes anything very good very well. What I discovered was that not only do critics disagree about what postmodernism is, but that modernism itself is a bird whose field-identification marks are only very approximately agreed upon. I should have known.

Emboldened by this anarchy of critical opinion, I proceeded to legislate what postmodernist fiction ought to be, if it's to be anything worth taking seriously. I shall omit here both the documentation and the wit of my essay and encapsulate its simple argument, which implies, if not a definition of postmodernist fiction, at least a program for it. By extension, it implies as well my sentiments about the proper and seemly role of authorial self-consciousness and narrative self-reflexiveness in P.M. fiction.

> A worthy program for postmodernist fiction, I believe, is the synthesis or transcension of these antitheses, which may be summed up as premodernist and modernist modes of writing. My ideal postmodernist author neither merely repudiates nor merely imitates either his twentieth-century modernist parents or his nineteenth-century premodernist grandparents. He has the first half of our century under his belt, but not on his back. Without lapsing into moral or artistic simplism, shoddy craftsmanship, Madison Avenue venality, or either false or real naïveté, he nevertheless aspires to a fiction more democratic in its appeal than such late-modernist marvels . . . as Beckett's *Texts for Nothing* or Nabokov's *Pale Fire*. . . .
>
> The ideal postmodernist novel will rise above the quarrel between realism and irrealism, formalism and "contentism," pure and committed literature, coterie fiction and junk fiction. Alas for professors of literature, it may not need as much *teaching* as Joyce's or Nabokov's or Pynchon's books, or some of my own. On the other hand, it will not wear its heart on its sleeve, either; at least not its whole heart. . . . My own analogy would be with good jazz or classical music: One finds much on successive listenings or close examination of the score that one didn't catch the first time through; but the first time through should be so ravishing—and not just to specialists—that one delights in the replay.

Well, now: If part of the energy of such a novel happens to come from a "performing" authorial self, as it conceivably might, we shall look

---

* "The Literature of Replenishment: Postmodern Fiction," the preceding Friday-piece.

for that self to be at least as self-knowing and self-controlled, perhaps even as self-effacing, as it is self-conscious. Its presence will be at once as functional and as finally beside the point as the novel's being set on the Mississippi, say, or in Macondo. And we shall be able to say of it, with Huck Finn: "That ain't no matter. That is nothing."

Revenge

. . . SHORT AND SWEET.

The novel *LETTERS* took a considerable beating from U.S. book reviewers, a number of whom found the story too complicated and difficult for their enjoyment and too dependent upon the reader's familiarity with the author's earlier fiction. Against the former charge there is no defense: The story *is* complicated, but difficulty is in the mind of the beholder. The latter charge I understand but respectfully disagree with, it being a rule in our house that one may echo or reprise one's former fiction, but must not presume that any reader knows that fiction even slightly. I believe that *LETTERS* meets that rule.

More tongue-tiskish than the reviewers' reservations about the novel was a recurring note of impatience, in a few cases even of sweeping anger, directed less at the work in hand than at the author himself, who seemed to have become in the minds of some critics the embodiment of an avant-garde literary experimentalism which they deplored.

Tant pis. By the fall of 1981 I had finished a new novel, *Sabbatical: A Romance,* to be published in June of the following year. Though it is a shorter and altogether simpler story, which I hoped might recoup some of my publisher's investment in *LETTERS,* I suspected that it too would get banged on the head not solely for whatever its own demerits but for its author's having been generally badmouthed, along with other American "postmodernist" writers, by the likes of John Gardner (in his treatise *On Moral Fiction*) and Gore Vidal (in the essay "American Plastic," in *The New York Review of Books*). Even a little blood will sometimes fetch the sharks—and the sharks in turn fetch rescuers—when all the swimmer has in mind is to go on swimming.

That suspicion must account for my agreeing to Rust Hills's merry proposal that I contribute to an *Esquire* Magazine "Revenge Symposium," in which a number of writers would settle scores with some particularly scathing reviewer. Payment was to be six bottles of one's favorite booze, with which to toast one's sweet revenge upon the son- or daughterofabitch.

But it is another shop rule hereabouts that one does not reply to critics of one's work, and so when the Friday came to take revenge, I found myself taking it upon a reviewer who (so far as I can remember) has never reviewed a book of mine, but whose attacks upon some authors I admire had had that familiar ad hominem tone.

The Revenge Symposium project was set aside by its conceivers, revived, set aside again, and finally published two years later, in the June 1983 number of *Esquire*. By the time it appeared, *Sabbatical: A Romance* had had *its* drubbing—and its praise—from the reviewers, and I was at work upon its successor and this *Friday Book*.

My favorite booze? I asked for a half-dozen bottles of 1970 Château Pauillac, on sale just then at about $65 the bottle: better Bordeaux by a factor of ten than anything in our cellar. There was an embarrassed shuffling of feet in New York City. Okay, then: Make it six bottles of Dom Perignon (then about $50 the bottle), a champagne particularly admired in our house, where it has almost never appeared. More shuffling of feet: What they'd had in mind was, um, Jack Daniel's bourbon, J & B Scotch—like that. But unless guests are in for cocktails, nearly no hard liquor is drunk chez nous. Who, I wondered, is taking revenge upon whom? I settled finally for six quarts of Mount Gay Sugar Cane rum in memory of my first romantic Caribbean visit, twelve years earlier, when Shelly and I had run off from Boston to Barbados. Six quarts of Mount Gay Sugar Cane, I reckoned, would make six summersworth of nostalgic rum punches at Langford Creek, and I feared that further dickering might leave me with a six-pack of Miller Lite. What the liquor store finally delivered was six *fifths* of Mount Gay *Eclipse* (not the same rum at all as Sugar Cane): presumably neither *Esquire*'s fault nor the subtle revenge of the critic here criticized. Whom I have never met; against whom I have no personal grudge; and who, I learned after the piece appeared (minus its final sentence, here reappended), is my present editor's brother-in-law.

Eclipse, anyone?

My fiction has so excited the spleen of so many and various reviewers over the past quarter-century that while I can still be instructed by intelligent criticism, I am proof against invective. My revenge is to *forget who it was,* say, who dismissed *The Sot-Weed Factor* and *Giles Goat-Boy* as "mere inflated spoofs"—though the word *spoof,* which anyhow sounds like an imperfectly suppressed fart, retains its malodor in my house. And who was that other imperfectly suppressed fart who, in the columns of *The New York Review of Books,* called the author of *Chimera* a "narrative chauvinist pig"? Gone from my memory, though I relish the phrase.

There are worse; I have forgot them. The dogs bark, says the Arabian proverb, but the caravan moves on.

About splenetic assaults upon the art of other writers whom I admire, however, I remain thin-skinned. I neither forget nor forgive, e.g., Roger

Sale's savaging, ten years ago—also in *The New York Review of Books*—
of John Hawkes's novel *The Blood Oranges*: an attack which opened with
the sentence "*The Blood Oranges* fails because it is the work of a con-
temptible imagination." There are earlier and later novels of Hawkes's
which I myself prefer, but in *The Blood Oranges,* as in all his fiction, John
Hawkes is one of our purest and most memorable verbal artists, whereas
Roger Sale is a mere inflated spoof. *There* is a reviewer whom I will not
shrive until he recants by writing of some future Hawkes novel, "Whatever its apparent flaws (and they are only apparent), this is a luminous,
transcendent work of art, not least because it proceeds from a luminous,
transcendent imagination. . . ."

Tales Within Tales Within Tales

BACK TO BUSINESS.

Science-fiction writers are not like you and me; they have more fun. This truth was revealed to me at the Second International Conference on the Fantastic in the Arts, held at Florida Atlantic University in Boca Raton in March, 1981. One of the fun things SF writers do is organize convention after convention— regional, national, international, intergalactic—among which they hop like drivers on the auto-racing circuit, reinforcing one another's enthusiasm for their genre, enlarging their personal acquaintance with its practitioners, and enjoying one another's company with a high-spirited camaraderie hardly to be found for example at a meeting of the American Academy and Institute of Arts and Letters.

My reservations about science fiction are much the same as my reservations about historical fiction, as set forth in that blue-crab Friday-piece earlier on: The more it is *about* science, the future, other worlds, etc., the less it is likely to be about the proper subject of literature: ''human life, its happiness and its misery.'' Fantasy is another matter: a mode of literature as old as the narrative imagination.

Florida Atlantic University's annual International Conferences on the Fantastic in the Arts are unusually well organized, well funded, and well attended affairs, ecumenical enough in spirit to include among their principal speakers each year one ''mainstream'' writer whose works at least occasionally involve fantasy. I accepted their lecture-invitation partly because it gave me a chance to think again about my friend Scheherazade and partly because Shelly and I planned to spend our vacation that spring sailing in the Caribbean; the Boca Raton stopover would help pay for the cruise and give us a few beach-days to shape up for it. The SF people, however, turned out to be as enjoyable in their way as the British Virgin Islands in theirs; at conference's end, as we took off for Tortola, our fellow fantasts were calling to one another ''Next month in Cincinnati . . . next summer in Vancouver . . . next year in Adelaide. . . .''

This lecture was published in amended form in the Autumn 1981 number of the quarterly *Antaeus*. The figures and footnotes are reprinted here as they were printed there.

It is an honor to follow Isaac Bashevis Singer as your guest at this Second International Conference on the Fantastic. Mr. Singer has been called by one critic a modernist in traditionalist's clothing: I approve equally of the disguise and of the thing disguised, and sometimes suspect my own case to be simply the reverse. Like a good Cabalist, Singer understands God to be a kind of novelist and the world to be His novel-in-progress; as a fellow storyteller, he is therefore able to appreciate the great Author's masterstrokes and to sympathize with, if not excuse, His lapses. As Horace says, Sometimes even good Homer sleeps. What's more, the story is not done yet: Who knows what plot-reversals the Author may have up His/Her sleeve for the denouement?

I second that attitude, too; I have remarked elsewhere that I regard the Almighty as not a bad novelist, except that He is a realist.

It is remarks like that, I suppose, that have fetched Mrs. Barth and me to Boca Raton so that I can speak to you about a certain standard device of fantastic literature: stories within stories. I have begun by invoking two other storytellers: I. B. Singer and God. I trust that neither of them would disapprove of my pausing here, or anywhere, to tell you a little story.

Once upon a time—it was 1971—I made up a story about Scheherazade's younger sister, Dunyazade, who sat at the foot of the royal bed for 1001 nights (so we're told in the Arabian version) watching her sister and the king make love and listening to all those beguiling, usually fantastic, old stories. In my version, Scheherazade is assisted in her exhaustive narrative enterprise by an American genie of sorts from the second half of the twentieth century: He has always been half in love with her and inspired by her situation, and he contrives, by a certain arrangement between them, to supply her from the narrative future with those stories from the narrative past which she needs to deal with her present danger.

My genie gets these stories, needless to say, from his copy of *The 1001 Nights*. And, like bread cast upon the waters, his assisting Scheherazade solves *his* problem, too, which is hers and every storyteller's: What to do for yet another and yet another encore? How to save and save again one's narrative neck? The genie's next story, we learn toward the end of my story,* will be the story of his interlude with Scheherazade.

How I wish that that fantasy were a fact: that I could be that genie, and meet and speak with the talented, wise, and beautiful Scheherazade.

One part of it *is* a fact: Dunyazade, the narrator of my story, recounting the genie's first appearance to the sisters, says, "Years ago (the genie told us), when he'd been a penniless student pushing book-carts through the library-stacks of his university to help pay for his education, he'd contracted a passion for Scheherazade upon first reading the tales she beguiled King Shahryar with, and had sustained that passion . . . powerfully ever since. . . ." What Diotima was to Socrates in the *Symposium,* Scheherazade has always been to me; her name stares at me from a 3 × 5 card above my writing table, both to encourage me when the critics are working me over—for I've never doubted since first meeting her that she is my true sister—and, contrariwise, to chasten me when my stories are overpraised, for I've never doubted that that true sister is immeasurably my superior.

Nevertheless, there are two white lies in the genie's protestation. First, Scheherazade's is not the only name on that 3 × 5 card: My very big brothers Odysseus, Don Quixote, and Huckleberry Finn, towards whom I harbor similar feelings, join her in buoying me up and staring me down. And second, it was never Scheherazade's stories that seduced and beguiled me, but their teller and the extraordinary circumstances of their telling: in other words, the character and situation of Scheherazade, and the narrative convention of the framing story.

Of that situation I have written elsewhere†: the significance of there being 1001 nights rather than 101 or 2002; the ritual of sex before storytelling; the terrifying but fertilizing relation between the storyteller and her audience; the primordial publish-or-perish ultimatum and its familiar consequence (after the king, on the 1002nd day, awards Scheherazade the relative tenure of formal marriage and orders a deluxe hardcover edition of her work, the woman evidently never tells another story); the crucial role of little Dunyazade at the foot of that bed; the even more intriguing and emblematic problem that *she* must deal with on *her* bridal night, etc. I won't speak further of those things here.

---

* "Dunyazadiad," in *Chimera* (N.Y.: Random House, 1972).
† "Muse Spare Me," in *Book Week,* Sept. 26, 1965; reprinted in *The Sense of the 60s,* ed. Quinn (N.Y.: Free Press, 1968).

Let's look instead at the phenomenon of stories within stories. A contemporary of mine, the novelist John Gardner, distinguishes between what he calls "primary fiction," which he defines as fiction about life, and "secondary fiction," which he defines as fiction about fiction. There are several grounds on which one might question this distinction, especially when its inventor turns it into a value judgment and even into moral categories. For the moment let's simply be reminded that the phenomenon of framed tales—that is, of stories within stories, which always to some degree imply stories *about* stories and even stories about story*telling*—that this phenomenon is ancient, ubiquitous, and persistent; almost as old and various, I suspect, as the narrative impulse itself.

Perhaps this is the place to review some elementary propositions about reality and fantasy, which I'm sure have been discussed in a sophisticated way in various sessions of this conference. Ludwig Wittgenstein, in the *Tractatus Logico-Philosophicus,* defines the world (which is to say, reality) as being "everything that is the case." The Cabalists, whom writers as different as I. B. Singer and Jorge Luis Borges have found to be a rich source of literary metaphor, maintain that this reality, our reality, is God's text, his significant fiction—I believe Mr. Singer might even say God's executed fantasy. Arthur Schopenhauer, whose importance to Borges I'll come back to, goes farther and declares that our reality, whether or not it's God's fiction, is our representation, as it were *our* fiction: that relations, categories, concepts such as differentiation, time and space, being and not-being—all are ours, not seamless nature's. Eastern philosophy teases these paradoxes out; their bottom line is that capital-R Reality—to a greater or lesser extent, but strictly speaking—is our shared fantasy.

I trust that this conference will agree, in the main, that the difference between the fantasy we call reality and the fantasies we call fantasy has to do with cultural consensus and with one's manner of relating to the concept-structure involved: What we call the real world, we relate to as if it were the case. Psychopathological fantasies are more or less individual concept-structures markedly at variance with the cultural consensus and related to as if they were the case: If you conceive yourself to be Napoleon and act upon your conviction, the rest of us will put you away. "Normal" fantasies are more or less individual concept-structures significantly at variance with the cultural consensus but not related to as if they were the case: e.g. night-dreams (from our waking point of view), daydreams, and aesthetic fictions both "realistic" and "fantastic." On this ontological level, all fiction is fantasy. (The electronic-computer microworlds dealt with by investigators in the field of artificial intelligence would seem to belong to some third category: perhaps secondary fiction in a sense different from Gardner's. The AI computer constructs a world along parameters laid down by its programmer—a microworld often at considerable variance indeed with the programmer's cultural consensus—and it relates to that microworld as if it were real; but we don't call either the computer or the programmer psychopathological—at least not ipso facto. I confess to not having thought this aspect of the matter through very carefully: I'm a storyteller, not a philosopher.)

Aesthetic realism, then, is any set of artistic conventions felt by people on a particular level of a particular culture at a particular period to be literally imitative of their imagination of the actual world. It goes without saying that one generation's or culture's realism is another's patent artifice—witness for example the history of what has passed for realistic dialogue and characterization in Hollywood movies from Humphrey Bogart to Robert de Niro. It likewise goes without saying that what the inexperienced find realistically convincing, the experienced may not, and vice-versa: The birds peck at Apelles's painted grapes (almost the only thing we're taught about classical Greek painting); the innocent frontiersman rises from his seat at a nineteenth-century showboat melodrama to warn the heroine against the villain's blandishments. On the other hand, zoo zebras ignore a life-size color photograph of a zebra—they don't know what it represents—and the Colombian novelist Gabriel García Márquez tells us that what we gringos take for surrealism in his fiction is everyday reality where he comes from.

As for *aesthetic irrealism*—fantasy of the sort addressed by international conferences on the fantastic—it must consist of any set of artistic principles and devices, conventional or otherwise, felt by people on a particular level of a particular culture at a particular time to be enjoyable and/or significant though understood to be *not* literally imitative of their imagination of the actual world. Consider the ghost of Hamlet's father. For most of us and for many Elizabethans, that ghost in Shakespeare's play is/was a device of fantastic literature. For many other Elizabethans and some of us—those who believe in ghosts—it was/is a device of realistic literature. We don't know which it was for the playwright or for particular players of the role. For the character Hamlet, the ghost is no device of any sort; it is reality, as it may well have been for some innocent rube scared out of his skin in the stalls of the Globe. Hamlet's mother Gertrude calls the ghost Hamlet's fantasy ("... the very coinage of your brain": III, iv), even his psychopathological fantasy ("Alas, he's mad": III, iv): She neither sees nor hears the ghost when Hamlet does, in her presence. But there's the complication that not only the watchmen but also the antisupernaturalist university student Horatio all see what Hamlet sees but apparently don't hear what he hears (this after the guard Marcellus had complained, "Horatio says 'tis but our fantasy": I, i)—etc., etc. We are in the paradoxical world of realistic fantasies like Kafka's and fantastic realities like Edgar Poe's version of Scheherazade's last tale: the one that King Shahryar refuses to swallow, having to do with steamboats and railways and other preposterosities. I shall add that I myself find the fantastic device of Hamlet's father's ghost a good deal more believable than the realistic device of the accidental exchange of poisoned swords in midst of Hamlet's duel with Laertes in Act V. So it goes—and it is time to wander back to our subject.

I remarked that the devices of aesthetic fantasy may be conventional or otherwise. In the opinion of Jorge Luis Borges, the most ubiquitous devices of fantastic literature are four: the double, the voyage in time, the contamination of reality by irreality, and the text within the text.

Of this last, my topic, we're all familiar with such classic examples as *The 1001 Nights*, in which Scheherazade entertains King Shahryar with stories in which the characters sometimes tell one another stories in which (in a few cases) the characters tell further stories. Closer inspection reveals that the real "frame" of *The 1001 Nights* is not the relation between Scheherazade and Shahryar, but something "farther out" and more ancient: the relation between the reader, or listener, and the unspecified teller of the story of Scheherazade. I mean this literally: The opening words of the tale (after the invocation to Allah) are "There is a book called *The 1001 Nights*, in which it is said that once upon a time ..." etc. In other words, *The 1001 Nights* is not immediately about Scheherazade and her stories; it is about a book called *The 1001 Nights*, which *is* about Scheherazade and her stories. That book is not the book we hold in our hands, with wonderful notes by Richard Burton; nor is it quite the book that Shahryar on the 1002nd morning orders to be written. I don't know what, exactly, that book is, or where. I have asked my friend William H. Gass—a professional philosopher as well as a professional storyteller— please to locate that book for me; he's not sure where it is either. To think about that book very long is to invite vertigo.

The classical invocation to the muse of Greek and Roman epic literature can be regarded similarly as a radical framing device. The "outside" or ground-story of the *Odyssey* may be said to be, not the situation of Odysseus striving home from Troy, but the situation of the bard who in the opening lines sings (in Albert Cook's translation) "Sing, Muse, of that man of many turns, the wanderer," etc.; "begin anywhere you like." To which the Muse in effect replies: "Since you ask, the story goes this way: All the other Greeks had got home long since," etc. My experience and intuitions both as a professional storyteller and as an amateur of frame-tale literature lead me to suspect that if the first story ever told began "Once upon a time," the second story ever told began "Once upon a time there was a story that began 'Once upon a time.' " Furthermore—since storytelling appears to be as human a phenomenon as language itself—I'd bet that that second story was no less about "life" than the first.

But let me tell you the story of my romance with this second sort of stories: tales within tales. You've heard its beginning: that student, once upon a time, pushing his book-cart through the stacks of the Johns Hopkins classics library and surreptitiously reading the fantastic literature he was supposed to be filing: *The 1001 Nights, The Ocean of Story,* the *Panchatantra,* the *Metamorphoses,* the *Decameron, Pentameron, Heptameron,* and the rest. A good many years later, that student found himself metamorphosed into a storyteller as well as a story-reader, and a professor at The State University of New York at Buffalo to boot, one of whose perquisites (this was the palmy mid-1960s) was a graduate-student research assistant. How I could have used one earlier, at Penn State, when I was writing *The Sot-Weed Factor*! How I could have used one later, at Johns Hopkins, when I was writing the novel *LETTERS*! But as it happened, my fiction just then in progress required no particular research.

To keep the situation honest, I therefore resolved to implement my old affection for frametale literature with a reasonably thorough, if nonprofessional, investigation of the genre—of which, in fact, there seemed to be little in the way of general examination beyond some useful checklists in German* and some side-glances by Chaucerians.† My objective

---

* e.g., Löhmann, Otto: *Die Rahmenerzählung des Decameron* (Halle/Salle: Max Niemeyer Verlag, 1935), and the more specialized Goldstein, Moritz: *Die Technik der zyklischen Rahmenerzählungen Deutschlands. Von Goethe bis Hoffmann.* (Berlin, 1906?)

† e.g., Bryan & Dempster's *Sources and Analogues of Chaucer's Canterbury Tales* (Chicago: U. of Chicago Press, 1941); H.B. Hinckley's "The Framing-Tale" (*Modern Language Notes,* Vol. XLIX no. 2, Feb. 1934), etc.

was neither to publish an essay on the subject nor to teach a course in it: simply to ask certain questions of the existing corpus of such literature in order to satisfy a long-standing curiosity and, perhaps, to discover something about that ancient narrative convention which might inspire a story of my own: a story which, whatever else it was about, would also be about stories within stories within stories.

I shall digress again briefly here to remark that it does not appear to matter to the Muses whether a writer invokes them out of a heroic wish like Alexander Solzhenitsyn's, to expose and destroy an oppressive system of government, or a decadent wish like Flaubert's, to write a novel "about nothing": Their decision to sing or not to sing seems based on other considerations. The Muses are a less responsible committee, in the moral sphere, than is the Swedish Academy.

Well. We proceeded to interrogate literature, fantastic and otherwise: I mean that research assistant, the Muses, and me. Here, briefly, are some of the findings of our leisurely and gentle interrogation and some of the things that those findings suggested to me.

First, as might be expected, we found it necessary in designing our questionnaire to distinguish categories of frametale literature. Our first distinction was between incidental or casual frames and more or less systematic frames: It is in fact more of a spectrum or continuum than a distinction. In the first category we put such unforgettable but incidental stories-within-stories as Pilar's story of the killing of the fascists in Chapter 10 of Hemingway's *For Whom the Bell Tolls,* or Ivan's tale of the Grand Inquisitor in Book V, Chapter V of Dostoevsky's *The Brothers Karamazov;* also the incidental romances with which Cervantes interrupts the adventures of Don Quixote; and, for that matter, such classical retrospective expositions as Odysseus's rehearsal to the Phaeacians of his story thus far (Books IX–XII of the *Odyssey*) and Aeneas's ditto to Dido (Books II and III of the *Aeneid*). More fiction than not, I suppose, frames *some* incidental anecdote or delayed anecdotal exposition. We decided to confine our attention to the other end of the spectrum: stories that programmatically frame other stories.

There we soon found ourselves making further taxonomical distinctions, which I shall merely illustrate. There is for example what I think of as the Dante/Chaucer continuum: on the one hand, stories like *The Divine Comedy,* in which the frame (Dante's impasse in the Dark Wood and his detour through Hell, Purgatory, and Heaven) is at least as con-

spicuous and as dramatically developed as the stories told along the
way, most of which in Dante's case are plotless moral exempla or extended epitaphs; on the other hand, stories like Chaucer's *Canterbury
Tales* or Boccaccio's *Decameron,* in which the framed stories are dramatically complete, but the frame-story—the pilgrimage to and from Canterbury; the retreat of ten young Florentine ladies and gentlemen from
the plague of 1348—is vestigial, rudimentary, incomplete, or dramatur-
gically static. I wish now that we had also kept tab of comparatively realistic frames for comparatively fantastic stories—pretty much the case
with the *Odyssey* and the *Nights,* for example—and vice-versa. But
we didn't.

Next, it seemed useful to distinguish between frame-stories with a
single frame—such as Dante's, Chaucer's, and Boccaccio's, and in fact
almost all frametale literature at the first level of its framing—and the
very much rarer cases of serial primary frames: as if for example the pilgrimage to Canterbury were but the first in a series of linked Chaucerian
ground-narratives whose characters proceed to tell their several stories.
Two conspicuous examples of this rarer species are the eleventh-century
Sanskrit *Ocean of Story,* a mammoth work of great structural complexity
involving a series of *very* intricate primary frames,* and Ovid's *Metamorphoses,* whose armature is an extraordinarily subtle and graceful series of
linked primary frametales.

Further, we saw fit to ask of each of the several hundred specimens of
frametales and quasi-frametales that we buttonholed whether it comprises merely two degrees of narrative development—tales within a tale,
such as Dante's and Boccaccio's—or three or more such degrees: tales
within tales within a tale, etc. In the oriental literature, we found, it is not
uncommon at all for the characters in a second-degree story to tell stories
of their own. Where this movement to the third degree occurs more
than once—e.g., in *The 1001 Nights*—the second degree of narrative
(Scheherazade's stories) becomes a serial frame within a single frame
(the story of Scheherazade). Where the characters on the *third* level of
narrative involvement more than once tell further stories, as in the
Panchatantra, we have stories serially framed within serial frames
within a single frame. The *Panchatantra* in fact moves to as many as

---

* See my essay "The Ocean of Story," in *Directions in Literary Criticism,* eds. Weintraub & Young (University Park, Pa.: Pennsylvania State University Press, 1973).

five degrees of narrative involvement, as does *The Ocean of Story*—whose primary frame, we remember, is itself serial. Indeed, *The Ocean of Story* manages to engulf the whole *Panchatantra* as one of its serial frames, and the *Vetalapanchavimsati* (*25 Tales by a Vampire*) as another.

Such oriental complexity is uncommon in occidental literature, if we ignore that sort of quasi-framing which I spoke of earlier: invocations to the muse and formulae like "There is a story about a man who" etc. But there are pleasant exceptions: Ovid shifts his *Metamorphoses* to at least four degrees of narrative involvement—e.g., in Book VI, where in the course of Ovid's ongoing story the Muse tells Minerva the story of the contest between the Muses and the daughters of Pierus, in course of which story the muse Calliope tells the jury of nymphs the story of the rape of Proserpine, in course of which story Arethusa tells Ceres the story of her own rape: a tale within a tale within a tale within a tale. It is managed so subtly that it goes almost unnoticed unless one happens to be reading a translation with conventional English punctuation and sees such strange accumulations of double and single quotation-marks as ' " ' ". *The Saragossa Manuscript,* Tzvetan Todorov points out, reaches no fewer than five degrees of narrative involvement: a veritable Sargasso Sea of Story. Even more remarkable, though vestigial, is the frame of Plato's *Symposium.* We all remember that the guests at Agathon's banquet take turns making speeches or telling stories about love, and that the climactic speech is Socrates's famous description of the Ladder of Love, whose final rung he says was explained to him by a lady named Diotima. Many of us will have noticed or had it pointed out to us that the story of Agathon's banquet itself is not told us directly by Plato, but by a fellow named Apollodorus, who is telling it to an unnamed friend. In fact, Plato writes that Apollodorus reports that *he* has the story from a disciple of Socrates's named Aristodemus, who was among Agathon's party guests. We are given the conversation between Apollodorus and this Aristodemus. However, Apollodorus is not telling his unnamed friend directly what Aristodemus told him: Apollodorus tells his unnamed friend the story of his being importuned in the street two days earlier by yet another friend, Glaucon, who wanted to hear what Aristodemus had reported to Apollodorus of Socrates's speech at Agathon's party. When we sort it all out, we discover that:

1. Apollodorus is telling his unnamed friend
2. the story of Apollodorus's telling Glaucon
3. the story of Aristodemus's telling Apollodorus
4. the story of Socrates's telling Agathon's company
5. the story of Diotima's telling Socrates
6. the story of the Topmost Rung on the Ladder of Love.

That is, we are about as many removes from Diotima's story as there are rungs on the Ladder of Love itself, even before we add the next frame out—Plato's telling all this to the reader—and the next frame out from there: my reminding you what Plato tells the reader. If, as I hope, some of you tell your lovers tonight the story of these remarks of mine, you will be involved in a frametale of nine degrees of narrative complexity, unapproached in the actual corpus of frametale literature.

To return to that corpus: Its formal possibilities can be visualized, and actual specimens schematized, by conventional outline format, if we ignore the rule of logical outlining that forbids a *I*, say, unless there's a *II*, an *A* without a *B*, etc. We are dealing here not with logic but with spellbinding. The *Canterbury Tales* or the *Decameron* we might begin to schematize as in Figure 1—

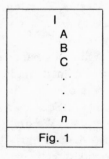

Fig. 1

—where *I* represents the pilgrimage from Canterbury or the Florentine aristocrats' retreat from the plague, and the upper-case letters represent the several tale-tellers and their tales. Where a character tells two or more tales serially, we might improve the notation as in Figure 2:

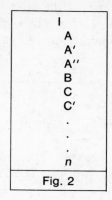

Fig. 2

Note that there is no *II* in nonserial primary frametales such as these.

Such elementary notation can be modified to indicate major returns to the frame, as distinct from the merely formulaic returns between each of *The 1001 Nights*. Figure 3, for example, schematizes the ten storytellers and ten days of the *Decameron*—where *I* represents the framing story, its exponents represent the several evenings of tale-telling with their fore- and afterplay, and the letters represent particular tellers in the successive orders of their telling:

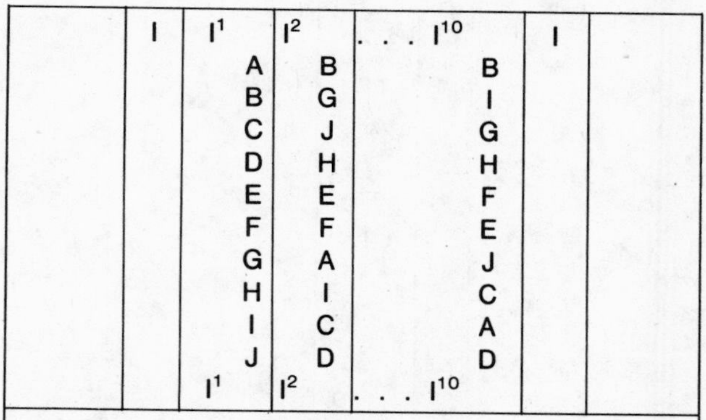

	I	I^1	I^2	. . . I^{10}	I	
		A	B		B	
		B	G		I	
		C	J		G	
		D	H		H	
		E	E		F	
		F	F		E	
		G	A		J	
		H	I		C	
		I	C		A	
		J	D		D	
		I^1	I^2	. . . I^{10}		

Fig. 3

Again there is no *II*.

Where narrative involvement exceeds the second degree but returns to it between third-degree tales, we may simply extend this modification of conventional outlining (as does the orientalist N. M. Penzer in his schematic table of contents to Tawney's translation of Somadeva's *Ocean of Story*). A hypothetical example, indeed a model, might look like Figure 4—

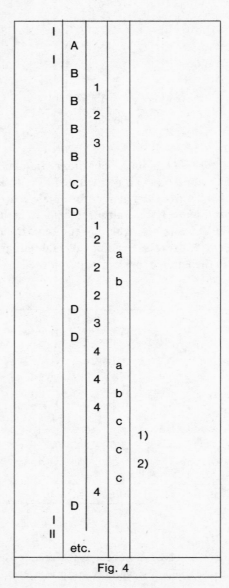

Fig. 4

—where the columns indicate degrees of narrative involvement, and *II* indicates that the primary frame is itself serial, as in *The Ocean of Story*.

Notice that the symbols for conventional outlining are exhausted at about the fourth or fifth degree, just as narrative involvement tends to be in the actual corpus: The peculiar example of the *Symposium* excepted, we found in our primitive explorations no frametale more involved than five degrees. No doubt there is a message here, a warning, as in Hindu cosmology: It is enough to know that (1) my hat sits securely on the head of (2) a man whose feet are more or less on the ground of (3) an earth borne securely upon the back of (4) an elephant standing securely upon (5) four tortoises. To press the inquiry further may be impious or boring. But one person's caution is another's challenge: Why stop at four or five degrees—tales within tales within tales within tales within tales—when, given the model, one can so readily imagine more? Why not press on, press on, like Kafka's Hunger Artist, to "a performance beyond human imagination"? I shall return to this challenge.

Please notice two things further about my hypothetical specimen, Figure 4, that in fact are rarely to be found together in the actual literature. First, the degrees of narrative involvement are not random but incremental, in an order of increasing complexity. The primary frame and then the secondary frames are returned to systematically, as if for orientation, and there are "retreats" (*IC* and *ID3*) before each escalation of narrative involvement. This is a typical feature of such analogues to frametales as Baroque musical themes-and-variations, for example, or jazz improvisation, or the common (and common-sense) design of juggling, tumbling, trick diving, and acrobatic routines, of fireworks displays, and of very many other things: No sensible magician will likely open his performance with his cleverest trick. But I am anticipating my conclusion.

Second, the most complex point of narrative involvement having been attained—ID4cl) and ID4c2) in the model—the narrative returns without delay to home base. Who wants to see three more simple somersaults after the triple-double-1½-inverse whammy? Alas, the standard frametales seldom recognize this simple principle of both showmanship and dramaturgy.

I mean, of course, the principle of climax and anticlimax. Give Figure 4 a quarter-turn counterclockwise, and you will see the Gibraltarian profile of Freitag's Triangle: exposition, complication, rising action, climax, denouement. Now the order of climax, when applied to dramaturgy, implies more than the simple saving of your best stunt for last and then your getting offstage in a hurry. It implies *dramatic logic:* a denouement which not only follows the climax but is its effect, just as the climax was the effect of its preceding complications. Imposed upon the genre of frametales, an order of climax suggests the possibility of a dramaturgical relationship among the several degrees of narrative involvement: a narrative strategy in which the inner tales bear operatively upon the plot or plots of the outer ones, perhaps even precipitating their several complications, climaxes, denouements.

Back to the questionnaire: We also asked of the existing body of frametale literature what sorts of relations obtain between the framed and framing stories. We found, unsurprisingly, three main kinds of relationships, which shade off into one another and sometimes occur in combination.

First and by far the most frequent is the gratuitous relation: little or no connection between the contents of the framed and the framing stories. The *Decameron,* most of *The 1001 Nights,* most of the *Canterbury Tales,* even most of *The Divine Comedy,* I would assign to this category, the formula for which is:

"Tell me a story." "Okay. Did you ever hear the one about [etc.]? Now you tell *me* one."

Or:

"What are *you* in here for? And you? And you? Mm *hm.*"

Or:

"Today let's all tell stories about people reduced from great fortune to great misfortune; tomorrow, vice-versa."

This is the gratuitous relation.

Second, there is the associative, thematic, or exemplary (or cautionary or prophetic) relationship: "You're not the only person ever deceived by a faithless lover; let me tell you about [etc.]"; or, "That reminds me of the one about the chap who [etc.]"; or, "Here but for the grace of God go you; I too, when I walked the earth, loved a certain lady, until one day [etc.]." Quite a lot of frametale literature is in this category, at least occasionally. Dante's interview with Paolo and Francesca in the circle of the lustful, for example, surely bears on his own situation—his adoration of Beatrice—more directly than does his interview with Count Ugolino in the circle of the traitors, howevermuch Hell might be argued to be all of a piece. Scheherazade's stories about faithless and faithful spouses bear more upon the future of her own story than does "Ali Baba and the Forty Thieves" or "Sinbad the Sailor."

Finally there is the dramaturgical relation, which we subdivided into low-level, middle-level, and high-level pertinencies—understanding these to be not categories but points on a scale.

1. "Aha," Shahryar might be said to say to himself here and there in the *Nights:* "I see now that my own cuckolding is as nothing compared to X's; moreover, the story of Y suggests that my misogyny may have been an overreaction, particularly given such a brave, wise, and beautiful storyteller. Perhaps I should consider not executing my bed-partners *every* morning." This is the low-level dramaturgical relation, distinguished from the thematic only because it portends a general course of action in the frame-story.

2. "Why does Demodocus's song of Troy make you cover your face and weep, stranger?" Or, "The more I see and hear this wise and beautiful storyteller telling her stories and giving birth to my children, the more it occurs to me that I really ought to rescind my murderous domestic policy and marry her." This is the middle-level dramaturgical connection: The framed stories specifically trigger the next major event in the frame-story.

3. "If that trick [or password, or whatever], which I have overheard this talking bird speak of, worked for X, whose predicament was not dissimilar to mine, then it should work for me as well; I'll give it a try." Or, "If that messenger's story is correct, and that shepherd's story, and Tiresias's story, then I have unwittingly murdered my father and sired children upon my mother. That being the case, there is nothing for it but [etc.]."

This last, high-level dramaturgical relation (the "inside" story's climaxing or reversing the action of the "outside" story) is common in stories which, like Sophocles's *Oedipus the King*, are not properly frame-tales; in such cases it is no more than the narrative device of operative delayed exposition, laid on in anecdotal or confessional fashion. In actual frametales, where the material and characters of the framed story are not normally those of the framing story, the high-level dramaturgical relation is almost nonexistent. And once one goes past the second degree of narrative involvement, any relation at all between the third or fourth level, say, and the first is almost certain to be gratuitous.

Yet the model teases us with the possibility not only of breaking the

Five-Degree or Under-the-Tortoise Barrier, but of discovering or imagining a frametale so constructed that the plot of the inmost tale, far from
merely bearing upon the plot of the next tale out, actually springs that
plot, which in turn springs the next, etc., etc., etc., etc., at the point of
concentric climax to which the whole series has systematically been
brought. Indeed, I think that any gutsy writer who happens to be afflicted
with a formalist imagination would, in the face of these observations, feel
compelled to go the existing corpus one better, or two or three better—not
simply in that *Guinness Book of World Records* spirit which leads to
eighty-foot pizzas and fifty-page palindromes, but also—turning now
from the number of degrees of narrative involvement to the dramaturgical potential of the model—in order to actualize an attractive possibility
in the ancient art of storytelling that one's distinguished predecessors
have barely suggested.

Scheherazade herself, I am confident, would approve. I made bold to
have little Dunyazade report, in the novella aforementioned, vis-à-vis her
sister and the Genie:

> They speculated endlessly on such questions as whether a story
> might be framed from inside, as it were, so that the usual relation
> between container and contained would be reversed . . . and (for my
> benefit, I suppose) what human state of affairs such an odd con-
> struction might usefully figure. Or whether one might go beyond the
> usual tale-within-a-tale, beyond even the tales-within-tales-within-
> tales-within-tales which our Genie had found a few instances of . . .
> and conceive a series of, say, *seven* concentric stories-within-stories,
> so arranged that the climax of the innermost would precipitate that
> of the next tale out, and that of the next, et cetera, like a string of
> firecrackers or the chains of orgasms that Shahryar could sometimes
> set my sister catenating.*

It is safe to suppose that the author of that passage must have been
imbued with that very ambition. The fact is, between the time of these
frametale researches in the middle 1960s and the *Chimera* novellas of
circa 1970, I had already written the tale that Scheherazade and her genie
speak of. It is in the series *Lost in the Funhouse;* it is about the Greek general Menelaus, Helen's husband, still in love with his errant wife despite
the Trojan War, of which she impossibly declares herself innocent. It is a
good story, I believe, though not uncomplicated.

---

* *Chimera*, pp. 23–24.

But I want to close by addressing Dunyazade's question: What human state of affairs *might* such odd, even fantastic constructions usefully figure? Why in fact have human beings in so many cultures and centuries been fascinated by tales within tales within etc.? I shall mention two interesting speculations and then venture a homely one of my own.

The first speculation is that of Jorge Luis Borges. Borrowing from his beloved Schopenhauer, Borges declares* that stories within stories appeal to us because they disturb us metaphysically. We are by them reminded, consciously or otherwise, of the next frame out: the fiction of our own lives, of which we are both the authors and the protagonists, and in which our reading of *The 1001 Nights,* say, is a story within our story. This speculation of Borges's strikes me as wise and unexceptionable.

The Bulgarian/Parisian formalist/structuralist critic Tzvetan Todorov,† mentioned earlier, draws a less philosophical but equally interesting parallel between the formal structure of stories within stories, which he calls "embedded stories," and that of a certain syntactic form, "a particular case of subordination, which in fact modern linguistics calls *embedding.*" He illustrates the parallel with a wonderful sentence in German:

> Derjenige, der den Mann, der den Pfahl, der auf der Brücke, der auf dem Weg, der nach Worms führt, liegt, steht, umgeworfen hat, anzeigt, bekommt eine Belohnung.

Richard Howard's translation of this sentence seems to me to miss Todorov's point:

> Whoever identifies the one who upset the post which was placed on the bridge which is on the road which goes to Worms will get a reward.

A word-for-word translation reveals clearly the six degrees of "embedding":

> Whoever the man who the post which on the bridge which on the road which to Worms goes, lies, stood, knocked over, identifies, gets a reward.

---

* e.g., in the essay *"Partial Enchantment in the Quixote,"* in *Other Inquisitions* (Austin, TX: U. of Texas Press, 1965).
† In the essay "Narrative-men," in *The Poetics of Prose,* tr. Richard Howard (Ithaca, NY: Cornell University Press, 1977).

In the German sentence, Todorov remarks,

> ... the appearance of a noun immediately provokes a subordinate clause which, so to speak, tells its story; but since this second clause also contains a noun, it requires in its turn a subordinate clause, and so on, until an arbitrary interruption, at which point each of the interrupted clauses is completed one after the other. The narrative of embedding has precisely the same structure, the role of the noun being played by the character: Each new character involves a new story.

To this fascinating analogy I would add the observation that Todorov's German sentence is constructed much more dramatically than most frametales. What gets postponed in that sentence are the verbs: If the nouns are characters and the subordinate clauses are tales within the frametale of the main clause, the verbs are the dramaturgical climaxes, and the sentence exemplifies the structure not only of frametales but of that high-level dramaturgical relation I spoke of earlier. It is Dunyazade's string of firecrackers.

Todorov asserts that this analogy is no accident; his implication is that narrative structure in general is an echo of deep linguistic structure, and that frametaling reflects, even rises out of, the syntactical property of subordination. He suggests further that the "internal significance" or secret appeal of frametales is that they articulate an essential property (Todorov says the *most* essential property) of all narrative: namely, that whatever else it is about, it is always also about language and about telling; about itself. All fiction, in short, even the most "primary," is "secondary fiction."

Further yet, Todorov argues (with splendid examples from *The 1001 Nights*) that narrating almost literally equals living. Here he joins Borges, but on linguistic rather than metaphysical grounds: We tell stories and listen to them because we live stories and live in them. Narrative equals language equals life: To cease to narrate, as the capital example of Scheherazade reminds us, is to die—literally for her, figuratively for the rest of us. One might add that if this is true, then not only is all fiction fiction about fiction, but all fiction about fiction is in fact fiction about life. Some of us understood that all along.

Whether or not the relation between frametale structure and syntactic structure is causal, as Todorov declares, his examples make clear that the two are isomorphic. Earlier on I remarked, apropos of that hypothetical model of an ideal frametale (Fig. 4), that it reminded me of some common musical forms and of magicians' and acrobats' routines, for example. I conclude, less daringly than Borges and Todorov, by suggesting that frametales fascinate us perhaps because their narrative structure reflects, simply or complexly, at least two formal properties not only of syntax but of much ordinary experience and activity: namely, regression (or digression) and return, and theme and variation. The two are not mutually exclusive, as the structure of this essay itself exemplifies: Digression and return is a variation on the theme of theme and variation. I wish I had time and space to show you how the frametale model reminds me of, for example, trampoline exercises, meal preparation, taxonomy, lovemaking, scientific research, argumentation, psychoanalysis, crime detection, computer programming, court trials, and my grandson's progress from crawling to walking unassisted. If the supposition is valid, these isomorphies will not be hard to see.

But I cannot resist one example from recent personal experience: what I call the horseshoe-nail subspecies of multiple-delayed-climax structures. It will illustrate the shared formal properties of, among other things, tales within tales, the pursuit of happiness, and the painting of sailboat bottoms. Here is the story:

Once upon a time I wished, and indeed I wish still, to lead a reasonably full, good, useful, and therefore happy life. In pursuit of this objective I have made up the best stories I can to entertain and instruct myself and others, and have assisted numerous apprentice writers in the same activity, and have refrained from becoming e.g., a CIA agent, a book reviewer, or an author of either romans à clef or nonfiction novels. On another front, I have fortunately managed to secure a wife whom I enjoy living with, a house on the water that I enjoy living in, and a sailboat to sail on that water from that house with that wife for our innocent recreation when our more serious work is done. All that remains is to cast off.

But before we can cast off we must get launched for the season; and before we can launch for the season we must get fitted out; and fitting out includes the chore of applying new bottom-paint to the hull. But before we can bottom-paint we must wet-sand, mustn't we, and wet-sanding requires both a certain sort of sandpaper, of which we are out, and lots of water, which won't be ours until we have turned on the outside faucet for the spring and rigged up the garden hose. But before I can turn on that faucet I must repack its leaking valve, a chore that requires valve-packing material of which we are also out; and so we must drive into town to the hardware store for valve-packing material and wet-sanding paper; but while we're in town we certainly ought to do the grocery-shopping and stop at the local marina to have a look at the sailboards they've just picked up a dealership in. Which reminds me that I ought to consider adding one more off-campus lecture to my schedule, to cover the cost of the Windsurfer which I promised my sailing-companion for her last birthday and have yet to come across with: Perhaps I shall take time to write a lecture on—well, this whole phenomenon of tasks within tasks, it occurs to me en route to town, as I pause to refuel the car and, while I'm at it, to check the tire pressures and tisk my tongue about the price of fuel and shake my head at the narrative connection, so to speak, between the gasoline in my tank and the American hostages in Teheran—it occurs to me, I say, as I correct my tire-pressures and make a joke with the service-station attendant about inflation, that this whole business is a regression isomorphic not only to the pattern of many mythical heroes' tasks (to marry the princess you must slay the dragon, to kill whom requires the magic weapon, to acquire which requires knowing the magic word which only a certain crazy-lady can tell you, to bribe whom requires etc., etc.), but also to the structure of certain sentences, e.g., this one, and, come to think of it, to a great many other things (are the capers on the grocery list, that we need for the tuna sauce to serve with the cold veal and cham-pagne to celebrate the semester's end and the launching of a new sailing season?) including gourmet cooking, broken-field running, navigation by deduced reckoning, and at least a certain category of frametale litera-ture—*any activity or process, let's say, whose progression is suspended by, yet dependent upon, digression and even regression of an ultimately enabling sort;* et voilà mon essai, which I shall either postpone pursuing till the boat is launched or postpone the launching to pursue, depending upon which—as we prepare the capers to prepare the sauce to prepare the vi-tello tonnato to celebrate the season—seems to us to be the framing situa-tion and which the framed.

Ah, isomorphy! Ah, Scheherazade!

On with the story.

The Prose and Poetry of It All,
or,
Dippy Verses

THIS Friday-piece needs no introduction.

Some seasons ago I published a novel called *Sabbatical: A Romance.*
It is about love and spies and sailing on Chesapeake Bay and deciding not
to have children at this late hour of the world. I myself think well of the
story, and so did numerous of its reviewers, but a number of others
decidedly did not.

Now, it happens that for nearly thirty years I have been pleased to be
a professional teacher as well as a professional writer. Since it behooves a
teacher to be an ongoing learner, still at my age I try to learn from sympathetic critics how to practice my storytelling art better. If it's somebody
else's art they want me to practice—even the art of other writers I admire,
and those are many and various—I shrug my shoulders: The leopard may
polish up his spots, but he can't change them; he may well not wish to.
Moreover, like any battle-wise veteran, I've learned to dismiss criticism
which itself is merely dismissive: hired hatchet-jobs, literary kneecapping,
exercises in the venting of spleen, for which the work under review is
merely the trigger. Such attacks are worth one exasperated sigh and no
more: The world is the world; one is who one is.

Even so, an occasional sand-grain gets under my shell and irritates
my imagination into pearling it over. The novel *Sabbatical: A Romance*
opens with 3½ lines of verse, the last of which modulates into the prose of
the story like this:

There was a story that began,
Said Fenwick Turner: *Susie and Fenn—*

Oh, tell that story! Tell it again!
Wept Susan Seckler. . . .

Graybeard Fenn would be happy to give it another go; we have
fiddled with our tale through this whole sabbatical voyage: down the
Intracoastal in the fall in our cruising sailboat, *Pokey, Wye I.,* from
Chesapeake Bay to the Gulf of Mexico and across to Yucatán; all
about the Caribbean, island-hopping through the mild winter of
1980; and in May through our first long open-ocean passage, from
St. John in the U.S. Virgins direct for the Virginia Capes, Chesapeake Bay, Wye Island, the closing of the circle, sabbatical's end.

One unfriendly reviewer—I have forgotten which; that's my revenge—called these verses "dippy." What he or she said was, "Barth's
new novel begins with some dippy verses. . . ."

Dippy verses!

Well, of course they're dippy. If the reviewer-person had used that
adjective as neutral description, I wouldn't have minded. Those couplets,
both of them, are spoken by the hero of the novel, the male of the couple,
Fenwick Scott Key Turner: a 50-year-old ex-CIA officer currently between careers; ardent sailor and husband; lineal descendant of the author
of "The Star-Spangled Banner"; and himself the author of a troublemak-
ing book about his former employer. Fenwick Turner is now an aspiring
novelist who hates spy novels as much as he loves his wife of seven years,
his Black-Eyed Susan. The verses are a kind of standing joke between
him and that same wife, Susan Rachel Allan Seckler: a sharp young asso-
ciate professor of classical American literature—part Jewish, part Gypsy,
and possibly descended from Edgar Allan Poe. Fenwick is, in fact, as he
repeats this versified standing joke, standing—at the tiller of the couple's
33⅓ foot cruising sailboat *Pokey, Wye I.,* in which they are just complet-
ing that aforementioned nine-month sabbatical voyage, beset by a number of large problems and small adventures. The verses are dippy.

But they are not *simply* dippy. For one thing, they are understood by
speaker, listener, author, and reader (if not by that nameless book-re-
viewer) to be . . . *ironic.* Fenwick Turner *says* "There was a story that
began," etc., but in fact he has not yet begun the story he knows is there
to be told. For another, one of the few things that Fenwick and the author
of *Sabbatical: A Romance* have in common is that neither of us is a
poet—not that professional poets are incapable of perpetrating dippy
verses. Fenwick and I don't even aspire to poetry, much as I, at least,

value much of it. William Faulkner's infamous remark that all novels are failed poems strikes me and Fenwick as far from the truth: Leaving aside all the poems that are failed poems, there are surely a great many novelists who never aspired to serious verse. I am of that number, and so is Fenwick Scott Key Turner. Indeed, much later in the novel, having shared with Susan a flashback-dream that flashes all the way back to the Big Bang that began the story of our universe, the couple experience separate but equal flash*forward* dreams, different in content but similarly apocalyptic, and Fenwick's includes an acknowledgment of his poetical incapacity. Here's Susan's dream first:

Her night's mare has flashed forward from the night before's, and is for the most part impersonal. Our marriage having failed along with the Democratic coalition, the NATO alliance, the U.S. dollar, and Fenwick's heart, to the strains of "The Star-Spangled Banner," Susan witnesses the physical collapse in turn of the continental United States (which splits anticlimactically at the San Andreas fault), then of the solar system, the galaxy, the universe—for some reason all because she and Fenn will have no children. From Fort McHenry's ramparts, which are also *Pokey*'s cockpit, Susan sees the West sink into the sun, the sun into the galactic vortex like Odysseus's ship-timbers into Charybdis, or whatever-it-was into Poe's Maelstrom. *Pokey* himself is now become our galaxy, now our universe, rushing headlong into one of its own Black Holes like that legendary bird that flies in ever-diminishing circles until it vanishes into its own fundament; like [Arthur Gordon] Pym's canoe rushing into the chasm at the foot of the cataract at the southern Pole: a black hole aspirating, with a cosmic shlup, us, U.S., all.

And here's Fenwick's flashforward dream:

His was about failure: professional, personal, physical. Sitting next to him yesterday in the Amtrak coach to Baltimore had been a paunchy self-important late-sixtyish man in soiled summer worsteds—string bow tie, loose dentures, florid face, dandruff on his shoulders like shaken salt from his ill-kempt salt-and-pepper hair—who turned out to be a leading figure in the Virginia Poetry Society, a compulsive self-promoter even unto strangers on a short train ride, and the very odor of failure. In Fenn's dream, Fenn was that man, losing obscure battles with the right-wing Poet Laureate of Maryland. Susan was long since gone, god knows where: She'd left him, and with good reason. Every dollar counted. He had no friends. [His ex-wife] Marilyn Marsh, thriving, prospering, was thick as thieves with [Daughter-in-law] Julie and Grandson Marshall Marsh Turner, named in her honor. But [his son] Orrin's career was going ill, and even Marshall Marsh was doing poorly in school. [Fenn's parents] Chief and Virgie were dead; Fenn himself was sick and sore; every movement was painful; Key Farm was falling down; there was no money to maintain it. Even Wye Island was disappearing, and that circumstance was somehow Fenn's fault. An aide to the President-elect was on the telephone, but Fenwick could find no other rhyme for inaugural than doggerel. He smelled death: It smelled like the breath of that Virginia Poetry Society man.

Now, that is not a dream that I have ever had—and anyhow, Fenwick Scott Key Turner n'est pas moi. He is a better sailor than I am, for one thing, with a bigger boat. Charles Darwin once praised Charles Dickens for "[giving] us heroes we can admire and heroines we can love." Another function of art, surely, is to provide us with larger sailboats than we can in fact afford. But I am a better novelist than Fenwick is; if he has a longer boat, I have a longer bibliography, and enough experience in the medium he aspires to to know that doggerel and other varieties of dippy verse have an ancient and honorable place in that medium. Two wonderful things about the capital-N Novel are that of all the genres of literature—maybe even of all the forms of art—it is 1) the most hospitable to amateurs and 2) the most accommodating to contamination of every sort.

Let us consider the first of these: It would strain plausibility, if not possibility, to imagine a 50-year-old with no previous real experience in the medium making a successful debut as a Wagnerian Heldentenor, I think, or a director of Chekhov's plays, or a sculptor of bronzes. A character in a novel who aspired to such a debut would almost have to be drawn with dramatic irony: *He* may think he'll make it, but *we* know that probably nobody ever picked up a violin, say, or a stonecutter's chisel and did it right the first time. Yet it is a famous blessing of the Novel, to the chagrin of many professional novelists and the despair of agents and editors buried under over-the-transom manuscripts, as they're called in the trade, that numerous amateurs *have* done it more or less right the first time, and numerous professionals have never equalled their first published effort. The list is long, and it runs the length of the genre's history, from those middle-aged beginners (as novelists) Cervantes and Defoe and Richardson, through the great flood of nineteenth-century amateurs like Lewis Carroll (but *everybody* in the nineteenth century wrote novels), down to such modern late starters and out-of-practically nowherers as

Joseph Conrad and Amos Tutuola, let's say—not to mention such mainly popular successes as William F. Buckley, Jr., John Erlichman of Watergate fame, and the Margarets—from Margaret Truman back through Margaret Mitchell to Marguerite the Queen of Navarre.*

Well, okay: Margaret of Navarre's *Heptameron* of 1558 isn't really a novel; it's a frametale cycle on the order of Boccaccio's and Chaucer's and Giambattista Basile's and Scheherazade's. That brings us to the other characteristic of the form which I mentioned admiringly a while ago: its almost anarchical flexibility and its capacity not only for absorbing but for thriving upon all sorts of extrinsic input, as it were, like immigrant America once upon a time, or the folkloristic recipe for stone soup. If I don't go along with Faulkner on the matter of novelists as failed poets, I very much sympathize with his stated wish to be reborn as a turkey-buzzard; I even take his remarks on that subject to be descriptive of the art he practiced. Faulkner said he'd like to come back as a turkey-buzzard because the animal has no natural enemies and can feed on anything. *I* say that the novel is your great turkey-buzzard of art.

What's more, it is a protean turkey-buzzard, which can pass itself off as everything from a hummingbird to an ostrich. What do the following objects have in common: Flaubert's *Madame Bovary;* Capote's and Mailer's "nonfiction novels"; Alex Haley's whatyoucallit novel *Roots;* Dino Buzzati's comic-strip novel of the late 1960s; Marc Saporta's unbound, unpaginated, randomly packaged novel-in-a-box of about the same vintage; Nikos Kazantzakis's long verse-novel, as some have called it, *The Odyssey: a modern sequel;* the latest pornographic photonovel from Hamburg, Paris, or Rome; Marcel Proust's zillion-word *roman fleuve, The Remembrance of Things Past;* and Robert Coover's very short new novel *Spanking the Maid,* which could have been published as a long short story?†

Damned if I know. Even Randall Jarrell's wonderful definition of the novel—a prose narrative fiction of a certain length that has something wrong with it—has several things wrong with it, as can be seen by apply-

---

* I am delighted by the news (Friday, January 13, 1984) that my American publisher, Putnam's, has just bought a 1176-page novel by an eighty-eight-year-old resident of a nursing home in Xenia, Ohio, who has spent the last half-century settling the narrative score with Sinclair Lewis for poor-mouthing the midwest in *Babbitt* and *Main Street.* "I wanted to do as artistic a piece as possible," declares the author, Ms. Helen Santmyer of Hospitality Home East in Xenia. And I'll bet she did, too.

† And in fact was, in *The Iowa Review,* before the Grove Press version appeared.

ing it to the list above: Some of those items aren't prose, some can scarcely be called narrative, some aren't fiction, and their length is wildly uncertain. It doesn't even quite fit *Madame Bovary,* which Nabokov among others declares has nothing wrong with it. The novel is an essentially existentialistic form whose existence not only precedes its essence, but keeps redefining its essence right out of existence. It is a (usually, mainly) verbal Watts Towers, a backyard cathedral made sometimes out of whatever wretched refuse lies to the builder's hand. It is a literary osprey's nest, which may *look* thrown together like a pile of pick-up-sticks, but which in the best cases will withstand storms of criticism and the shifting winds of fashion.

I shall now digress at length upon the subject of ospreys' nests: Faulkner had his favorite bird; I have mine. The osprey, or fish-hawk, a cousin of the eagle, builds its big ramshackle rickety-looking nest in the crotch of a dead tree in or near tidewater when it has to rely upon nature for a homesite. However, it much prefers the osprey platforms built for it by conservationists: a $10 square of marine-grade plywood mounted well above the highwater line on a $125 piling driven into a river bottom not far from shore. And even more than an official osprey platform, it likes a U.S. Coast Guard navigational day beacon as a building site: Since their purpose is to mark shoals, day beacons satisfy all the osprey's basic requirements—a sturdy platform on a sturdy post well above the highwater mark in shallow water not far from shore—plus the bonus of the beacon's dayboards, which serve as windbreaks and side braces for the nest. Having a very bright light flash every 2½ seconds or so all night long a few inches from his head doesn't seem to bother your osprey: So ideal is a Coast Guard day beacon as a nesting site that you are unlikely ever to see one without a grand osprey-house upon it, and so enthusiastically do the ospreys build there that very frequently their nests come to obscure the lights which mariners depend upon to identify day beacons by night. The notice *Light obscured* (*osprey*) is a refrain even today in the list of "Discrepancies in Aids to Navigation" in the Coast Guard's weekly bulletin *Local Notices to Mariners,* and it used to be even more so.

For decades and decades, what the Coast Guard did, assisted by local mariners, was routinely to destroy such ospreys' nests; and the ospreys, being ospreys, routinely rebuilt them. Everybody was unhappy. The Coast Guard was unhappy because destroying osprey nests is expensive, disagreeable, time-consuming nuisance work that could never really be kept up with even in the make-work 1930s. The mariners were unhappy because day-beacon lights were still very often obscured, and when you're sailing at night and can't find a day-beacon light that is supposed to be there, you're likely to pile up on a shoal, either because you've made a serious navigational error or because you haven't but erroneously conclude that you have. The ospreys were unhappy for obvious reasons. And the conservationists, in their increasing number, were unhappy because the ospreys in their decreasing number were unhappy. Everybody's claim was legitimate, but the claims seemed irreconcilable.

We are not done with this digression.

Attempts to design a day beacon uninviting to ospreys failed: You need a platform on that pile to support those day boards and that battery box with its light. Attempts to lure the ospreys away from the day beacons with those special platforms built exclusively for ospreys failed: The osprey population quickly correlates exactly with the nesting sites available to it. The number of ospreys went up, but the number of obscured day-beacon lights did not go down. Surprisingly late in the day—just a few years ago, I believe—some anonymous genius was inspired to a simple, cheap, permanent solution to this dilemma that made all parties happy: Instead of them obscuring our lights and us destroying their nests, why not leave the day beacons and the osprey nests exactly as they are and *raise the light?* Raise the light a meter or so above the battery box on a simple, sturdy, skinny length of pipe, and all problems vanish; all claims are reconciled. The ospreys are as happy as it is given to ospreys to be. The conservationists are as happy (on this one subject) as it is given to conservationists to be. The mariner knows that if the light that ought to be visible by now in fact is not, the fault is very probably his; we cannot call that condition happiness, but at least it's a less equivocal and less frequent misery. And the Coast Guard—that most beneficent, most useful, most pacific, most deserving, least well funded of our more or less armed services*—its resources diminishing even as the ospreys' resources increase, can now turn its strained attention to higher priorities. If we still see the notice *Light obscured (osprey)* in the *Local Notices to Mariners,* that is because the USCG can't afford to make even so cheap and easy a modification right across the board. They fix a few every year.

Meanwhile, I never sail past such a modified day beacon without admiring both the osprey's crazy nest with that wonderful piece of pipe

---

* The U.S. Coast Guard is not, strictly speaking, a branch of the military, though its cutters are lightly armed.

sticking up beside it, through it, anyhow well above it, and the simple elegance of the Coast Guard's solution to a seemingly irreconcilable dilemma—a solution which may have taken the human imagination decades to come up with, but which the osprey imagination couldn't equal except perhaps in evolutionary time. In my innocence I can't help wondering why Israelis and Arabs, for example, or Iraqis and Iranis, or (to take a really thorny example) modernists and antimodernists, don't simply somehow raise the light a little higher above their conflicting and more or less legitimate claims. No doubt there are good reasons other than insufficient imagination—but the example of the day-beacon lights makes me wonder.

Back now to the important subject of dippy verses as a legitimate contaminant of novels. My wife and I rounded one particular Chesapeake Bay day beacon last summer closely enough for us to observe, while Ma and Pa Osprey circled our mast, kvetching about invasion of privacy, that in addition to the usual sticks, straws, battery box, and very homely baby ospreys, their nest incorporated several odd lengths of fishline, one with plastic float and hooks still attached, a strip of what looked like toilet paper, a ribbon of Dacron sailcloth (probably a furling gasket from somebody's mainsail), a twisted chrome-plated piece of what was doubtless Detroit automobile trim, and other, less recognizable odds and ends. It had also become a sort of polyglot condominium, in whose lower reaches noncompeting species such as house sparrows and beach swallows had built their own small nests, while over all rose the beacon on its pipe—and I thought about the Novel.

I wish some book reviewers, too, would raise their lights a bit. Verses, I repeat, even dippy ones—perhaps especially dippy ones—have an ancient and honorable place in booklength works of prose fiction. I shall not presume to judge the dippiness of, e.g., Lisa Erdman's long poem which comprises the "Don Giovanni" section of D. M. Thomas's novel *The White Hotel,* or Warren Penfield's long poem "Loon Lake" in E. L. Doctorow's novel of the same title, or John Shade's 555-line poem which Charles Kinbote annotates to make Nabokov's novel *Pale Fire,* or even Stephen Dedalus's villanelle composed in the closing chapter of Joyce's *Portrait of the Artist as a Young Man.* If you happen to enjoy those poems straight, on their own merits—as I rather do—the novelist is ahead of the game (Doctorow's "Loon Lake" poem appeared in the *Kenyon Review,* over Doctorow's name, before the novel was published). But as a rule you won't find such poems-within-novels excerpted for separate publication or included in serious anthologies of poetry: Lewis Carroll's "Jabber-wocky," "The Walrus and the Carpenter," etc. are wonderful exceptions to this general rule. If on the other hand you find such poems as those just mentioned less than immortal as poems in their own right, all the way back to Rabelais's avant-garde pattern-poem "Ode to a Bottle" in *Gargantua and Pantagruel*—even if you find some of them a touch dippy—the novelist's tracks are covered. For a poem incorporated into the text of a novel—or a page of musical score so incorporated, or a play, a line drawing, a photograph, even a political or philosophical idea—is no longer its innocent existential self, any more than that bit of fishline worked into that osprey's nest is still a line for catching fish. Now: If such a line should happen also to dangle accidentally into the water at flood tide, say, and accidentally catch fish for the ospreys to eat, we are permitted to be charmed by that coincidence; but if it doesn't, we shall not therefore call it a dippy piece of fishline.

No need to belabor this simple point, except to say that unlike day beacons and osprey nests, which can be said each to have a single "true" function and other accidental ones (such as serving as symbols in a lecture on the novel), a novel may be an osprey-nest of intentions as well as of materials. We know that certain novelists take their political, social, philosophical, even mystical-religious ideas quite as seriously as they take their literary ideas, and may even regard their novels primarily as launching platforms for those ideas, the way the osprey regards the day beacon as a launching platform for fledgling ospreys. To such novelists—whose ranks include not only mediocrities and cranks but many great artists as well, from Charles Dickens to Gabriel García Márquez—I think we may say, "Go to it—so long as you don't obscure the light." Which is to say, so long as we are permitted to admire your work for other reasons.

Back to dippy verses. My own mentor in that art, as in some others, is Scheherazade. *The 1001 Nights,* in Richard Burton's ten-volume 1885 edition, comprises, in addition to the great primary frametale of Scheherazade and King Shahryar, 169 secondary tales, by my count, told by Scheherazade to the King (plus one told to her by her father the Grand Vizier), 87 third-level tales told by the characters in Scheherazade's second-level tales, and 11 fourth-level tales told by the characters in those third-level tales told by the characters in the second-level tales told by Scheherazade, the heroine of the nameless author's primary tale: some 268 tales in all. The work also includes, by Burton's estimate, about 1,400 poems or parts of poems: approximately 10,000 lines of verse in all, very

many of which—in translation, at least, and across the centuries and cultures—strike *this* admiring reader as fairly dippy. But I couldn't care less,
and I can't imagine that magnificent catch-all work without those bright
bits of bunting worked into its construction. King Shahryar himself, at
the end of those 1001 nights, describes Scheherazade's fiction as consisting of "proverbs and parables, chronicles and pleasantries, quips and
jests, stories and anecdotes, dialogues and histories and elegies and other
verses. . . ." In short, the works. And it works.

As for dippy verses in my own fiction: I'm pleased to find that I can
virtually review my life's work under that aspect, and now I virtually
shall. My first published novel, *The Floating Opera,* contains a few, in the
showboat-show from which that novel takes its name. My original intention, in fact, had been to do the whole novel in the form and format of the
turn-of-the-century American blackface minstrel show, but by the time
this particular osprey's nest was built, the show was reduced to part of
one chapter and the poetry abridged to a single quatrain in the show,
spoken by Mister Bones to Mister Tambo. Never mind that quatrain: It's
apprentice dippy; mere fledgling dippy.

Two novels later, in *The Sot-Weed Factor,* I was able to spread my
wings much farther, dippy-versewise, since that novel's hero is a real-life
Colonial American poet, Ebenezer Cooke of Maryland, whose real-life
poem, so to speak—"The Sot-Weed Factor"—is the armature of my
novel. Cooke was one of our earliest American poets and would be one of
our dippiest were it not that his medium is satire. Indeed, I believe him to
have been the first American satirist. He was an Augustan poet much influenced by Samuel Butler's *Hudibras;* his characteristic vehicle is Butler's mock-heroic couplet. E.g., from Cooke's original "Sot-Weed Factor"
of 1708:

> The Indians call their wat'ry Wagon
> *Canoe:* a Vessel none can brag on.

Pretty dippy. Or the luckless tobacco-dealer's closing malediction
upon the province of Maryland, which has used him so ill:

> Embarqu'd and waiting for a Wind,
> I leave this dreadful Curse behind.
> May *Canniballs* transported o'er the Sea
> Prey on these Slaves, as they have done on me;

May never Merchant's trading Sails explore
This cruel, this Inhospitable Shoar;
But left abandon'd by the World to starve,
May they sustain the fate they well deserve:
May they turn Salvage, or as Indians wild,
From Trade, Converse, and Happiness exil'd;
Recreant to Heaven, may they adore the Sun,
And into Pagan Superstitions run
For Vengeance ripe—
May Wrath Divine then lay these Regions wast
Where no Man's Faithful, nor a Woman Chast!

The hudibrastic couplet, like Herpes simplex, is a contagion more easily caught than cured. It was my pleasure to compose a great many hudibrastic couplets for my fictionalized Ebenezer Cooke, of which two brief specimens, the first and the last, will serve here. The first is from early in the novel, when, as the opening paragraph declares:

In the last years of the seventeenth century there was to be found among the fops and fools of the London coffee-houses one rangy, gangling flitch called Ebenezer Cooke, more ambitious than talented, and yet more talented than prudent, who, like his friends-in-folly, all of whom were supposed to be educating at Oxford or Cambridge, had found the sound of Mother English more fun to game with than her sense to labor over, and so rather than applying himself to the pains of scholarship, had learned the knack of versifying, and ground out quires of couplets after the fashion of the day, afroth with *Joves* and *Jupiters,* aclang with jarring rhymes, and string-taut with similes stretched to the snapping point.

These particular dippy verses Cooke writes at Magdalene College, Cambridge, after an undergraduate lecture on philosophical materialism. He leaves the lecture hall, we're told, with no more in his notebook than:

Old *Plato* saw both Mind and Matter;
Thomas Hobbes, naught but the latter.
Now poor Tom's Soul doth fry in Hell:
Shrugs *GOD,* " 'Tis immaterial."

In the course of the story Cooke perpetrates many another hudibrastic, for which I am responsible—on love, innocence, sea-voyaging, the fall from innocence—as well as the rough draft of "The Sot-Weed Fac-

tor" poem itself. And since no one knows when the historical Ebenezer
Cooke died or where he's buried, it was my privilege to close the novel
with a dippy epitaph, which I have the disillusioned old poet compose for
himself:

> Here moulds a posing, foppish Actor,
> Author of *The Sot-Weed Factor,*
> Falsely prais'd. Take Heed, who sees this
> Epitaph; look ye to *Jesus!*
>
> Labour not for Earthly Glory:
> *Fame's* a fickle Slut, and whory.
> From thy *Fancy's* chast Couch drive her:
> He's a Fool who'll strive to swive her!
> E.C., Gent, P^t & L^t of M^d

Well. Since art is long—some of my art particularly—and life is short
(as Horace remarks in one of *his* verses), I shall spare you my dippy-verse
satire of Sophocles in *Giles Goat-Boy.* Also the dippy effusions of my
stranded, nameless Homeric bard in *Lost in the Funhouse* (in the story
"Anonymiad"), who is reduced to making love to empty wine-jugs and
inventing alternative endings to the Trojan War, which he writes on goat-
skins and publishes by floating them off in the empty amphorae from his
desert island. Oh well, I will read you one dippy lyric of his; it's called
"The Minstrel's Last Lay," and it's written in extremis—a favorite verse-
form of dippy poets. First he invokes his muse:

> Twice-handled goddess! Sing through me the boy
> Whom Agamemnon didn't take to Troy,
> But left behind to see his wife stayed chaste.
> Tell, Muse, how Clytemnestra maced
> Her warden into song, made vain his heart
> With vision of renown; musick the art
> Wherewith was worked self-ruin by a youth
> Who'd sought in his own art some music truth
> About the world and life, of which he knew
> Nothing. Tell how ardent his wish grew
> To autograph the future, wherefore he
> Let sly Aegisthus ship him off to see
> The Wide Real World. Sing of the guile
> That fetched yours truly to a nameless isle,
> By gods, men, and history forgot,
> To sing his sorry self.

And die. And rot. And feed his silly carcass to the birds.

But not before he'd penned a few last words,

inspired by the dregs and lees of the muse herself, at whom, Zeus willing, he'll have a final go before he corks her for good and casts her adrift, vessel of his hopeless hope. The Minstrel's Last Lay.

> Once upon a time
> I composed in witty rhyme
> And poured libations to the muse Erato.
>
> Merope would croon,
> "Minstrel mine, a lay! A tune!"
> "From bed to verse," I'd answer; "that's my motto."
>
> Stranded by my foes,
> Nowadays I write in prose,
> Forsaking measure, rhyme, and honeyed diction;
>
> *Amphora*'s my muse:
> When I finish off the booze,
> I hump the jug and fill her up with fiction.

You shall likewise be spared the occasional verses floating through the ample waters of the novel *LETTERS,* some of them allegedly composed by a contemporary lineal descendant of Maryland's original Poet Laureate, Ebenezer Cooke. Instead, I shall now end my lecture twice: first with the ending of *Sabbatical: A Romance,* which closes as it opened, with you-know-what. The good ship *Pokey, Wye I.,* has come to anchor behind Cacaway, an uninhabited island off Chesapeake Bay. Susan and Fenwick have not resolved all the problems and mysteries that beset their sabbatical voyage; almost certainly they will not have children of their own. But they have decided to write their story, the story of their literal and figurative voyage. (The text throughout, I ought to explain, has been appropriately star-spangled with footnotes—Susan being a working academic and Fenwick the descendant of F. S. Key—and the couple will append their names to its bottom line in a final such note.) Susan says:

> If that's going to be our story, then let's begin it at the end and end at the beginning, so we can go on forever. Begin with our living happily ever after.

Fenwick says he doesn't quite get it and then cries I get it! Oh Susan!

Yet we both know that not even a story is *ever* after. Here come more storms toward Cacaway, and we've yet to retrieve that dinghy. No matter, there's light left. Happily after, Susan prompts, unfastening. Come on. Right readily her grateful mate complies; we commence as we would conclude, that they lived

Happily after, to the end
Of Fenwick and Susie. . . .*

---

* Susan.
Fenn.

Finally, as a kind of footnote to that footnote, I shall read you the opening of my work in progress. A sort of opposite-sex twin to *Sabbatical: A Romance,* this novel, too, involves a couple of Chesapeake sailors: a man rather younger than Fenwick Turner, named Peter Sagamore; a woman somewhat older than Susan Seckler, named Katherine Sherritt. But their situation, as shall be seen, is rather the reverse of Fenwick's and Susan's. If I am spared to write it, the book will be called *The Tidewater Tales: A Novel.* It will be divided into two parts, the first called "Our Story," the second called "Our Stories." And Part I, "Our Story," will begin with the following dippy verses, after its opening subtitle. The subtitle is:

KATHERINE SHERRITT SAGAMORE,
THIRTY-NINE YEARS OLD AND NINE MONTHS PREGNANT,
BECALMED IN OUR ENGINELESS SMALL SAILBOAT
AT THE END OF A STICKY JUNE CHESAPEAKE AFTERNOON
AMID EVERY SIGN OF THUNDERSTORMS APPROACHING FROM ACROSS
THE BAY,
AND SPEAKING AS SHE SOMETIMES DOES IN VERSE,
SETS HER HUSBAND A TASK.

The dippy verses are these:

Tell me a story of women and men
Like us: like us in love for ten
Years, lovers for seven, spouses
Two, or two point five. Their house's
Increase is the tale I wish you'd tell.

Why did that perfectly happy pair,
Like us, decide this late to bear
A child? Why toil so to conceive
One (or more), when they both believe
The world's aboard a handbasket bound for hell?

Well?

Sentimentality, was it? A yen
Like ours to be one person, blend
Their flesh forever, so to speak—
Although the world could end next week
And that dear incarnation be H-bomb-fried?

Maybe they thought that by joining their
(Like our) so different genes—her
Blue-blooded, his blue-collared—they'd make
A blue-eyed *Wunderkind* who'd take
The end of civilization in his/her stride?

What pride!

Or maybe they weren't thinking at all,
But (unlike us) obeyed the call
Of blind instinct and half-blind custom:
"Reproduce your kind and trust 'em
To fortune's winds and tides, life's warmth and frost!"?

Perhaps they considered all the above
(Like us, exactly)—instinct, love,
The world's decline from bad to worse
In more respects than the reverse—
And decided to pay, but not to count, the cost . . .

Fingers crossed.

Well:

Tell me their story as if it weren't ours,
But *like* ours enough so that the Powers
Which drive and steer good stories might
Fetch *them* beyond *our* present plight,

And navigate the tale itself to an ending more rich and strange
than everyday realism ordinarily permits; a bottom line that will
make art if not sense out of the predicament your sperm and my egg,
with a lot of help from their producers, have got us into; in short, yet
another rhyme as it were for *cost* to end this poem with, even if we

have to abandon verse for prose or prose for verse to reach it: a rhyme less discouraging, more pregnant so to speak with hope, than *lost.*

Okay?

The American New Novel

IN OCTOBER 1982, New York University and the French Embassy co-sponsored a celebration of the *Nouveau roman* and a reunion of several of the French New Novelists themselves, who dominated the French literary scene not so long ago and are still vigorously productive: Nathalie Sarraute, Alain Robbe-Grillet, Claude Simon, Robert Pinget, and the younger writer Monique Wittig. As a diplomatic afterthought, the university invited a few U.S. novelists to discuss the influence of the *Nouveau roman* upon American fiction or, alternatively, the question whether there is an American literary phenomenon comparable to that French one: an American New Novel. The French writers—every one of whom I admire—politely attended the American discussion, which opened with statements and brief readings by Jonathan Baumbach, Robert Coover, John Hawkes, and myself.

I have come all the way from Baltimore to New York to report to you that to the best of my understanding there is no such animal as the American New Novel: not in anything like the sense that we speak of the French *Nouveau roman* of the 19-late-50s and 60s.

Certainly among new American novels there is no sign of the American New Novel. I myself have published a new American novel in this calendar year, and as is my custom when that occurs, I keep a little list of who else has done likewise among those of my countrymen upon whom I maintain a watchful eye. That little list includes all three of my fellow panelists: Mr. Baumbach (*My Father, More or Less*), Mr. Coover (*Spanking the Maid*), and Mr. Hawkes (*Virginie: Her Two Lives*). It includes, in chronological order, Saul Bellow, Paul Theroux, John Cheever, Jerzy Kosinski, Thomas McGuane, Anne Tyler, John Gardner, Bernard Malamud, and Joyce Carol Oates, as well as story collections by I. B. Singer and Ann Beattie. This has been a bountiful American literary

year, and there is still a big quarter of it to go: new novels by Kurt Vonnegut, Don DeLillo, Alice Walker, and a good many more. But I do not
detect among these books, several of which are no doubt both good and
important, anything resembling a noteworthy new general direction in
the U.S. novel.

Nor do I when I think about what we U.S. novelists have been up to
over the last dozen years or so. I suppose that the term *Black Humorists*
described something reasonably real and reasonably significant back in
the American 1950s. Such later labels as *Fabulators* and *Metafictionists*
have a certain descriptive power, but what they describe strikes me as
comparatively special and minor, rather than a general energizing
spirit—though some individual works tagged with those labels are good
works.

Then there is the adjective *postmodern,* the meaning of which I have
done my best to help confuse. I continue to believe that that adjective describes a very approximately shared inclination among numerous writers
and other artists in the second half of our Western twentieth century: an
inclination to work out in their individual ways, as I have put it elsewhere, not the next best thing after modernism, but the *best next* thing
after modernism. However, that inclination cuts across national lines;
what's more, smarter people than myself have let me know that what *I*
mean by postmodern fiction isn't what the term really means at all. So
forget it.

What else is there? In a conversation recently with a newly notable
younger U.S. realist/minimalist short-story writer, who happens also to
be an ex-alcoholic, I spoke of another younger U.S. newly notable mini-
malist/realist short-story writer, whom I learned was also a former alcoholic; our conversation then turned to a third writer, a sometime student
of mine, now also a younger ex-alcoholic minimalist et cetera. Since I had
been seeing their names lumped together now and then in the *Times* book
supplement, I was moved to coin the term Post-Alcoholic Blue-Collar
Minimalist Hyperrealism to describe this potentially significant new literary phenomenon. I suppose Gore Vidal would be pleased; he has frequently sneered at what he calls the Alcoholic American Republic of
Letters. But it is not my mission in life to please Gore Vidal. In any case,
one of those three authors-on-the-wagon, or on the bandwagon, has unfortunately since relapsed, and anyhow they're all mainly short-story
writers, not novelists. (In fact—setting aside the alcohol, the "hyper," and
the hype—I believe the new flowering of the American realist short story,

as represented by the likes of Frederick Barthelme, Ann Beattie, Raymond Carver, Stephen Dixon, Barry Hannah, Mark Helprin [a hyperromantic, that one], Bobbie Ann Mason, and Mary Robison, to be the most noteworthy recent development in American fiction. But so rapidly does the literary weather change, I feel impelled to date this observation *3 P.M., October 2, 1982,* and fix the latitude and longitude as well.)

My friends, what I believe is this: That when it comes to movements, coherent ideologies, and the issuing of articulate position papers, the French arrange these things better. That now and then an authentic phenomenon appears, even in non-Gallic literatures, interesting and homogenous enough to make a few nonridiculous generalizations about; and that the appearance of such phenomena makes life easier for teachers, art historians, and culture watchers—for anybody interested in understanding and registering what's going on around us, since we can think and talk only with the aid of categories. But I take the tragic view of categories (that they are, though indispensable, more or less arbitrary); and I believe further that inhomogenous, nondescript ideological interregnums, such as novelistic North America may be enjoying presently, may also be fecund for the production of great individual works of art, which are at least as valuable as general aesthetic movements. Since the novel is, of all the genres of literature, perhaps the least categorizable, I believe that it is as likely to thrive in an incoherent period as in a coherent one.

Therefore I advise the culture not to worry if there is no American New Novel. The culture has more important things to worry about. More to the personal point, I believe that the odds against my writing an excellent new American novel myself, which I aspire to do, are not worsened in such an interregnum, if we are in fact in one. Those odds may even be improved.

And so I wish the old French New Novel good luck and good health, as I wish the newer Latino literary boom good luck and good health—with an admiration uncontaminated by envy.

Don't Count on It

A NOTE ON THE NUMBER OF *THE 1001 NIGHTS*

THIS latest Friday-piece was written after my fiction currently in progress was firmly under way—a book called *The Tidewater Tales: A Novel*—and just before I decided to spend a year's Fridays reviewing and assembling these pieces.

Scheherazade again, examined intimately indeed. It seems a fit note to end the book upon.

I delivered this as a lecture on a warm evening in June 1983 on an outdoor basketball court at the American School in Tangier, Morocco—the city which inspired Rimsky-Korsakov to write his *Scheherazade Suite* and Matisse to paint his odalisques—while over us hung the new crescent moon which signaled the end of the holy month of Ramadan. There was even a bright planet in the moon's embrace: the very sign of Islam. At one point I was obliged to pause in my reading while from the lighted minarets of nearby mosques the muezzins cried the faithful to evening prayer. It was a moving and a cautionary moment: Here as elsewhere, I have checked my amateur scholarship with experts where I could, but I am no Arabist. On the other hand, my long infatuation with Scheherazade has little to do with the egregious Western "orientalism" deplored by Edward Said and other Arabists: It is simply one storyteller's professional (in this instance, all but inexhaustible) interest in another. I may well, some future Friday at Langford Creek, come back to her yet again—but I don't count on it.

After centuries, we still haven't settled on an English name for the thing. Its Arabic title, *Kitab Alf Laylah Wah Laylah,* means literally *The Thousand-Night-One-Night Book.* Usually it's Englished into *The Book of the Thousand Nights and a Night,* or just *The Thousand and One Nights.* About as often it's called *The Arabian Nights' Entertainment;* popularly it has always been *The Arabian Nights.*

What's more, few of us have actually *read* it, in anything like its entirety, though the image of Scheherazade, spinning out tales for 1001 nights to amuse the king and save her life, is surely among the top ten or a dozen on anybody's great-literary-image list. *The Arabian Nights,* among other reasons because it belongs to Islamic rather than to Western literature, is not to be found on American high school and college reading lists. Unless we have sought it out on our own, we are likely to know it if at all from a children's version, radically expurgated as well as heroically abridged, and probably illustrated by N. C. Wyeth. Most moderately cultured Americans are more familiar with Rimsky-Korsakov's Scheherazade Suite and Marc Chagall's illustrations than with the actual text that inspired them. All, however, have heard of Aladdin and of Ali Baba (both of whose stories, by the way, are rejected by Richard Burton as late-comers and excluded from his authoritative ten-volume 1885 version of the *Nights*); all remember that the nights numbered 1001; and nearly all remember that telling those stories over all those nights was a life-or-death matter for Scheherazade, though fewer recall just why.

Not much has been written in English *about* this wonderful book, either, and so I propose to review the framing-situation of the *Nights* in some detail and make a few general remarks upon the work as a whole before addressing the particular question why there are 1001 nights' entertainment—rather than, say, 101, 999, or 2002—and speculating a bit upon Scheherazade's narrative-sexual strategy as it is implied (but never made explicit) in the text.

According to Burton's famous Terminal Essay (X:93), the frame-story of the *Nights* is "purely Persian, perfunctorily Arabised," and in its present form dates from about the thirteenth century, though its archetypes are older (the tales themselves are from all over the oriental map and date from as early as the eighth century—the beast fables—to as late as the sixteenth—Ali Baba, Aladdin, & Co.). It is a much more elaborately developed frame-story than the frames of the *Divine Comedy,* the *Decameron,* or the *Canterbury Tales.* It is also, like many of the stories Scheherazade herself tells, at once funny and terrifying, fantastic and realistic, delicate and scabrous—Goethe, like the rest of us, was particularly taken by this mixture of qualities in the *Nights,* which he registers in a journal entry on the tale "How Abu Hasan Farted," Night 410—and the mainspring of this frame-story is frankly sexual.

Once upon a time there were two kings, brothers, each of whom thought himself happily married. One day the younger brother, Shah Zaman of Samarkand, inadvertently discovers that his wife is having a vigorous affair with a filthy kitchen-slave. Shocked, the young king kills the lovers in flagrante delicto, deputizes his vizier to administer the kingdom, and takes psychological refuge in the court of his older brother, Shahryar, King of "the Islands of India and China."

Shahryar recognizes that Shah Zaman is traumatized, but cannot induce him to say what his trouble is. Presently, by another accident, Shah Zaman discovers that Shahryar's wife is cuckolding *her* husband even more massively and revoltingly than his own wife cuckolded him—with a gibbering, slavering, hideous giant of a blackamoor named Sa'ad al-din Saood, who swings down from the trees like an ape at her signal and humps her ferociously in the palace courtyard while all her maidservants and mamelukes go to it as well. This spectacle cheers the young king right up; he tells his own misfortune now to Shahryar—who swears ominously by Allah that if *his* wife ever did that to *him,* he'd kill a thousand women in revenge, despite the fact that "that way madness lies." Shah Zaman obligingly arranges for Shahryar to witness what he himself has just witnessed (it happens every time the king leaves the palace), and Shahryar, interestingly, is too shocked at first to take any revenge at all. Like Shah Zaman, he turns the affairs of government over to his grand vizier, and the brothers withdraw together to wander the world in chaste and appalled incognito.

Thus might their story have ended, but for a grimly funny sexual adventure just a few days later in which they are the unwilling participants. In effect, a young woman rapes them both, under threat of death if they don't service her, in order to revenge herself upon an evil Ifrit who keeps her under septuple lock and key—seven chests within chests, each padlocked—for his exclusive sexual pleasure. She adds the brothers' sealrings to those of 570 other men with whom she has cuckolded her terrible captor (the Ifrit, who stole her from her betrothed on her bridal eve, habitually falls asleep after unlocking the seven chests and raping his prisoner; though she dare not flee, she obliges any passing male to mount her, on pain of waking the demon up). The episode demonstrates to the brothers that their wives were no exceptions to the general rule: a rule which they interpret misogynistically, in the spirit of John Donne's "Go and catch a falling star,"* but which may certainly be interpreted otherwise. Each resolves to go back to his kingdom, resume direction of the government, take a virgin to bed every night, and have her executed in the morning, before she can cuckold him.

---

* "And swear / No where / Lives a woman true and fair," etc.

Of Shah Zaman we hear no more until the end of the story, ten volumes later, by when, presumably—the text gives no numbers, but internal evidence permits certain estimates, as shall be seen—he will have deflowered and decapitated some 2002 Samarkandian virgins. As for Shahryar, he first executes his wife and her twenty wanton maidservants, half of whom were those male mamelukes in harem drag. It is not stated whether he gets the blackamoor Sa'ad al-Din Saood down out of the trees. He then commands his vizier to procure for his pleasure a fresh virgin every night and to decapitate her in the morning.

In this wise he continues, the text tells us, "for the space of three years," thus more than making good, we may note in passing, his casual earlier oath. Here too the text gives no specific number, nor does it remind us explicitly of that vow to Allah; but it is tempting to round down the body count from approximately 1062—three Islamic yearsworth of victims—to the aforethreatened thousand. Whether or not "that way madness lies," the result is political and social chaos in the Islands of India and China: The whole populace prays to Allah to destroy Shahryar and his regime; by the three years' or thousand-plus nights' end, so many parents have fled the country with their daughters that there remains in the city, we are specifically told, "not . . . one young person . . . fit for carnal copulation."

Except, notably, the daughters of the vizier himself, and here the plot thickens. The younger daughter, Dunyazade (Burton spells her name *Dunyázád:* in Persian, "World-freer"), is safely not yet nubile, though she will be by the end of the story. The elder, however, Scheherazade (Burton: *Shahrázád* = "City-freer"), is nubile, beautiful, extraordinarily accomplished in all the polite and liberal arts and massively so in some (she has collected "a thousand books of histories," we're told, and she knows "the works of the poets . . . by heart"); she is also, as her name implies,* resolved to deliver the city from the slaughter of its women and the king from his own madness—Scheherazade uses that term herself. Shahryar, we learn, has deliberately spared this eminently eligible young woman out of respect for his chief counselor; on the other hand, that counselor must produce the virgin-du-soir on pain of his own life, and after three years he is out of virgins.

---

* In Burton's Persian, at least. Another expert tells me that the names translate into "World-*born*" and "City-*born*."

At this critical moment, Scheherazade volunteers herself. She has a stratagem, she says, which she won't disclose to her father, to end the carnage. There is just a hint that if it fails she is prepared, in Burton's footnoted phrase, "to 'Judith' the King." ("These learned and clever young ladies," Burton's straightfaced note adds, "are very dangerous in the East.") The vizier attempts to dissuade his daughter by telling her a story: the cautionary Tale of the Bull and the Ass, the only "second level" tale in the *Nights* besides the ones which Scheherazade will tell to the king. It is clear to us that the young woman comes by her particular stratagem honestly—she's her father's daughter—but here as elsewhere the nameless authors of the *Nights* leave the connection implicit, the foreshadowing unremarked.

The vizier's story doesn't work ("I shall never desist, O my father, nor shall this tale change my purpose"): an ill omen in itself, one would think, but the fact goes unnoticed. And to her plea for self-sacrifice, Scheherazade now adds a canny threat: If her father says no, she'll go straight to Shahryar and report that she wants to go to bed with him, but his vizier won't allow it.

It is an offer that her father can't refuse; nor can Shahryar, though he is astounded when his "most faithful of Counsellors" now tells him the whole story of Scheherazade's mad resolve. Is the vizier aware of what must happen tomorrow morning? He is; can't do a thing with the willful girl. One senses a moment of real male sympathy between the king and his prime minister (Scheherazade seems conveniently to have no mother to complicate the emotional situation). One may imagine also that the king is given pause: Here is a role for which none of Scheherazade's one thousand predecessors can be supposed to have volunteered. Be that as may, when he has satisfied himself that both the young woman and her father understand the consequences of her proposal, Shahryar "rejoices greatly" and orders the show to go on.

Here is the place to notice, though Burton doesn't notice it, that the thousand and one nights of Scheherazade's upcoming liaison have been foreshadowed by the thousand-odd nights of Shahryar's deadly policy, and those in turn by his earlier vow by Allah to take his revenge on "a thousand women" if his wife ever cuckolded him. They are even foreshadowed by Scheherazade's "thousand books of histories." Perhaps such symmetries go without noticing. But we notice also that the vizier's daughter, unsurprisingly, has been fully aware of the plight of her country, of her sister virgins, and of her father; that she is insightful or sympathetic enough to diagnose the king's misogyny as a madness that he must and can—perhaps that by now he even wishes?—to be freed from; that she is shrewd enough to exploit others' vulnerabilities to her ends, as in her dealings with her father. She has had three years to formulate and prepare her strategy; she will surely have been aware, and may suppose the king aware, that a number of factors, none explicitly stated, make the moment propitious for action and reduce somewhat her nonetheless terrifying personal risk.

Consider: The vizier has told Shahryar "all about his dispute with his daughter from first to last." Will that account not also have included the information that except for her there remains in the city not a young person fit for carnal copulation, partly because Shahryar has exhausted the supply and partly because his subjects are "voting with their feet"? Won't all parties then have been exquisitely aware that when Shahryar has deflowered and killed this last one, the game is over in any case? That should he nevertheless do so, he will most certainly have lost the loyalty of his "wisest of Counsellors," whether or not he puts the vizier to death for nonprocurement of what can no longer be procured, and that that final atrocity might well be the last straw for an already outraged populace? Finally, and most directly to our purpose, won't the king, the diplomatist, and the diplomatist's daughter all have recognized that (if we round down that "space of three years" as aforeproposed from 1062 to 1000 nights) this critical day, when no nubile virgins remain except the most eligible one of all, coincides with the day when Shahryar's rash original vow will have been fulfilled? Despite all his dire face-saving protestations to the contrary, if Scheherazade is Shahryar's 1001st sacrificial virgin (not to say his 1063rd), he should be free to rescind without loss of face a policy that there is every political reason to rescind in any case— particularly if its absolute and public rescindment be preceded by a tacit moratorium . . . of a certain duration.

I like to imagine that all these unmentioned but perfectly reasonable things are so, and that this coincidence of numbers is among the reasons for Scheherazade's waiting till just now to put into action the stratagem for which she has long since prepared herself. It is surely also one of at least three reasons why the success of the critical initial phase of that stratagem (not being killed on the first morning after) is followed by a second phase (the consolidation of her position) lasting exactly 1000 rather than more or fewer nights, before the third phase (rescindment of the vow and formal marriage to the king) ends her storytelling and our story.

The second of those three reasons—and the only one noticed by the indefatigable but unpredictable Burton in the Terminal Essay to his edition of the *Nights* (X:75)—is a matter of cultural numerology. "Amongst the Arabs," he says, "as amongst the wild Irish, there is a divinity . . . in odd numbers" and bad luck in even ones; ". . . the number Thousand and One," in particular, "is a favourite in the East. . . ." He cites e.g., the Cistern of the Thousand and One Columns at Constantinople, the "mille et unum mausolea" of the Dervishes near Iconium, and the seventeenth-century Dervish *Book of a Thousand and One Days,* which echoes the *Nights* as it in turn echoes the earlier *Hazar Afsanah,* a book of tales told over a thousand nights from which our *Kitab Alf Laylah Wah Laylah* derives. In some such instances, as when Edward Lear's owl and pussycat sail away for a year and a day, or when somebody writes the book of *101 Uses for a Dead Cat,* the number means no more than "plenty and then some"; but Burton also cites a curious Hindu practice of determining hundreds by affixing the required figure to the end—for 100 writing 101; for 1000, 1001, etc.—since "the number of cyphers not followed by a significant number is indefinite. . . ." On this view (Burton says the Hindu practice is to be found "throughout Asia where Indian influence extends"), the number 1001 means not only a lot and then some; it means specifically 1000. He does not report how the Hindus write the number 1001 when they mean a thousand plus one.

In any case, 1001—not "plenty" or 1000 or 1002 or any other number—is the number of formulaically subtitled nights in Burton's translation, which he justifies at some length as faithful to the consensus of the manuscript versions. Some of those nights are but two or three pages long and contain as little as one one-hundredth of whatever story is in progress; some are many times that length and contain more than one complete sub-subtale or sub-sub-subtale as well as an installment of the subtale in progress. But when at last we read in Volume X the formula "Now when it was the Thousand and First Night," the number that Scheherazade and Shahryar (and Dunyazade and we) have spent together is—count 'em—exactly that.

And for this fact I believe there to be yet a third circumstance, or set of circumstances, beyond cultural numerology and the formal symmetry—not to mention the dramatical foreshadowing and strategical opportunity, which we shall return to—of there being just as many nights of narrative creation as there were nights of programmatic defloration-murder and of threatened victims in Shahryar's idle vengeful vow.

Some aspects of this third factor are incontrovertibly given in the denouement of the frame-story; indeed they *are* its denouement. Others are the merest enchanted speculation on my part. I shall make clear which is which after digressing to review, again in some detail, how the sexual-narrative formula of the *Nights* develops from the crucial First Night—on the eve of which we left our principals (all but the vizier) each eager in his/her own way to get on with it—into the routine which is then sustained for just under 36 lunar months, or about two years nine months by the Gregorian calendar (two years ten months by the Islamic).

On that first night, after giving Dunyazade certain careful instructions, Scheherazade presents herself to Shahryar. They go to bed; he "falls to toying with her" and prepares to mount. She weeps; he asks what ails her; she says she can't bear to be parted from her little sister on this last night of her life. The king sends for Dunyazade at once and seats her at the foot of the bed; then he "[rises] and [does] away with his bride's maidenhead"—the term "bride" is of course euphemistic—and the three fall asleep. At midnight, per plan, Scheherazade wakes Dunyazade, who by prearrangement complains of sleeplessness and asks her sister for a story to while away the hours till dawn. The text takes no note of what an odd request this is to make of one about to die; perhaps Dunyazade has not been told. In any case, Scheherazade cheerfully declares her readiness and asks the king's permission; he grants it, happening to be "sleepless and restless" himself. Is it the politically delicate prospect of ordering his chief counselor to kill his own daughter, we wonder, that spoils his sleep? Or the unnerving equanimity with which this pearl of the city, for no apparent reason, has volunteered herself to die and now confronts that imminent prospect? Is the king, instead of counting sheep, perhaps counting nights and realizing that Night 1 with Scheherazade is Night 1001 of his vow? We are not told.

Scheherazade begins her first story: In all editions, it is The Tale of the Trader and the Genie. What she tells, in fact, on this first night, is half of her first story, to be continued, and half of the first of three subtales which will be framed by that first story: subtales narrated in turn by the characters in it. At the first sign of dawn she falls silent in mid-sentence, leaving not one but two plots suspended as a kind of narrative insurance. (Both plots, by the way, have to do with innocent victims under imperious and imminent threat of death, the first of whom, like Scheherazade herself, is playing for time by telling his would-be executioner a story! We are reminded for the 1001st time that "self-reflexivity" is as old as the narrative imagination.) Dunyazade now dutifully praises the tale thus far, as she has been instructed to do; Scheherazade shrugs off the praise with what will become a refrain of authorial self-deprecation—"What is this [compared] to what I could tell thee on the coming night, were I to live and the King would spare me?"—and Shahryar makes the fateful remark to himself which will become *his* dreadful, hope-giving refrain: "By Allah, I will not slay her, until I shall have heard the rest of her story."

We have speculated already what motives, beyond his pleasure in the young woman and her stories, might lie behind Shahryar's new vow: As day dawns, it may well be dawning ever more clearly upon him that Scheherazade's indirect plea for a stay of execution is his opportunity not only to save face but to save his political ass as well. We are not told; we are not told. What we *are* told is that the two now sleep in *mutual* embrace—the emphasis is mine, but the phrase is the text's—until day is fully dawned. The king, having said nothing to Scheherazade, rises and goes forth to hold court. The vizier approaches with a shroud under his arm, expecting to be commanded to lead his daughter to the chopping block. Again the king says nothing—an exquisite saving of face indeed!—but proceeds with the day's business. The vizier "wonder[s] thereat with exceeding wonder," and no wonder.

At day's end Shahryar returns to his bedchamber and to a no doubt secretly jubilant Scheherazade. When the time comes, Dunyazade, in her role of primer of the pump, in effect says On with the story, and in a burst of narrative virtuosity Scheherazade completes the first and tells entirely the second and third of the subtales framed by her first main story (she has arranged these subtales, I ought to add, in an order of increasing marvelousness, and has made very sure that the trader, the genie, and all hands in the main tale acknowledge and applaud that increase). The main tale itself, however, she leaves strategically suspended as before, virtually guaranteeing the king's consent when Dunyazade repeats her praise and Scheherazade her deprecation of what she has produced thus far by comparison to what she's capable of producing. Again they lie in mutual embrace till full daylight; the king goes forth; the vizier comes forward; nothing is acknowledged; business is done—and the formula is established for the 999 nights to follow.

That formula, as made clear on the third night, is this: Each evening the king retires and "has his will of the vizier's daughter"; Dunyazade then asks her sister to continue the unfinished story-in-progress; Scheherazade does so, always addressing it to the king. (Some commentators assume the storytelling to take place immediately after the sex. Burton argues, on the evidence of the detailed first night and the ritual of Scheherazade's ceasing when she "perceives the dawn of the day," that it's done after their postcoital sleep, anytime between midnight and the crack of dawn.) Whenever she actually completes one of her primary stories, as she does on this third night, she immediately begins another. This first time she says, "And yet this tale is not more wondrous than the fisherman's story," and waits for the king to ask, "What is the fisherman's story?" Later, more confident of his permission, she'll simply say "And there is also the story of" etc.—and launch forthwith into the next main tale without even indenting for a new paragraph. Always she interrupts it in mid-plot, not infrequently in mid-sentence, when she perceives the first light of dawn.

Once established, the formula becomes increasingly perfunctory in all the manuscript versions (in many translations it is dropped altogether, as is even the numbering of the nights): Only occasionally now will Dunyazade's praise be repeated, Scheherazade's deprecation of her oeuvre to date, the king's silent vow, the mutual embrace, the king's going forth, the vizier's approach with shroud, the king's return at evening, the sex, the sleep, the request. There is however one startling anomaly, unnoticed by Burton: About five months along, on Night 145, Scheherazade winds up The Tale of King Omar bin al-Nu'uman and His Sons, the longest story in the *Nights* (it has taken her exactly 100 nights to tell it)—and, mirabile dictu, she does *not* begin a new one! Instead, the king says to her, in Burton's English, "I desire that thou tell me somewhat about birds," and having so said, promptly falls asleep. Instead of applauding the long tale just done, little Dunyazade declares to her sister that she's never seen the man cheerful before this night; she even dares to hope, aloud, that his good humor bodes well for the outcome between them. It is a deviation from the formula without precedent or succedent, until the last night of all, which however it certainly foreshadows, from an extraordinarily long remove. On Night 146, Scheherazade comes up with the requested bird-story (which happens to be the oldest story in the *Nights*), and the abbreviated formula is resumed.

Abbreviated or not, we are to understand that the ritual is essentially maintained right through a thousand nights. Indeed, at the end of Night

1000 it is repeated in its entirety, by way of preparation for the denouement, and Burton is at pains to footnotice that in thus fully reprising it he
is following the originals: The king still vows not to slay Scheherazade
until he has heard the end of her story; even the vizier, like a figure out of
Kafka now, still presents himself on that thousandth morning-after,
shroud under arm, waiting for his dread instructions; once again the king
says nothing to him, but proceeds as always to "bid and forbid between
man and man"; then on this last of the nights he "return[s] to his Harim*
and, according to his custom, [goes] in to his wife Scheherazade." After
the sex, Dunyazade asks as always for the continuation of the story-in-
progress; as always Scheherazade asks Shahryar's permission; as always,
he grants it; and she winds up the tale of Ma'aruf the Cobbler and his
wife Fatimah the Turd (Burton's word is Dung, but that was 1885), a
story which she has been spinning out for the past eleven nights. It is an
exemplary tale of a cobbler's shrewish and deceitful wife who fully deserves to be killed and is, thus permitting her injured spouse, by this time
a king, to marry guess whom, his vizier's excellent young daughter. . . .

It is also the end of a truly staggering narrative production. Burton
himself declares that there are "upwards of 400 stories" in the several
manuscript versions of the *Nights.* In his own ten-volume edition, which
(not counting the seven volumes of *Supplemental Nights* which Burton
published later) is shorter than the less reliable of the manuscript versions, Scheherazade tells by my count 169 primary tales; she moves to the
second degree of narrative involvement on no fewer than nineteen occasions, to tell 87 tales within the primary tales, and to the third degree on
four occasions, to tell eleven tales-within-tales-within-tales—267 complete stories in all, which by the way include about 10,000 lines of verse,
by Burton's estimate (I:xv). To appreciate the scale of this accomplishment, one might remember that the Homeric bards are supposed to have
required a mere four evenings to sing the *Odyssey.* And the fabled *Brihat
Katha,* or Great Tale—which the god Siva once told his consort Parvati
in return for an especially good copulation, and which reputedly came to
700,000 distichs, and of which Somadeva's huge eleventh-century
Sanskrit *Katha Sarit Sagara,* or *Oceans of Streams of Story,* is but a radical abridgement—if recited at Homeric pace, would require by my calcu-

---

* The Arabic word means "forbidden" and refers simply to the women's quarters, off-
limits to outsiders, not necessarily to a collection of wives and concubines.

lation a mere 509 evenings, it being no more than 64 times the length of the *Iliad* and the *Odyssey* combined. Scheherazade—indefatigable, inexhaustible Scheherazade—has doubled the performance of the god of destruction and creation himself.

Let us say, rather, *all but* indefatigable; all but inexhaustible. For now, the tale of Ma'aruf the Cobbler done, she makes obeisance to the king and for the first time asks, not for his permission to begin another story, but for a favor in return for those 1001 nights of past narrative production. Shahryar immediately grants her anything she might ask. Burton notes that some French recensions of the story have the king add ungratefully at this point, ". . . inasmuch as your last several stories in particular have bored me to death." Apparently this cynical reading is not without basis in some of the manuscripts; Burton rejects it, however, and so do I, as insulting to my favorite storyteller and inconsistent both with Shahryar's subsequent lavish praise of her narrative talent and with his freedom to kill her anytime he gets bored.

At least his apparent freedom: for now we learn for the first time that stories are not the only thing Scheherazade has produced in these 1001 nights. She calls out to the nurses and eunuchs "Bring me my children!" and they fetch forth three sons whom she has borne to her imperious auditor: "one walking," the text specifies, "one crawling, and one suckling." It is on their behalf that she pleads now for her life: to be exempt forever from his decree of execution, without (it is implied but not stated) having to earn each day's reprieve with another night of narrative output. The king grants her wish: not on those grounds, but out of respect for her moral character, for her family, and, it is presently made clear, for her stories, which, after the double marriage of himself to her and of his brother Shah Zaman to her sister Dunyazade, he orders transcribed into thirty volumes, which are to include the story of himself and Scheherazade.

I shall return to this last detail, the implications of his *imprimatur,* after reflecting upon the surprise revelation of these three children and their bearing on the number of the *Nights.* The unknown authors of the *Kitab Alf Laylah Wah Laylah* are not interested in the *middle* of their frametale. Indeed, it has no middle: only the ingenious and elaborate headpiece, the climactic and ceremonious tailpiece, and the formulaic transitions from night to night in between. Scheherazade's three pregnancies and deliveries, and any menstruations before, between, and after

them, are not mentioned, nor as we have seen is any gradual softening of
Shahryar's attitude, except for that anomalous and momentary lapse on
Night 145. Though the coital motif is not explicitly reprised night by
night, the conceit itself requires us to presume that the pair (the trio) have
at least slept together every night of the 1001—this despite strict Moslem
injunctions against e.g., coition during menstruation, which Burton declares many Islamites to believe responsible for leprosy and elephantiasis
(VIII:24).

Very well, then: We are obliged to infer that there must have been
nights of narrative without sex—at least without sex between the king
and Scheherazade (and we may safely exempt little Dunyazade, inasmuch as she was non-nubile on Night 1 and is still virginal on her and
Shah Zaman's wedding day). We have seen what a canny strategist
Scheherazade is: Without asking of this marvelous story an inappropriate
degree of verisimilitude, I believe we may presume that, its mainspring
being sexual, Scheherazade would not likely for example have volunteered herself to Shahryar while she was in mid-menstruation, or on the
verge of menstruation. To do so would have been suicidal. It seems reasonable further to imagine that she'd want to conceive by the king as
early in the game as possible, both to insure her sexual availability for at
least some months in that critical first stage of her strategy and to bind
herself to him with a child-in-progress: There is no mention, either in
headpiece or tailpiece, of Shahryar's having children by his unfaithful
first wife or by other members of his harem, if there are any. Human biol-
ogy being rather less various across the centuries and cultures than some
other things, I have set to work with my pocket calculator, a standard
manual of gynecology, obstetrics, and pediatrics, and a few assumptions
and constraints (notably the phrase "one walking, one crawling, and one
suckling"); I have come up with some results and speculations which, if
they do not further illuminate the number of the *Nights,* may at very least
shed some light upon the great ground-symbol of Scheherazade the storyteller.

I have presumed already that Scheherazade will have timed her ultimatum to her father for a period between periods, so to speak. If, as
seems reasonable, she plans to get herself pregnant as fast as possible before menstruation puts her dangerously out of action, she will have
scheduled her liaison with Shahryar to begin not long after her last virginal menses, both to preclude an inconvenient and counterstrategic

menstruation on, say, the second or third night, and to guarantee her fertility early on in their connection. Her ultimatum takes her father by surprise, but his plight will not have taken *her* by surprise: Just as she's been boning up in her library for the task ahead, I see Scheherazade cannily monitoring the moon and her menstrual cycle with an eye to the most opportune "window," as the NASA people say. It cannot be too much emphasized that this young woman is *smart:* When she tells the tale of the slave-girl Tawaddud, for example—a beautiful and sexy polymath who confounds all the sultan's experts with her mastery of syntax, poetry, jurisprudence, exegesis, philosophy, music, religious law, mathematics, scripture and scriptural commentary, geometry, geodesy, medicine, logic, rhetoric, composition, dancing, and the rules of sex—Scheherazade gives us the complete 27-night oral examination (Nights 436–462); and all that Tawaddud knows is only part of what Scheherazade knows.

To get down to it, between no fewer than seven and no more than thirteen days before Night 1, she will have begun her final maiden menses, and will have put them tidily by from one to seven days before her ultimatum. She can then expect to ovulate somewhere from one to four nights into this first sexual affair of hers, though ovulation could possibly occur later: by Rhythm Method calculations, anywhere from Night 1 to Night 10, if she began her last menses on Night Minus 7. (I use the phrase "expect to ovulate" as a manner of speaking: The people of *The Arabian Nights* do not speak of sperm and ova as such, but they are rich in folk wisdom about fertility and barrenness. A number of Scheherazade's stories are concerned with the subject.)

I'm going to presume further that Scheherazade did indeed conceive successfully upon this first post-virginal ovulation. Just as in Greek mythology "the embrace of a god is never fruitless," so there is ample precedent in Arab storytelling for the idea that powerful or favored men get their women pregnant on the night they deflower them: One need look no farther than Scheherazade's Tale of Núr al-Dín Alí (Nights 20–24), in which two brothers, sons of the vizier, both impregnate their brides on their joint wedding night and become fathers on the same day exactly nine months thereafter. If conception occurred between Nights 1 and 10, our storyteller will have guessed the fact by Nights 14 to 21, when she will have skipped her next menses; she will know it pretty certainly by Nights 42–49, when she will have missed two straight periods and begun to show the other early signs of pregnancy. By Night 145, the night of that startling lapse from the formula, Scheherazade will have been plumply half through the second trimester of her first pregnancy: I think I know why the king dozes off cheerfully, and I feel as relieved as little Dunyazade at the way things are working out between them.

Now, assuming the average normal human gestation of 266 days plus or minus two weeks, Scheherazade will have delivered her #1 son no earlier than Night 253 (if she conceived on Night 1 and delivered a fortnight early) and no later than Night 290 (if she conceived on Night 10 and delivered a fortnight late). Her median EDC, as the obstetricians call it (Estimated Date of Confinement), would be about Night 271: i.e., 266 days after Night 5. Considerations of storytelling lead me to prefer conception on Night 1 and confinement on Night 267, right on the button.

Thereafter, *The Merck Manual* reports, it would be possible though gynecologically inadvisable for her to conceive #2 as early as fourteen days after delivering #1: i.e., on Night 281 if she delivered #1 on Night 267. She would thereby postpone menstruating in the king's company for another nine months. But surely she has by now passed successfully the critical test of narration without copulation, in the period immediately prior to, during, and after her first childbirth. What's more, if she conceives #2 on Night 281 and delivers him exactly 266 days later (Night 547), the boy will be fifteen months old on Night 1001: very late indeed to be "crawling," as the text specifies (the average healthy baby, Dr. Spock reports, begins to walk between twelve and fifteen months of age). And she could conceivably conceive #3 as early as fourteen days after delivering #2 and deliver *him* 266 days thereafter (Night 827); but then by Night 1001, while he'd still be nursing, at just under six months he'd very possibly be crawling as well (the average crawler is six to twelve months old) while his two older brothers walked.

The phrase "one walking, one crawling, and one suckling," together with the presumption of even minimal consideration on Shahryar's part for the welfare of his chief source of sexual and narrative entertainment, suggests that the king permitted Scheherazade a more reasonable interval between her pregnancies—though it cannot in the best of cases have been as long as the "several months" recommended by modern gynecologists for complete recovery from uterine wear and tear. Further reflection (and a bit of exercise with the calculator) suggests that if on Night 1001 Child #1 is walking (i.e., is at least a year old; but given the existence of two younger brothers he must be at least eighteen months old), and Child #2 is crawling (i.e., is between six and twelve months old; but given the existence of one younger brother he's more likely between ten and twelve months old), and Child #3 is suckling but not yet crawling (i.e., is comfortably under six months old), then the three pregnancies were indeed spaced about equally through the period. It suggests further that if—as Child #1's age and Scheherazade's likely strategy argue—her first conception occurred within the first ten nights and her third sometime between nights 552 and 735 (any earlier and #3 would likely be crawling; any later and he'll have been premature)—then these intervals between her three pregnancies and/or following the third of them will have been long enough virtually to guarantee her having menstruated at least once, and most likely more than once, by Night 1001: If she is not reimpregnated at her first postpartum ovulation, declares the *Merck,* a woman normally resumes menstruation six to eight weeks after childbirth.*

So what? you ask. I'll tell you so what, after adding one final presumption: that Scheherazade is *not* pregnant again, or in any case does not know that she is, on Night 1001. If she were, she'd surely add that circumstance to her plea for her life: one walking, one crawling, one suckling, and one in the oven. Let us proceed.

From these several considerations and constraints, plus the Arab storyteller's fondness for formal regularity and symmetry, a sensible pattern suggests itself: Scheherazade first conceives at that first ovulation; she ovulates and menstruates once after each of her successful deliveries; and she is reimpregnated promptly upon her next ovulation following each of those menstruations—at least following the first and second. Assuming a perfectly average fourteen days between the onset of menses and ovulation (and another fourteen, where applicable, between ovulation and the next onset of menses) and perfectly average 266-day pregnancies, and assuming further that her first conception occurred on Night 1, we can generate a large number of feasible schedules for Scheherazade's gynecological-obstetrical events, depending on the interval we allow between deliveries and the resumption of menses. I shall consider here only three of those schedules, and then choose my favorite.

The *low* limit of that normal interval (six weeks, or 42 days) gives the following result:

---

* Nursing may delay this resumption. But those nurses summoned by the king's favorite on Night 1001 may be presumed to have been wet nurses.

JOHN BARTH

SCHEDULE 1

```
Night        1: 1st conception
      +  266
Night      267: 1st delivery
      +   42
Night      309: 1st menstruation
      +   14
Night      323: 2nd conception
      +  266
Night      589: 2nd delivery
      +   42
Night      631: 2nd menstruation
      +   14
Night      645: 3rd conception
      +  266
Night      911: 3rd delivery
      +   42
```

Night 953: 3rd menstruation		Night 953: 3rd menstruation
+ 14		+ 28
Night 967: 4th conception?	Or	Night 981: 4th menstruation?
+ 34		+ 20
Night 1001		Night 1001

The children are in their proper age brackets: The walker is four days past two years old, the crawler thirteen months and seventeen days (just a touch tardy, but you know how it is with Middle Children), the suckler three months. But the "end-game"—while it has a remarkable feature about it that I'll come back to—is finally uninteresting: Whether Scheherazade is 34 days pregnant with her fourth child or twenty days past her fourth menses, Night 1001 is, except for its portentous number, a night like any other. And the point of these investigations is to ask of Night 1001 what the Jews ask of the first night of Passover: How is this night different from all other nights?

Increasing the normal delivery-menstruation interval to its *upper* limit (eight weeks, or 56 days) produces the following interesting result:

SCHEDULE 2

```
Night        1: 1st conception
      +  266
Night      267: 1st delivery
```

```
        +    56
Night   323: 1st menstruation
        +    14
Night   337: 2nd conception
        +   266
Night   603: 2nd delivery
        +    56
Night   659: 2nd menstruation
        +    14
Night   673: 3rd conception
        +   266
Night   939: 3rd delivery
        +    56
Night   995: 3rd menstruation
        +     6
Night  1001
```

The kids are still in the right age brackets: two years four days; thirteen months three days; two months. Scheherazade, just winding up the third postpartum menstruation of her career, is ready to resume sex with the king, as indeed the frame-story tells us she does: ". . . according to his custom, [Shahryar] went in to his wife Scheherazade" (it has been yet another constraint upon these calculations not to have her menstruating at bedtime on Night 1001). If things continue according to Shahryar's custom, Scheherazade can look forward to a fourth conception on Night 1015, a fourth confinement on Night 1281, etc. almost ad infinitum, or until the king tires of her. Her plea for exemption from his deadly vow will by this schedule have been prompted by the coincidence of three factors, none mentioned in the text but two already discussed here: (1) The turning up on the tale's odometer of the magic number 1001, signifying both "plenty and then some" and the inauguration of another cycle. (2) The circumstance of that number's equalling (perhaps exceeding by one) the number of nights through which Shahryar has enforced his murderous policy. Each morning that he hasn't killed Scheherazade is symbolic penance for his having killed one of her predecessors; on the 1001st night that penance is complete. It is as opportune a moment for Scheherazade to ask for rescindment of his vow as Night 1001 of that vow was opportune for her entering his life. And (3) to clinch the matter: her having borne his third child, duly menstruated, and faithfully re-presented herself for his further sexual pleasure. It is a fortuitous coincidence indeed: *Dayenu,* as the Passover song declares: The first two factors alone "would have been enough"; the third adds an appropriate dimension of sexual fidelity to the resolution of a plot which begins in sexual infidelity.

But to arrive at this happy coincidence we have departed from our principle of strict averages. What happens to the schedule if, along with exact average ovulation and gestation times, we apply the exact average interval (seven weeks, or 49 days) between childbirth and the resumption of menstruation? In my opinion, the result is even more interesting*:

SCHEDULE 3

```
Night        1: 1st conception
      +   266
Night      267: 1st delivery
      +    49
Night      316: 1st menstruation
      +    14
Night      330: 2nd conception
      +   266
Night      596: 2nd delivery
      +    49
Night      645: 2nd menstruation
      +    14
Night      659: 3rd conception
      +   266
Night      925: 3rd delivery
      +    49
Night      974: 3rd menstruation
      +    27
Night     1001
      +     1
(Night    1002: 4th menstruation)
```

The children remain of appropriate ages: two years four days; thirteen months ten days; two and a half months. The coincidence of the number 1001 with the number of Scheherazade's predecessors and the rest remains in force. But a new element, dramatic and unprecedented in the story, presents itself: For the first time in nearly three years, Sche-

---

* I have checked all three of these schedules against the content of Scheherazade's stories on the nights involved, in search of conspicuous correspondences, discrepancies, and irrelevancies. There are all three: A little jiggling here and there with Schedule Three, in particular, can produce some remarkable happy echoes—but not remarkably more than the others, jiggled, can be made to produce. And the whole arrangement of the tales and division of the nights is too inconsistent among manuscripts to permit us to adduce as evidence anything between Night 2 and Night 1001.

herazade has completed a menstrual cycle in the normal lunar month! For the first time since her maiden night with Shahryar 1000 nights ago, the king has *not* impregnated her upon her first ovulation after her preceding menstruation. And although any number of premenstrual symptoms may have forewarned Scheherazade of this circumstance, the king himself must be apprised of it no later than Night 1002, when he will find that by Moslem practice he cannot "go in to Scheherazade," as their whole past history will have led him to expect to do, because—a mere 28 days since her previous menses, instead of the accustomed 329 (14 + 266 + 49)—she's menstruating again! (Granted, the same thing might have happened e.g., in Schedule 1; but there the moment came meaninglessly on Night 981.)

It is a delicate moment indeed. (We need not assume, by the way, that she is "a day early": If, as Burton argues and the crucial first night attests, Scheherazade does her storytelling in the hours between midnight and dawn, then the "1001st night" is actually the 1002nd morning, and our schedule is intact.) We recall another element in the formula: At first light, Scheherazade normally breaks off her story in progress and sleeps with the king "in mutual embrace till day fully breaks." If, as may be imagined, this unprecedented, abnormally normal menstrual period or some unequivocal sign of its immediate onset comes upon her as she winds up the tale of Ma'aruf the Cobbler and Fatimah the Turd, there is no time to be lost. Scheherazade must either launch at once into another story—and it had better be a good one—or do something as extraordinary as her menstruating twice in a row.

Here is the place to wonder how it may be that this extraordinary thing has come to pass. Has the king become infertile? Or—after deflowering at least 1002 virgins (his first wife, presumably, plus the murdered 1000, plus Scheherazade)—has he become impotent, as the sexologists tell us Don Juan would likely have become? Can it be that his appetite for the pleasures of narrative has supplanted more physical appetites? Alternatively, and more alarming, can he in these latter weeks, except for this 1001st night, have turned his sexual attentions elsewhere, coming in to Scheherazade only for his pre-dawn narrative fix?

The text will not help us: So outspoken on all matters physical regardless how delicate or indelicate, it is silent on this. In the absence of any supporting evidence, all such speculations as the above are far-fetched, though any would constitute a danger which Scheherazade's new menstruation would serve to focus and perhaps bring to a head—*her* head. So too, possibly more so, would a less farfetched imaginable state of affairs predicated from this hypothetical menstruation: an alternative case that much appeals to my own imagination, and which will fetch us to the moral of these impolite investigations.

Perhaps Shahryar is as potent a potentate as ever, as fertile as ever, as faithful as ever in his sexual attentions to Scheherazade. Perhaps even—though this is imagining much of a storybook sultan—he has, except in the neighborhoods of her previous menses and deliveries, "gone in to" no other woman besides Scheherazade (the text mentions no other); perhaps he has come to expect that her production of children by him, like her production of stories for him, will go on forever, or at least until "the Destroyer of Delights and Severer of Societies," as the wonderful Arab formula puts it, "translates them both to the ruth of Almighty Allah, and their houses fall waste and their palaces lie in ruins." Perhaps at very least he has come in all these nights to extend his unspoken vow from "By Allah, I will not kill her until I shall have heard the end of her story" to "By Allah, I will not kill her until I have heard the end of her *stories*." And perhaps our Scheherazade—this very fountain of narrative production and biological reproduction—has gone dry.

Oh, not forever, of course; not *yet* forever. If one swallow does not a summer make, or a drunkard, one swallow the less doesn't mean that winter's here and the bar is closed. If Child #4 is not in the works this month, very likely he will be next, or the one after that. And there may be only thirty-six basic dramatic situations, as Georges Polti claims (in *The 36 Dramatic Situations* (1916): very close, by the way, to the number of coital positions recognized by the *Kama Sutra*—thirty-nine—and that, as Burton himself notes, to the "Quarante Façons" of French erotic tradition), but the number of interesting stories and copulations that these can generate is surely very very large, if after all not infinite. Polti calculates for example from his thirty-six situations that there are exactly 1,332 ways to be Taken by Surprise: Scheherazade could go on for another childsworth of nights yet on surprise-stories alone, even if she'd been telling no other kind at the rate of one a night since Night 1. As for biological fertility, I have no figures for well-born Moslem women of Scheherazade's time and place—the time and place themselves are uncertain enough—but *The Merck Manual* informs me that a healthy modern American woman, in the years between her menarche and her menopause, will produce about the same number of ova as Scheherazade produces stories in the combined manuscript versions of the *Nights:* just "upwards of 400." If we assume, as tradition permits, that precocious Scheherazade will not have been many years past puberty when she volunteered herself to the king, she has a good number of childbearing years left her beyond that 1002nd morning.

So unless Shahryar is just looking for an excuse to be rid of her, neither Scheherazade's (speculative) first failure to conceive nor (what I'm just for a moment speculating further) her first inability to come up with the opening of her next story immediately upon the close of her last—neither of these doubtless temporary lapses constitutes a grave present danger after all, if either of them "actually" occurs. Let us not forget that she survived Night 145, when the king fell asleep at intermission time.

What they do constitute, however, either or both of these lapses, is a warning, a foreshadow, which no one as percipient as our Scheherazade would likely ignore; which we ourselves may do well to perpend; and which I'm happy to imagine might—coincident with those two other, more evident special aspects of the number 1001—have prompted Scheherazade's petition for tenure; for exemption from the publish-or-perish ultimatum under which she has lived (and produced) for so long.

The most fecund woman in the world will eventually reach her climacteric, if she lives so long.* The most potent man (no statistics available) will one day fail to get it up, if anybody's still interested. And the most fertile, potent narrative imagination—out of which has come, in Shahryar's own words, a whole world of "proverbs and parables, chronicles and pleasantries, quips and jests, stories and anecdotes, dialogues and histories and elegies and other verses . . ." (X:56)—even so fertile a narrator as Scheherazade, if she live long enough and produce long enough, must one day find herself in a case the reverse of what young John Keats feared: not that she "might cease to be / Before [her] pen hath gleaned [her] teeming brain," but that she might continue to be *after* her pen hath gleaned her teeming brain. More precisely, the omen of her very first failure to conceive—a kind of biological Writer's Block—could well serve to remind Scheherazade that on any morning after the night when her teeming brain shall finally have been gleaned, she might peremptorily cease to be.

---

* According to the 1981 *Guinness Book of World Records,* the most fecund woman in the world was the first Mrs. Feodor Vassilyev of Shuya, near Moscow. In 27 confinements, between c.1725 and 1765, Mrs. Vassilyev bore 69 children, at least 67 of whom survived infancy: sixteen sets of twins, seven sets of triplets, and four sets of quadruplets.

I like to think that that night was *not* Night 1001. I like to imagine that on that night, of whose fateful number Scheherazade will certainly have been aware and no doubt the king as well, she was not even momentarily blocked; that up her sleeve, or wherever, Scheherazade still had in reserve at least the seven volumes of Burton's *Supplemental Nights* with which to follow the tale of Ma'aruf the Cobbler, if she wanted to. But that first repeated message of her blood, like a word to the wise, told her it was time for a change in the circumstances of her production.

"In the morning, study," Goethe advises; "in the afternoon, work." In the morning of Scheherazade's apprenticeship, we're explicitly told, this model storyteller did indeed study, taking unto herself massively the corpus of her literary predecessors: those "thousand books of histories"; all those poets committed to heart. In the afternoon—the 1001 "afternoons" of a night-shift worker—she has massively worked, in that terrifying but inspiring relation that all artists work in, with an audience whom at any time they may fatally cease to entertain; for whom it is never enough to have told one good story, or a hundred and one good stories. (The audience I refer to is of course Scheherazade's deflorator, impregnator, and absolute critic, the king. The role of Dunyazade—always applauding, praising, and begging for more from the foot of that bed—is another story.)

But there comes a time when this state of affairs mustn't be the case forever; when the threat of perishing if one does not publish, and publish pleasingly, no longer inspires and fertilizes but positively contraceives, detumesces, anaphrodizes. "In the evening, enjoy," Goethe's obiter dictum concludes. Enjoyment, for a woman like Scheherazade, is not likely to mean idly resting on the laurels of her past production: those three young sons and the deluxe uniform hardcover edition of her works which the king orders after the double-marriage ceremony. (Indeed, there's a wry implication here that her next massive narrative labor will have to be telling all those stories over again, to the scribes, plus the one about herself and Shahryar, unless she or Dunyazade has been writing them all down between nights. It is a bit like your interviewer's discovery—at the end of a long, difficult, but successful interview, in which you have managed to articulate your entire *Weltanschauung*—that his tape machine wasn't working. Would you mind awfully running through that again?) But enjoyment ought to mean the right to rest there if she wants to, bearing no more children, telling no more stories ever. After a certain amount and level of accomplishment—an impressive amount and level; nay, an awe-inspiring amount and level—removing the ax from over the narrative neck is not only a fit reward but probably the best guarantee of further good production. Not endless, mind, but further, at the producer's rate and discretion.

For a natural like Scheherazade, that is almost certainly what "enjoying the evening" will include, if not consist of: going on with the story. We are permitted to hope that it will. But after that first second menstruation, we may not—and Scheherazade herself must absolutely *need* not—count on it.

Enjoy your evening.